£7.50

THE PILGRIMS' WAY

Seán Jennett

THE PILGRIMS' WAY

from Winchester to Canterbury

CASSELL · LONDON

CASSELL & COMPANY LTD
35 Red Lion Square, London WC1
Sydney, Auckland
Toronto, Johannesburg

First published 1971

I.S.B.N. 0 304 93755 X

PRINTED IN GREAT BRITAIN
BY THE CAMELOT PRESS LTD,
LONDON AND SOUTHAMPTON
F.471

Whan that Aprille with his shoures soote
The droghte of March hath perced to the roote,
And bathed every veyne in swich licour
Of which vertu engendered is the flour;
Whan Zephirus eek with his sweete breeth
Inspired hath in every holt and heeth
The tendre croppes, and the yonge sonne
Hath in the Ram his halve cours yronne,
And smale foweles maken melodye,
That slepen al the nyght with open ye
(So priketh hem nature in hir corages);
Thanne longen folk to goon on pilgrimages,
And palmeres for to seken straunge strondes,
To ferne halwes, kowthe in sondry londes;
And specially from every shires ende
Of Engelond to Caunterbury they wende,
The hooly blisful martir for to seke,
That hem hath holpen whan that they were seeke.

The first lines of
The Canterbury Tales by Chaucer

Contents

Contents

Illustrations

Acknowledgements

No one can, or should, write about the Pilgrims' Way without reference to the pioneer work of Hilaire Belloc and Julia Cartwright (Mrs Adie) around the end of the nineteenth century. My own exploration has been assisted by information provided by the Countryside Commission, and by the county councils of Hampshire, Surrey, and Kent. I owe thanks to my wife Irene for her company along the Way, for her many practical contributions, for her recording of photographs and other details, and for her reading of the typescript, in which her better memory than mine has recovered details and corrected errors. I am grateful to my son Michael for his having acted as chauffeur on several occasions. Finally, I owe thanks to Mrs D. Bown for her patient filing of information and her typing and retyping of this book.

PART ONE

The Setting of the Pilgrims' Way

1 The Landscape of the Way

Chalk is king. To understand the landscape of the Pilgrims' Way and its changes from open heath to deep forests, from bare or wooded uplands to rich agricultural valleys and levels, one must pay homage to the chalk. The chalk uplands extend over England in a forked plan: from Dorset north-east to the Wash in Norfolk, and on to Flamborough Head in Yorkshire; and from Dorset eastwards to the South Foreland in Kent. It is with this second, more southerly branch that we are concerned in tracing and analysing the landscape and the route of the Pilgrims' Way, for the chalk and the sedimentary layers that lie under it have a great deal to do with what the eye sees and what the foot feels in journeying along the Way. So it is of interest to see and necessary to comprehend what the chalk is and how it came to be where it is.

In the Cretaceous period of the Mesozoic era Britain was part of a vast continent that included as dry land what are now the North Sea and the English Channel. Somewhere in this continent were high mountains with busy rivers on their flanks eroding their substance and carrying it down towards lakes or to the sea. Some of these rivers flowed into a large freshwater lake that extended, in terms of the modern map, from Haslemere to Romney Marsh, from Sevenoaks to Pevensey in Sussex, and across to the Bas Boulonnais in the Pas de Calais. In Sussex, the rivers, tearing away at the flanks of the mountains, brought down vast quantities of sand and silt and deposited their loads in the lake, forming first the clay and sands of the Hastings Beds and then the heavier clay of the Weald. This clay is a thick, sticky material; many ages later it hindered the steps of beast and man and drove travellers of the stone ages and the metal ages and the pilgrims who came after them to avoid it by making their way along the slopes of the chalk hills, where the going was dry and firm.

All geology is concerned with the massive movements and

caprices of the crust of the earth, movements either slow and perceptible only in cumulation over millions of years, or rapid and dramatic, as in the spouting of volcanoes and the tumbling of earthquakes. There is no evidence of sudden earth movement in the south-east corner of England, but what happened there is equally interesting. The land began to sink beneath the sea and continued to sink until it was far below the surface. Rivers continued to bring down the substance of their robbery of distant mountains and over the floor of the sea spread a layer of sandy strata mixed here and there with another kind of clay, the gault. The sand formed the lower and upper layers of the strata called by geologists the greensand. The greensand may have taken on a green colour when it was laid down and in some cases it is certainly greenish when first quarried, but on exposure it alters in colour from yellow to orange or brown, and even to red, and occasionally it bleaches to white or grey.

Perhaps after this the climate changed and our part of the world became warmer, for the water began to pullulate with myriads of tiny shelly creatures that lived out their minute lives and died and dropped to the floor of the sea. Their shells and skeletons, constantly drizzling down, formed a thick ooze, augmented by calcareous muds brought by rivers, which was concreted by the increasing pressure into a stratum of rock or chalk of varying density and hardness. If you suppose that that layer of ooze was well over a thousand feet thick, you may imagine, or fail to imagine, as well as I, how many creatures died in the making of the chalk and how long they were about it. Geologists are cautious about dating or even indicating the duration of such processes, yet in geological time it was very recent.

A leisurely uplift of the sea bed brought about the end of the Cretaceous sedimentation in our area as the chalk burst forth from the waves. The rise was considerable. What had previously been far beneath the surface now rose hundreds of feet and perhaps thousands of feet above it. Over the area of Kent and Sussex the thrust was like that of a fist pushing from below, a thrust that bent the Weald sands and clay and the greensand and the chalk above them into a great convex, riven dome, geologically an anticline. No sooner did this dome emerge than the winds and the weather began to play upon it. Rains gathered in streams that parted from the water-divide and rushed over the chalk, in which they cut trenches by the force of their fall and the solvent action of the water. As the mass rose further the elements scalped or stripped off the covering of chalk and of much of the greensand from the head of the dome and revealed the Weald clay and sands, lying as though in a circumferential rim of chalk and greensand. By this time the rivers had already made their beds through the chalk and they now remained in their courses, though in some instances yielding parts of their headwaters to more active streams.

This scalping of the dome and the tilt of the strata formed the North and South Downs. If the chalk had been a harder material, such as millstone grit, it would have formed sharp-edged scarps similar to those of the Yorkshire Dales or the 'edges' of the Peak. But chalk is comparatively soft and the continued action of the weather rounded off any such masculine acerbities into swelling, female curves. The steepness of the scarps remained on the inner edges of the broken dome, and you may see it today on the south face of the North Downs, where the Pilgrims' Way runs, and on the north face of the South Downs. The dip slopes, the outer slopes of the former dome, following the tilt of the strata, are more gentle, falling to the London basin in the north and to the sea in the south. Cut by the waves, the chalk presents great white cliffs between Bognor and Beachy Head and between Folkestone and Sandwich; between Eastbourne and Dungeness the sea has won through the chalk and has eaten into the earlier strata laid down in the former freshwater lake.

The outer slopes are, however, not everywhere gentle. In places they are breathlessly steep, and sometimes there is only the merest strip of the high chalk between the Eocene strata and the greensand, as for example on the Hog's Back; there the chalk falls off quickly to the London clay and the Bagshot Beds, with vast panoramas to the north.

The greensand and the Weald clay and Hastings Beds in that descending order, did not and do not form a plain or lowland between the scarps of the chalk. The Weald is that area between the North and South Downs that rests on these older strata and anyone who has travelled in the Weald will know that it is

Bpw

anything but level. It rises and falls and has its ridges and valleys, and in places it soars as high or nearly as high as the neighbouring chalk. Leith Hill, for example, is in the greensand, rising to a little short of 1,000 feet—its tower raises the observer to the 1,000-foot level—and south of East Grinstead the Hastings Beds, the earliest of our strata, reach 711 feet. Such ridges of the freshwater strata and of the greensand, covered with trees, are clearly seen from the Pilgrims' Way in Surrey and Kent.

To the west of Sussex and Kent the Weald and the chalk continue into Surrey and through to Hampshire, where there is a great mass of the chalk, not very high, over which the Pilgrims' Way runs to Winchester. Beyond that city the chalk forms the windy levels of Salisbury Plain and carries the Old Road, as the Hoar Way, on to Salisbury. If the Hoar Way went on through Devon and Cornwall to Marazion and the tin-mines, as some people say it did, it crossed over a geological tangle of rocks—sedimentary, igneous, and metamorphic—the unravelling of which and their connection with the scenery are material for a different book than this.

The Weald is all that wide area between the North and the South Downs, extending from Selborne and Farnham in the west to the sea at Dymchurch and Romney Marsh. All this, on the Weald sands and clay and partly on the greensand, was wild woodland and was so from times long before the knowledge of man. The Romans called it Sylva Anderida, but why they called it so is not as clear; it seems no help to suppose that 'Anderida' came from their name for a settlement and that that settlement is now Pevensey. *The Oxford Dictionary of English Place-Names* traces the name back to British *ande* and Celtic *rhyd*, a ford, and quotes Jackson as rendering it 'the green fords'. That seems to make no sense for a district far more notable for its forests than for its fords and in which, in any case, travel was minimal. A century after the departure of the Romans, the Saxons knew the district as 'Andredesleage', and later as 'Andredesweald'. Whatever 'Andred' may mean, 'weald' is a word for a woodland, and so near in connotation to 'wild', also a Saxon word, that it will do very well for a district the salient characteristics of which were woodlands and wilderness.

Wolves, boars, wild men, fugitives, and thieves and bandits

lived in the forest. It was probably so in the new stone age, it was so in the time of the Celtic British, in the time of the Romans, and again in the days of the Saxons and of the Normans. Peaceful men kept out of the forest, and if they had to journey from one place to another they passed along its margins, for there they had a double advantage. Not only could they more clearly see their way ahead, not only were they tolerably relieved of the danger of surprise, but also the way was dry along the edge of the chalk, while in the lower land there was sand and the thick clay that glued and gummed a horse's hoofs and made a man weary before he had gone a mile. So the Old Road on the chalk slope developed.

It will be seen from this account that the landscape of the Way is very varied and that to travel the Way is to experience many of the varieties of scenery that the south and south-east of England have to offer. Coming from Winchester, the Way passes through river valleys, upstream along the Itchen to the water-divide and downstream above the Wey, and over the sandy heaths around Compton, and does not really take to the hills (unless you count the Hog's Back as part of the Pilgrims' Way) until after it crosses the river Wey at Shalford. Then it climbs the loose sandy hill of St Martha's for its first high viewpoint, loses itself in the woods north-east of Shere and below Ranmore, and emerges decisively on to the high chalk above Dorking, on Box Hill, not to leave it again except for the river crossings and an occasional descent on to the greensand.

With few exceptions, the view is always to the south and the way is sheltered and warm under the sun. Though the forests of the Weald at last fell to the iron-foundries, which consumed the trees until legal restrictions had to be imposed to preserve timber for the king's navy, the quantities of trees are still notable in the view, standing in hedges or in spinneys or coverts, and filling or covering hollows and humps that are too difficult for the plough. Trees clothe the ridges of the greensand, sometimes called the Forest Ridges, and in places form woodlands that indeed might be remnants of the great forest of Anderida, of Andredesweald, forests such as Alice Holt in Hampshire, Abinger in Surrey, and Challock in Kent. The fields between the woodlands, in places apparently too poor for the plough and therefore grazed by sheep, in other places fertile and generous and in summer thick with wheat, barley, or oats, have those feminine curves and swellings that make such landscape, especially in Kent, peculiarly beautiful (*plate* 10). And the colours too are beautiful —not only the revolving colours of the varied trees in winter, spring, summer, and autumn, and of ripening crops, but also the colours of the ground, of the ploughed earth. There are the slatey green of the clay, the ochre of the sands, in places made pastel by the presence of chalk, and then of course the white of the chalk, which comes into almost every view in those curved cliffs, cut by the quarryman, that are a feature of the downs.

Many buildings along the Way, the older ones at least, reflect in their substance the nature of the land. On the sands and on the clay, timber frame with wattle or brick infilling is common, topped by heavy thatch. Where the chalk is hard enough to be quarried for building, cottages of clunch may be seen, and clunch may be found also in the interiors of some churches, e.g. Compton and Merstham, where its easily inscribed surface has for centuries attracted the attention of initial-scratching juveniles. Out of the chalk comes flint, and flint with quantities of mortar makes a durable, speckled building material for cottages and castle walls, and for many churches. In some districts the ironstone that attracted the iron-founders has been used for building, generally in irregular lumps, in house and church walls; it appears dark and rich, the colour of wet rust. Sandstones vary in colour from the yellow and browns of Kentish rag of the lower greensand to the green of Ightham stone. Sometimes, all these materials are mixed together in one wall, with a few Roman bricks or tiles added for effect or simply because they were at hand in one of the many ruined Roman villas neighbouring the Way. Earlier than any of these are the great chamber tombs of Addington, Coldrum, and Kit's Coty, built of enormous sarsen stones, a variety of sandstone occurring naturally in the earth, and sometimes called 'grey wethers' from their supposed resemblance to sheep.

Among the many trees of the Pilgrims' Way the yew is prominent, at times as a chequer of dark accents among the fresher green of birch, beech, and oak, at others forming groves through which the Way goes as through a cavern. Hilaire Belloc was convinced that the Way is distinguished by a line of yews and that where it is lost or uncertain one need only look for the yews to find it again. Other writers, following him, have emphasized the connection between the Way and yews, ancient yews that some suppose to have been there for many hundreds or even thousands of years, as though deliberately set in ancient times to mark the Way. I do not understand how Belloc could have come to the conclusion that yews have more than a fortuitous connection with the Pilgrims' Way, and I assert that not only do they not have any such significance but that there are few yews along the Way that are more than a hundred or two hundred years old, not counting those that may be found in churchyards. Yews grow in quantities along the Way, just as do many other kinds of trees, for no other reason than that they are native trees, this is their habitat, and they are not particular about soil. I am convinced that they would be found on the lower levels too, in the fields, if it were not that the leaves and the fruit are poisonous to cattle and farmers destroy the trees. The age of yews is greatly misunderstood. The girth of the bole is no good indication, for yews throw up several stems which fuse into one, and the thickness that results is misleading. The great boles impress, certainly, and the dark and cavernous growth and the wrinkled bark overawe the naïve, but experts doubt that yews are anything like as ancient as popular belief supposes, that, indeed, a yew a thousand years old is a rare exception.

2 The Antiquity of the Way

It is a curious fact of English topography and communications that there has never been, in historical times, a satisfactory continuous road running from west to east across the southern part of the country. This fact prevails today: you may drive from Penzance to Canterbury, but not on a continuous road— the route is rather a series of local roads, some minor, strung together and varying in width, surface, and quality. Sometimes, at junctions, you must sidestep north or south in order to recover once more your latitudinal trend. This lack of a main route is made more strange by the fact that Winchester was the capital of the Wessex kings, who came to govern the greater part of England, and that Canterbury was from an early date the headquarters of the Christian Church in this country. It might be supposed that kings and their courtiers, bishops, clerics, traders, common men, and herds with their beasts would have had frequent reason to pass from one to the other of these centres and would have trodden out a more distinct road, a road that should have become in our time a main highway. There is small evidence that they did, just as there is little to show that the Romans before them had any need of such a road. It may be that the Romans and the Saxons afterwards made use of the ancient track that Hilaire Belloc called the Old Road, and which is now called the Pilgrims' Way, between Winchester and Canterbury, and with the lack of better communication it is probable that they did, but it never became a paved road along its whole course. A number of Roman villas and other Roman buildings seem to have been connected with the Old Road by being built on sites that it would conveniently serve, just as many houses or farm-houses of the present day stand distant from a road but linked with it by lanes or drives.

The Pilgrims' Way, however, is far older than the time of the Romans or of the Christian pilgrims. This ancient way was trodden out first by the feet of neolithic tribes, the kind of men who left their sign manual in the form of megalithic burial chambers at Addington, Trottiscliffe, and Kit's Coty; and later by the men of the bronze age and the iron age, coming from the Continent or from various parts of the south-east of England to journey along a common line to Salisbury Plain and the great temples of Stonehenge and Avebury. Stonehenge, as it became in alterations a century or so after its first building, some sixteen centuries before the Romans became masters in Britain, was one of the greatest and most important temples in Europe. For John Aubrey in the seventeenth century and William Stukeley in the eighteenth century it was a temple of the druids, where, they supposed, savage rites were performed with pitiless sacrifices. But it is far older than the druids. This was the temple, the cathedral of an able and artistic people, the people of the splendid Wessex culture, whose achievements and ability we see only partially in their monuments, in the contents of their graves, and in artefacts. They were not boors islanded in their country as a Victorian peasant was islanded within the bounds of his parish. They knew of other countries and traded with them across the sea, importing and exporting copper and gold from Ireland, and bringing home, among other things, amber from the Baltic and faience beads from Egypt. They could not have built Stonehenge without capable architects, masons, and engineers, nor without a large force of labourers. Whether those labourers were slaves or free men we have no means of knowing, but the complexity of the structure, its size, and its sophistication imply a settled order in a country firmly governed by able kings or chiefs who had many men and ample wealth at their command. It implies also that these kings and their subjects had a religion in which their belief was as deep and intense and as ceremonial as that out of which rose the great medieval cathedrals of the Christian world. It is easy to say that they were ignorant and worshipped the sun or the moon—just as it would be easy but erroneous to declare that Christians worship the orient because their churches commonly point in that direction. It is by no means too airy a flight of imagination to picture the people of the later new stone age, of the bronze age, and of the iron age flocking from all directions, travelling along the flanks or the ridges of the several chains of uplands that converge on

Salisbury Plain, a convergence that may have been the geographical factor in the choice of the site of Stonehenge. One of these routes followed the line of our Old Road and that of the Hoar Way. This route would have been the one commonly used by people coming from the Continent—it entailed the shortest possible sea voyage, with land comfortingly in view throughout all or the greater part of the crossing. Then, around the Kentish coast there was a useful choice of landing-places if the wind, the weather, or the tides should prove difficult. For these landings around the shores of Kent an inland gathering place or settlement must be postulated, a place where travellers would congregate to begin their overland journey, in company or in caravan. Such a place was the site of Canterbury. The settlement that was to become the city of Canterbury may, then, have had its origins far back in the second millennium before Christ.

The ancient route did not go by way of Winchester. That part of the country was left aside, on the left hand, by those who set their faces towards Stonehenge. They left the present Pilgrims' Way at Farnham, where they took the track called the Harrow Way or Hoar Way, that is to say the ancient way, the grey or hoary way. Ancient it was and grey or whitish grey it may well have been, for from Farnham into Wiltshire and on into Dorset, far beyond Stonehenge, it runs over the chalk uplands. 'Old Road' and 'Hoar Way' are but names for different lengths of the one ancient road.

Farnham, it may be noted, is one of the few towns directly on the ancient way: elsewhere the Hoar Way and the Pilgrims' Way seem to avoid settlements. It would be more accurate to say that settlements, which came later than the Way, were built, with their churches, at a distance from it, some to the north and more to the south. The reason is not arcane or difficult. The chalk downs and plains are dry; that is why the ways keep to the chalk where they are able, in order to have dry going underfoot. But settlements must have water, and the springs are generally lower down, at the junction of the chalk and the greensand or where the impervious gault brings the water to the surface. So the settlements grew into villages, and the villages into towns along the southern slopes of the downs, where the sun was genial, and some linked themselves together by lower paths parallel with the Old Road, lower paths that in our era have turned into major roads.

From Farnham westwards the Hoar Way goes south of Basingstoke and then over lonely country to run between St Mary Bourne and Whitchurch, and so south-west along minor surfaced roads to pass north of Andover. So far it can be traced and walked. West of Andover the route is less certain and passes from the survey of this book. It is asserted that the ancient track ran to Marazion in Cornwall, and that it went there, in the bronze age at least, because in Cornwall tin was to be found. It may be that the Cornish tin-mines were as rich as any in the ancient world, comparing only with mines in Spain. Tin was a metal that made possible a great step forward in the history of mankind, a step from the crudity and difficulty of the stone ages and from the softness of copper in the first use of metal, to an age in which tools, utensils, ornaments, and weapons were made of that hard alloy of copper and tin that is bronze. Empires and kingdoms were founded on bronze, and for kings, princes, and soldiers the alloy became as necessary to the art of war as to the arts of peace. For such a commodity, never sufficient, traders would go far. The mines of Cornwall attracted the Phoenicians, the dark-eyed, dark-skinned, nautical Semitics from the east coast of the Mediterranean. These men sailed the length of that long sea to pass through the Pillars of Hercules into the Atlantic and braved the storms of the Bay of Biscay to buy tin in the Cassiterides, the islands of tin. The Cassiterides have been doubtfully identified with the Isles of Scilly, with St Michael's Mount, and even with the Isle of Wight. Where in reality the Cassiterides were you may guess as well as anyone, for nobody knows. That is as the Phoenicians wanted it to be: they kept their trade secrets strictly, and where they found their cargoes of tin or tin-ore was a secret worth keeping. With tin from Cornwall and tin from mines in Spain, both carried in their ships, the Phoenicians were the prosperous middlemen of Europe in a trade with little competition.

Within Britain ore or metal was probably exported to various parts of the country in panniers on the backs of asses or mules. Among the routes in use would have been the Hoar Way, all along to Farnham, and then by the Old Road along the downs to Canterbury or whatever depot may have stood there at that time. From there the metal could be exported by the short sea crossing to the Continental coast and to those markets out of reach of Phoenician influence or supply. This supposition brings a temptation to derive 'Hoar Way' from 'Ore Way', but both 'hoar' and 'ore' are Saxon words, not in use in Britain until nearly a millennium after the bronze age came to an end. For the Saxons the antiquity of the Hoar Way was as difficult to grasp as it is for us; it was simply the ancient road, made by men unknown in a time long past.

The Pilgrims' Way from Farnham eastwards through Surrey and Kent is really the continuation of the ancient Hoar Way. If medieval pilgrims coming from Winchester used it, it was because they found it there, marked out on the ground and conveniently leading to the best travel conditions, the best crossings of rivers, and the briefest practicable route. It might by the twelfth century have become partly overgrown and obscured, though it is probable that traders and drovers with their beasts kept it in being, just as they did centuries later, when they took to the hill paths to avoid the tolls of the turn-pikes.

We have, however, no documentary evidence of anyone regularly using the Way, drovers, traders, or pilgrims, no evidence of the generations of moving feet and the sharp hoofs of beasts, other than may be derived from the ground itself. The ground is not mute. Where many men tread throughout the centuries, the earth remembers. On hillsides with firm ground the passage of feet crumbles the material of the slope and shifts it downwards, where it is compacted by following feet, and in this way a shelf or platform or terrace is formed. The more this terrace is used, the more distinct it becomes, and the more strongly it attracts later travellers to follow it. There are many lengths of such terraces along the Way, with a sharp rise on one hand and on the other a sharp drop to lower ground. This drop is one of the factors that have deterred the ploughman from venturing upon the Way and which have helped to preserve it. Over many stretches the terrace runs, today, just within wood-land and forms easy, shaded paths.

Where the ground is softer the ancient way becomes a hollow way. Over certain stretches the Pilgrims' Way runs in a close hollow, a miniature canyon that you might suppose to have been formed by the rush and erosion of a stream; but there is no stream here. What has happened is that the earth has been rubbed to powder by the tread of feet, powder that has been lifted and blown away by the winds or swept away by the rains. As the process, once started, goes on, the path becomes more and more distinct, more deeply sunk in the ground, and later travellers follow exactly in the line of those who went before them, accepting gratefully the distinct path and the shelter from the winds (*plate* 3). In Weston Wood, where the Way passes uncharacteristically along the north side of a hill, and in some other places, terrace and hollow way are combined in one. Many generations have passed along the path to cut certain hollow ways several feet into the ground.

Throughout this book I have assumed that pilgrims used the Pilgrims' Way from Winchester to Canterbury. Though obviously many people have used the route, there is no factual evidence that pilgrims to the shrine of Saint Thomas of Canterbury did come along the Old Road. There is no mention of the Way as a pilgrims' route earlier than the eighteenth century, long after the dissolution of the monasteries and the decay of the pilgrim spirit in England. It was for this reason that Hilaire Belloc in his entertaining book spoke of the 'Old Road' rather than of the 'Pilgrims' Way', partly because of the uncertainty of its use by Christian pilgrims and partly, and more importantly, because the Old Road is indeed old and the pilgrims, if any, were mere latecomers who prevailed for a time historically brief, that is, for three centuries and a half. It may be said only that it is probable that pilgrims did use the Way, and that anyone travelling from Winchester to Canterbury in the twelfth century and long after would have had little choice but to use it; for the many miles of tumbled lowland and hill country to the south of the downs were covered with the great, deep forest of Andredesweald, thick woodland full of dangers real or imagined. The Way must have been the route taken by Henry II in July 1174, when he landed at Southampton and rode eastwards to make his belated but massive and painful penance at Canterbury. If the king himself took the Pilgrims' Way as one of the earliest of pilgrims to the Canterbury shrine, then surely others must have followed in his steps for the same end, the remission of sins to be found in worship and in penance at the tomb of a martyr, and the participation in glory at his shrine.

In this book I have used the terms 'Old Road' and 'Pilgrims' Way' for the same path or track. This usage is not indiscrimiate. Though I firmly believe that pilgrims did travel on this path between Winchester and Canterbury, it is absurd to speak of the Pilgrims' Way in reference to periods earlier than the pilgrimage. In pagan contexts I have therefore adopted Belloc's term the 'Old Road' and in Christian contexts the 'Pilgrims' Way'.

Belloc, it should be noted, does not everywhere agree with the indications of the Pilgrims' Way on the Ordnance maps of his day; nor is his route everywhere identical with that shown on present Ordnance maps, which nevertheless have been affected by his arguments.

3 Pilgrims and Pilgrimages

The word 'pilgrim' comes from a Latin word 'peregrinus', which means a foreigner. It is clear that this description originated, not from the point of view of the pilgrim, but from that of the people in whose countries he wandered. Even in his own country, travelling to native shrines, a pilgrim would have been regarded as a foreigner, an 'incomer', as soon as he had gone only a few miles from his hearth and dwelling, from his own village or town. This attitude is familiar even today.

The pilgrim would find customs and manners different from those he was used to, and the language or dialect not everywhere easily understood. Near or far on his journey, at home or abroad, he suffered inconvenience and expense, and often danger from disease, accident, theft, or violence, in order to visit and to be able to boast thereafter that he had visited places made holy by the historical presence of Christ or of one of his disciples or apostles, or of one of his saints. In such places, by reason of their special sanctity, miracles occurred and sins might be forgiven, whether of the past or the future, or, more immediately, a disease might be cured or a sorrow assuaged.

The prime pilgrimage was to the Holy Land, to those sites impregnated with wonder and with potency by the bodily presence of Jesus when he dwelt on earth. There the pilgrim saw the very places mentioned in the Bible: the village of Bethlehem where Jesus was born, Nazareth where he lived, Jerusalem, the Garden of Gethsemane on Mount Olivet, the lake of Galilee, the hill of Golgotha, the Holy Sepulchre, and all those other places he knew as names in Scripture and now saw as realities to which he could match and fire his imagination.

The journey to the Holy Land was fraught with difficulties and perils. The easiest and perhaps the most secure way, though it went in danger of storm, wreck, and pirates, was by ship through the Mediterranean, but many pilgrims had neither stomach nor money for such voyages and preferred to travel

overland on foot or on horseback, begging or buying their food
and shelter from the many hospices, monasteries, and castles
on the way. Such a pilgrimage would take months to accom-
plish, yet Chaucer's indomitable, gat-toothed Wife of Bath had
been to the Holy Land three times as well as to Rome, Boulogne,
Cologne, and Compostella, and others, too, made repeated
journeys. It may be that many pilgrims did not seek to travel
quickly; the word 'saunter' is reputed to have come from the
leisurely progress of pilgrims to the Holy Land, the 'Sainte
Terre', just as 'to roam' is said to come from pilgrimages to the
city of Rome, and 'to canter' from Canterbury. All these words
suggest a pleasurable outing rather than a hard duty.

The pilgrimage to Rome was the next best thing to that to the
Holy Land. When the Holy Land, despite the efforts of the
Crusaders, was closed to Christians, Rome attracted those who
would have made the longer journey. Rome was not only the
centre and heart of the Christian world, it was also the place
where Saint Peter and Saint Paul were buried, and these saints
must have been of more moment in the minds of pilgrims than
was the ecclesiastical pre-eminence of the Vatican.

Many other centres attracted pilgrims, with a catchment
local or international. From the thirteenth century the town of
Loretto in Italy was a special magnet because of its Santa Casa
or Holy House, the house, once in Nazareth, in which the
Virgin and Saint Joseph lived with the child Jesus. The Holy
House, it was believed, had been borne through the air by
flying angels and, after being deposited first in Dalmatia in
1291, came three years later, by the same despatch, to Loretto.
It survives there, a small, modest building of brick, but solidly
built, and it serves to show the muscular power of angels. The
same delivery staff carried the Holy Stair to its present resting-
place in Rome—twenty-eight broad, white marble steps
climbed by Jesus when he was brought to meet Pilate, and
which are now climbed by many pilgrims on their knees. These
examples of holy porterage serve to introduce the many
absurdities that entered into the business of pilgrimage in the
middle ages.

Outside Rome, the best-loved object of pilgrimage was in the
little town of Compostella in Galicia in north-west Spain. Here

lay the body, or perhaps only the skull, for Toulouse also claimed the body, of Saint James—'Sant Iago di Compostela'. Pilgrims who had been or were going to Compostella wore on their hats or as a brooch on their clothing a symbolic scallop shell, which marked them out as Companions of Saint James. Such was the popularity of this beautiful shell and the attraction of the shrine that in time the shell became a sign or emblem of pilgrimage in general. It was so when Sir Walter Raleigh, expecting to be beheaded next day, wrote his odd and beautiful poem on 'The Passionate Man's Pilgrimage':

> Give me my Scallop shell of quiet,
> My staffe of Faith to walke vpon,
> My scrip of Ioy, Immortal diet,
> My bottle of saluation:
> My Gowne of Glory, hopes true gage,
> And thus Ile take my pilgrimage

The shell was not, of course, exclusively used by Christian pilgrims. It appears in art and architecture from a time long before the birth of Christ and was used in secular or pagan associations long afterwards—Boticelli's Venus rising, anadyomene, from the waves will come to mind at once.

Not all churches could have bodies of saints, but it was laid down in 787 by the Council of Nicaea that every church ought to have a relic of some kind to justify its dedication or consecration. The rising fever of pilgrimage and the monetary benefits to be derived from it by churches and monasteries brought into being or brought forth a very varied range of objects, many of them unlikely, to attract the devotions and the donations of pilgrims and to offer a series of intangible benefits nearly as extraordinary. Nothing could be too far-fetched, too absurd, to satisfy the religious hunger for wondrous things evinced by pilgrims. One might accept that the True Cross was found in the Holy Land in the fourth century by that pious and indefatigable archaeologist the Empress Helena of Constantinople, and that it was afterwards cut into pieces and distributed far and wide; that the bodies of the Magi were discovered by the same lady and that in 1164 they were brought to Cologne; that the Crown of Thorns rescued by Saint Louis from Venetian moneylenders in 1238 and enshrined in the Saint Chapelle was the true crown (it is now in Notre Dame); that the three Marys (or the two Marys and Martha) were cast away in a small boat off the coast of Palestine and came ashore to die in Les Saintes-Maries-de-la-Mer in Provence; that the Seven Sleepers of Ephesus lie in Marseilles; that Saint Joseph of Arimathea came to Glastonbury and is buried there (after having previously brought his infant nephew Jesus on a brief visit); that the Holy Coat of Trier is the seamless garment Jesus wore to his Crucifixion; that the Holy Shroud of Turin wrapped his body and from that circumstance derives its mysterious negative image of the features and limbs of Christ: all these you may believe if you will because they are strange and potent, and may be possible, and because wonder and magic and faith have not quite disappeared from the world. But many other objects of pilgrimage are yet more improbable or fantastic. The brothers Felix and Thomas Platter, for example, medical students in Montpellier in the sixteenth century, whose separate journals I have translated,[1] saw several strange things in their travels in Languedoc and Provence. At Saint Siffrein in Carpentras there was a horse's bridle made from a nail of the True Cross; at Les Saintes-Maries-de-la-Mer the head of Lazarus; and at Marseilles the alabaster pitcher used by Jesus when he washed the disciples' feet, a tooth of Saint John, and the very thirty pieces of silver paid to Judas as the wages of betrayal, together with the lantern Judas carried into the garden of Gethsemane. In England there were the coals of Saint Laurence at Durham and at Walsingham and other places phials of the Virgin's milk— Erasmus was shown the Walsingham specimen and remarked that it looked like white of egg and chalk. Even more incredible, among a host of strange things, but nevertheless believed in by many pilgrims, were: the tears of Christ, in a phial; another phial containing some of his breath; yet another containing holy blood from his circumcision; the tip of Lucifer's tail lost in an altercation with a saint; the mark of Cain (how was that preserved?); and the sound of the bells of Solomon's temple (in

---

[1] *Beloved Son Felix* by Felix Platter, and *Journal of a Younger Brother* by Thomas Platter, both published by Fredrick Muller Ltd.

a bottle!). It is obvious that the supply of relics was an open
field for fakers, forgers, and confidence tricksters, a field
widened by the avarice for relics of the public in general: in the
market in Avignon the half-sceptical Thomas Platter bought a
bowl made from clay of the field in which God created Adam.
Churches gathered large collections of such things. Canterbury
had over four hundred relics and Wittenberg in Germany no
less than nineteen thousand. So many pieces of the True Cross
were scattered about that there were enough, as was remarked,
to supply several entire crosses. Even in the middle ages there
were sceptics who scouted the value of relics and their multi-
plication; but they had to meet such arguments as that the
True Cross, being highly miraculous, would obviously possess
the power to duplicate itself—if seven loaves and a few little
fishes could feed the multitude, how could one strain at too
many pieces of the True Cross? The vernicle or sudary of
Veronica, that is the towel with which she wiped the face of the
cross-burdened Christ, whose features were ever afterwards
imprinted upon it, was also multiplied, with examples in Rome,
in Jerusalem, and elsewhere. Mere folding, it could be
explained, could have brought this about, with the image
imprinting itself through layer upon layer.

It really does not seem to have mattered whether a relic
was genuine or not. What was important was that pilgrims
should have faith in it, for then it would serve its purpose, it
would earn money for the church in which it was kept, and it
might work miracles as well as any other. Nor was it important
that a relic should have close local connection or relevance.
Relics were brought from afar to endow a church or a chapel or
a monastery. Monks or priests who envied another house its
possession of some successful relic were not above attempting
to steal it or a part of it, as the bones of Bede were stolen from
Jarrow by the sacrist Earlfred of Durham, the crowning
achievement of a career of successful relic pilfering. Some of the
larger shrines in which relics were enclosed served not only to
enhance the glory of the object but also to keep it safe from
purloiners. There is evidence too that monks were not so awed
by the body of a saint, nor so reverent, that they were above
sawing the body in pieces to distribute the head here and sell an

CPW

arm there, as for example the body of Saint Louis of France was parcelled out thirty-eight years after his death.

The shrines were, indeed, most of them marvellous things. A small relic might be enclosed in a lavish and jealously guarded portable box or shrine, as was the Fíacal Phádraig, the tooth of Saint Patrick, lost by the saint in a little church in the west of Ireland and enclosed in a beautiful tabernacle that you may see today in the National Museum in Dublin. There, in Dublin, is also to be seen the equally precious Cross of Cong, made to enshrine a tiny piece of the True Cross. Larger relics and especially the bodies of saints, as for example of Thomas Becket, were enclosed in elaborate architectural constructions ornamented with gold and silver and many kinds of jewels. Some such shrines had rows of apertures in the base, round like portholes or trefoiled or quatrefoiled, through which the coffin of the saint could be seen and touched—there was a special virtue in touching the coffin. At Canterbury one slim and pliable pilgrim managed to get his whole body through one of these apertures in order to lie full length on the coffin. There was a great to-do, with the monks fearing that they would have to dismantle the whole shrine to get him out, but in the end the man emerged by the way he had entered.

Not many shrines of the architectural kind remain complete in the British Isles. Nearly all those that existed were destroyed in the fury of the Reformation by those fell commissioners of the king who are now hated with an intensity altogether unforgiving. Notable exceptions include the shrine of Saint Edward the Confessor at Westminster—Henry VIII shrank from destroying the tomb of a Saxon king, even as he shrank from damaging the fine Decorated tomb at Gloucester built by Edward III for his murdered father Edward II. At Holy Cross in Tipperary, in Ireland, there is a beautiful and delicate shrine probably built to house the piece of the True Cross from which the abbey took its name—the piece is still in existence in the Ursuline Convent at Blackrock, near Cork. In a number of churches fragments of a former shrine have been put together like a jig-saw puzzle— e.g., the shrine of Saint Frideswide at Oxford, of Saint Thomas de Cantelupe at Hereford, of Saint Werburgh at Chester, and of Saint Alban at Saint Albans. At Dorchester on Thames the shrine of Saint Birinus has been completely recreated. But of the most glorious of these shrines, perhaps not exceeded in richness and splendour even by the royal shrines at Westminster and Gloucester, that of Thomas Becket at Canterbury, not a piece remains, and all that is to be seen where it stood are the hollows in the terrazzo floor worn by the knees of a procession of pilgrims three hundred and twenty years long.

A picture in the thirteenth-century glass of the Miracle Windows in the cathedral shows what the shrine was like. We are lucky to have even that, together with the other windows in this series illustrating the life of Saint Thomas, for Henry VIII decreed that all pictures of the priest who had defied a king, and whom he therefore denounced as a traitor, should be broken down or expurgated. As a result, pictures, sculptures, and stained glass of the man who was once the country's most popular saint are rare in England and when found are often not complete. At Oxford, for instance, a figure of Saint Thomas in stained glass has the face broken out; a priest or bishop perhaps persuaded the king's destroyer that what was done would be enough. At Reigate murals of the life of Thomas were white-washed over.

Also gone is Winchester's more ancient shrine of Saint Swithun. The saint was the tutor of King Alfred, whose body also lay at Winchester. Saint Swithun at Winchester, Saint Thomas at Canterbury, and the Virgin at Walsingham were the objects of the most popular of English pilgrimages, each drawing its adherents from a wide area. Walsingham had a Holy House in the precincts of the monastery, which is now ruined, a house of uncertain origin but sharing by name the glory and the marvel of the airborne Holy House of Loretto. Henry VIII made a pilgrimage to it in 1511, and perhaps again later, walking barefoot the two miles from Barsham Manor. The unfortunate Catherine of Aragon presented to the shrine a full-size effigy of the king in wax, a costly substance at that time. Her hope, and his, was that a son and heir should be born, and indeed a son was born, the infant Prince Henry, a weakly boy who did not last long. The desperate Catherine would have given anything to be the successful mother of a prince. Her six children, except Mary, were all still-born or died in infancy.

Twenty-five years later Henry sent his commissioners to tear down the images and to dissolve the monasteries of Walsingham and to confiscate their possessions. It was not vengeance for his ill success in breeding an heir. Walsingham suffered only what every other religious order and building experienced.

Before the death of Becket, Winchester, with the tombs of Saint Swithun and of Alfred the Great, attracted many more pilgrims than did Canterbury, and it is possible that Christian pilgrims then travelled along the Pilgrims' Way in the reverse sense, to Winchester. The murder of Thomas and the patent offence against sanctuary focused the attention of all Europe on Canterbury and on the immediate miracles that occurred there —the cleverest of publicity officers could not have done more for the cathedral and its prosperity than Becket did by dying so perversely in it. There had been little to choose between the two great monasteries that were close neighbours in Canterbury, those of Christ Church and of Saint Augustine, even though Christ Church included the primacy of England. The murder, the martyrdom of Becket was too much for Saint Augustine's, which could never again compete. The shrine of Becket in Christ Church rapidly became the object of the most valued pilgrimage in all England, and those who would once have gone abroad to Rome or to Constantinople now made their way to Canterbury for the worship of this new and domestic saint.

From all parts of England pilgrim routes led to Canterbury. Inevitably they passed by churches and cathedrals, monasteries and nunneries, and many pilgrims paused to pray or to rest in these places. But the main streams of people and of money led to Canterbury and churches on the routes enviously took stock of their assets in order more fully to tap this flow. Rochester displayed the shrine of William of Perth, who had been murdered by his servant, and at Boxley there was the notorious Rood of Grace, a moving, frowning, and smiling figure that had fallen into the hands of the monks by a heaven-sent accident— or so the monks would have it.

Pilgrimages and the cultivation of relics did not come to an end with the declarations of Martin Luther or the destructive cupidity of Henry VIII. In the four centuries and more that have passed since Henry's reign and the time of Luther, many old pilgrimages have continued or have been revived and some new ones have come into existence. Lourdes, of course, is famous throughout the world. Walsingham has another Holy House, but not on the original site (and not delivered by angels!). In Ireland the ancient and curious pilgrimage to the summit of Croagh Patrick, in Mayo, where Saint Patrick once mused for forty days, was revived in the nineteenth century and now draws some eighty thousand people every July to climb the 3,500 feet of this handsome quartzite cone. Knock, also in Ireland, is visited yearly by half a million pilgrims, who come to worship in a church made holy by the surprising and inexplicable vision seen over a space of two hours in 1879, first by two women and then by the whole village, of Saint Joseph, the Virgin, and the Agnus Dei. In Dublin one of the most recent of saints—too recent to be yet declared officially sanctified—the labourer Matt Talbot, has his following already.

The pilgrims of the middle ages comprised all kinds and conditions of people. Many were poor and some were rich, but most seem to have been of the middle classes, of whom Chaucer's company was typical. Chaucer's people all rode on horseback, a fact that firmly removes them from the poorer pilgrims. In the middle ages there was a recognized pilgrim costume of broad-brimmed hat and russet gown drawn in about the waist with a belt, a rope, or a rosary. On the gown were sewn-on crosses of contrasting colour. The pilgrim furnished himself with a satchel or 'scrip' and a stout stick or staff. You may see a little carving of such a pilgrim at Lincoln, with his wide hat, slung like a shield on his back. Before he set out the pilgrim announced publicly what he meant to do, and went to his church for a service in which his accoutrements and his resolution were blessed by the priest. Chaucer's company, coming a little late in the noon of pilgrimage, were more diversely dressed, in accordance with their means and their position in life.

The aims of pilgrimage were manifold. There was the simple wish to visit a shrine, to enjoy the wonder and the display, and to be somehow conjoined with the sanctity of the past. Then there were the indulgences to be had, indulgences that in the later days became automatic, freely given, and conferring pardon for so many months or years and so many Lents; by the length of the period of indulgence one could measure the value of one shrine against another.

An indulgence was a document on which was written, in spaces left for the purpose, the name of the applicant, the date and the period of validity, and any other matter that might be relevant. The earlier indulgences were written out repetitively by scribes, but there was such a demand for these comforting documents that they were an obvious subject for the new process of printing perfected by Johann Gutenberg in Mainz. Indeed Gutenberg's first essay in commercial or 'jobbing' printing was an indulgence, which he printed in a small blackletter with appropriate spaces to be filled in, like any modern printed form.

There were several kinds of indulgences, distinguished by their duration and the range of their coverage of sins or of locality. Plenary indulgences, at first rare but later becoming as debased as bad coinage, conferred freedom from *temporal* punishment for sins already committed or that might be committed in future. I have italicized the word 'temporal' because it seems to suggest that criminals provided with an indulgence might escape punishment for their crimes. This, of course, was not so. The indulgence freed the holder from the compulsion to do penance in this world for the sins he had committed or might commit. The theory of the origin of indulgences and the justification for their use was that there existed a vast and inexhaustible reservoir of benevolent holiness derived from the deeds of saints, and a measure of this holiness might be conferred, through an indulgence, on any who had money to pay.

There were churchmen and scholars in the middle ages as sceptical of the value of indulgences as they were of the cult of relics in general, but they could do little about it; if they were incautious in their criticism they might find themselves disciplined or excommunicated. The practice was, of course, open to great abuse, abuse best exemplified by the pardoners, who became a notable adjunct to the scene of pilgrimage in its later days. The pardoner was no more than a hawker of indulgences, carrying his stock about by the dozen or the score. He sold his documents wherever he could and to anyone who had sufficient money, filling in the blanks on the spot. A pardoner, it will be remembered, was a member of Chaucer's company; he enhanced the sale of his pardons by a display of relics:

> For in his male he hadde a pilwe-beer*
> Which that he seyde was Oure Lady veyl:
> He seyde he hadde a gobet of the seyl
> That Seint Peter hadde, whan that he wente
> Upon the see, til Jhesu Crist hym hente.
> He hadde a croys of latoun ful of stones,
> And in a glas he hadde pigges bones.

With these things, says Chaucer, he earned more money in a day than a parson got in two months. Chaucer's characters are illustrated in delightful little drawings in the Ellesmere manuscript. Here the Pardoner is shown with his hat-brim turned up and on it a vernicle, a recognition sign that seems also to have been borne by palmers. It was the proliferation and abuse of indulgences that offended Luther and was an important factor in the Reformation.

A palmer was a kind of professional pilgrim, a homeless man who spent his life on the roads to this shrine or that, beginning another pilgrimage the moment a previous one was completed. He wore a palm leaf or part of one on his hat as a sign that he had been to Jerusalem, and from this sign derived his description. He might have been a deeply pious and religious man, or an inveterate and unwearying traveller, or simply a tramp, a drop-out covering his retreat from life under a convenient title. The palmer would offer his services to men rich enough to make a pilgimage by proxy, for this was possible and permitted. While the rich man remained comfortably at home the palmer trod the pilgrim ways in his name, visiting whatever shrine he had been directed to. Caspar Fry, a man Felix Platter met in Montpellier together with several Companions of Saint James, was such a proxy, making his fifth pilgrimage to Compostella on account of stay-at-home employers.

* pillow-case.

It is evident in the *Canterbury Tales* that by Chaucer's day a pilgrimage had become largely a holiday, an outing, a journey to be enjoyed for its own sake and for the company in which one travelled. Chaucer's company, starting from the Tabard inn in Southwark, agreed, under the chairmanship of Mine Host, to tell each other stories, some of which proved to be distinctly secular in character. But the journey was not aimless. At the end of it was the shrine of the murdered Becket, who had really lived and had really walked among Englishmen and was now a saint. A gift to the shrine, a prayer or two, and penance and true humility might well count for something in this world and for more in the next. The least reward would be the satisfaction of having completed a notable pilgrimage, with at heart perhaps a glow of piety and of faith.

That was not all there was to experience at a shrine. There were, of course, the miracles. Miracles were constantly happening at shrines, just as they are believed today to happen at Lourdes and at many other places. Those who suffered from incurable ailments hoped to find relief at a shrine such as that of Thomas Becket, while those who were whole might obtain a cure for someone else, for a wife or a child or a friend. I do not think it can be doubted that miracles, or what are taken for miracles, do occur at shrines, and not only at Christian shrines. It may be that such cures refer to maladies of psychological or psychosomatic description, maladies in which the mind is the cause and maybe the cure. There are many people who claim to have been cured and many doctors and physicians who can testify to such cures. But many more sufferers return saddened and in despair from pilgrimages on which they had set out in high expectation.

Chaucer and his thirty pilgrims never got to Canterbury—or rather, the book ends before the culmination of the journey. I do not think that it was left unfinished by accident or lack of interest. While we might have learned much of value about Canterbury in the fourteenth century, the return journey of the pilgrims to Southwark could not have been but a weak ending, an anticlimax, lacking object. There was, however, another man to take up the tale, an anonymous poet and a lesser one, who wrote a sequel to *The Canterbury Tales* in which he makes the company stay at the Chequer of the Hope, an inn that stood at the corner of the Mercery near the cathedral.

A successful pilgrim who had reached and worshipped at a shrine was glad to have a souvenir, a brooch or a badge to remind him of his achievement and to show to others that he had done what he had done. In every pilgrim centre there arose an industry to supply these things, or, as in the case of scallop shells, to prepare and stock them for sale. Many symbols were cast in lead or cut in tin or latten, and perhaps some were embroidered on cloth, though I have seen none of this kind. There was no limit to the number of symbols that might be bought and worn and some pilgrims returned rattling with the sound of swinging bits of metal or tinkling with dangling shells. At Canterbury there was a variety to choose from. There were little metal bells, to be hung on harness, from which the wild flower of the Canterbury bell derives its name—these flowers still grow plentifully beside the Pilgrims' Way. There were also several sorts of representations of Saint Thomas—busts, seated and standing figures, and the saint on horseback—and there were simple initials in blackletter. Then there were ampullae or phials, often mounted on some kind of decorative background. These represented the most potent of the wonders of Canterbury, the blood and brains of the saint, which the monks had hastily scraped from the floor of the transept in which he had been killed. This matter was deemed to perform miracles. It had another wonder too, that the monks were able to make it go so far, even though they mixed it with water to extend it, for they were still supplying it when the monastery was dissolved by Henry VIII in 1538.

There was no doubt a corpus of information and of advice on which a prospective pilgrim might draw before he began his journey. In the later days, at least, there was a printed guide, first issued in 1498 by Wynkyn de Worde, and reprinted at least twice, in 1515 and 1524. This was the *Informacōn for Pylgrymes into the Holy Londe*. It was a kind of medieval Baedeker or Michelin, giving routes and distances to various places, currency exchange rates, and modes of travel. There was practical advice on inns and kinds of beds, on hiring an ass and

on the best place to choose in a ship. The pilgrim was urged to
take on board a cage with half a dozen hens or chickens, 'for ye
shall haue nede of them many tymes. And bye you half a
busshell of myle sede at Venyse for theym.' The author gave
cautions about eating fruit, especially 'melons and suche colde
fruytes, for they be not accordyng to our complexyon & they
gendre a blody fluxe', and advises concerning the place where
Jesus fasted, because it is 'passyngly hote and ryght hyghe . . .
whan ye come downe agayne for any thynge drynke noo water,
but rest you a lytyll. And thenne ete brede and drynke clere
wyne wythout water, for water after that grete heete gendreth
a flyxe or a feuour, or bothe that many one have deyed therof.'
Gippy tummy was evidently as likely among travellers in the
middle ages as it is today. There are only three copies of this
enchanting book in existence, one of each edition, but a facsimile
was published in 1893.

4 The Hooly Blisful Martir

The story, the tragedy with every element of sombre inevitability, of Henry II and Thomas Becket is that of two men ushered by fate and their own obstinacy, obduracy, and simple native stubbornness to an end in violence and murder. Neither man would yield an inch to the other on the ground he chose to defend in the long argument concerning the rights and privileges of monarchs in relation to the jurisdiction and independence of the Church. Like a play, with peals of thunder from the wings and dark foreboding that holds the audience in their seats, who nevertheless already know the end, the conflict moves on and is intensified until with a flash of arms the more vulnerable of the two contestants is struck and dies. But that is not the end. The audience is about to rise when suddenly the drums roll and the curtain goes up on another scene in which the spirit of the murdered man is triumphant and acclaimed by all, even by his late enemy. Christopher Marlowe, who was born in Canterbury, might have made of it a resounding drama of high sentiment and fine phrase; or Shakespeare might have written a history full of love and grandeur and resolving the strange dichotomy of Thomas the principal character. Neither Marlowe nor Shakespeare chose this theme, however, and not because it was not a fit subject for their pens: they lived in a time when to glorify Thomas Becket could have cost them their heads.[1]

Henry II, the first of the Angevin dynasty of English kings, and Thomas Becket, the son of a Norman merchant in London, were for a season the closest of friends, such friends as it is possible for king and subject to be. Yet the two men were utterly different and diverse. Henry was some fifteen years the

---

[1] In 1653 Humphrey Moseley registered *Cardennio* by Mr Fletcher and Shakespeare, and added 'Henry ye first & Henry ye 2d, by Shakespeare and Davenport'. The manuscripts were burned by Moseley's servant Betsy Baker, who found some pages useful for lining 'pye bottoms'.

junior of the other, red-haired, unprepossessing, hot-tempered, violent, coarse, and given to outbursts of uncontrolled and savage ill temper, which he would as often repent. So he has been described, yet he was much more than this. He was a good and fearless soldier, a capable and ruthless organizer, powerful, persistent in his intentions, authoritarian, even totalitarian, and determined to govern his realm in the way he saw fit, with the Church subordinate and aiding. In his person he combined, with the resolution and determination, some of the worst features of his Norman and Norse forebears; he was ebullient, bullying, fell, and drastic, lascivious and libidinous, and though nominally a Christian king in a Christian country he behaved too often like a pagan and a savage. He was a man to beware of, a man not to fall foul of, if you valued your freedom and your life. He could dissemble when he chose, disarm and charm when it was profitable, and yet be genuinely kind and generous. And he could punish pitilessly, remember an affront or an insult until occasion arose for revenge, and persecute ceaselessly and unflinchingly any who opposed him.

Henry was one of the most powerful men of his time. He was King of England, and not only King of England, of this small island off the coast of Europe, which had been conquered by his great-grandfather and which had not yet fully absorbed its conquerors: he was also a powerful noble on the Continent, as Duke of Normandy and Count of Anjou, and through other inheritances and those of his wife Eleanor was master of lands that extended from the Scottish border to the Channel and from there down to the Pyrenees. Normandy, Brittany, Maine, Anjou, were his, with Poitou, Guienne, Gascony, and Auvergne, among other territories. He governed more of France than did the King of France himself, and yet owed homage and fealty for his French possessions to the French king, homage he might pay when it suited him and ignore when it did not.

Henry was born in 1133 in Le Mans, the son of Geoffrey Plantagenet, Count of Anjou, and of his wife Matilda, daughter of Henry I of England. His claim to the English throne was through his mother, who had battled and raised civil war in England against King Stephen and had at last arranged the succession so that Henry should succeed instead of Stephen's son Eustace. The death of Eustace later made Henry's accession certain.

Henry ascended the throne in 1154. He was the founder of that line of kings commonly called Plantagenets but by historians named Angevins (from Anjou). The line endured from 1154 until 1399, the longest tenure of any English dynasty.

It seems incredible that such a man as Henry, whose perception was acute and his judgement of character good, could so have misunderstood the man who at his instance was elected to the see of Canterbury; yet he did misjudge him and that misjudgement was at the root of the tragedy that followed.

Henry saw in Thomas Becket a capable and honest man, a loyal friend, and a faithful servant. He thought that as archbishop Becket would remain what he had been, a king's man. What he did not see was that Becket was and always had been an out-and-outer, a man who dedicated himself utterly to the service in which he found himself and made no exceptions to the demands he believed that service to impose. As chancellor and boon companion of Henry he was everything the king desired—able in his work, joyous in sport and in the chase, and brave in battle. As archbishop he was the servant and minister of God and the Church, and never what Henry had hoped he would be, a tool and an implement.

Thomas of London, later known as Thomas Becket or Thomas à Becket, was born in London in 1118, the son of Gilbert Becket and his wife Matilda. His parents were Normans, his father of a family that had come to England from Rouen, while his mother was from Caen. There is a pretty fable, not current until after the death of Becket, when it appeared in the *Legenda Aurea* printed by Pynson, that his mother was a Saracen princess. Gilbert Becket is supposed to have gone on a crusade to the Holy Land and to have been captured there. During his imprisonment he fell in love with his captor's daughter and she with him. One day he escaped and was able to make his way back to London. The girl immediately set off after him, with only two words of English to find her way. When she needed direction she cried 'London, London!' and miraculously she landed unharmed in England. In London she cried out to anyone who would listen 'Becket! Becket!' and so was brought to

Gilbert. The account does not suggest a joyful reunion. Gilbert was puzzled what to do with her, but on being advised that he should marry the girl he did so at once, and Thomas was conceived that very night.

Thomas received a good education at Merton and in the schools of London and then, in his teens, was sent to Paris to study theology. There he remained for five years. It is unlikely that he intended to become a priest, but rather to take what were known as minor orders. He became a cleric, which is to say that he became an educated man, a man who could read and write, for 'cleric' in his day meant little more than that—the modern word 'clerk' has the same derivation. Though he might not have intended to become a priest, Becket seems to have taken a vow of chastity during his sojourn in Paris, a vow that he kept throughout his life; it was the first important evidence of his tendency to take things to extremes.

When he returned home he found his family in financial straits and he took a job with a prosperous relative distinguished by the crisply commercial name of Osbert Huit Deniers. Later, Thomas came to the notice of Theobald, Archbishop of Canterbury, who took him into his household.

Theobald's was a brilliant household, full of clever and intelligent young men and some notable older ones—it has been said that it was like a university in miniature. Theobald liked the tall young man with the clear voice and engaging manners and showed him great favour, and in doing so made for Becket a jealous and life-long enemy, Roger Pont l'Evêque, who later became Archbishop of York. Theobald took Becket to Rome with him in 1143 and later sent him to study ecclesiastical and canon law at Bologna and Auxerre. Becket's next journey abroad was with Theobald to a council at Reims, where they went against the express wishes of King Stephen.

Theobald's relations with the king, were not, indeed, always happy, and they were at their worst when Theobald refused to crown Eustace, the king's son. Stephen, as did Henry II later, wished his son to be crowned during his, Stephen's, lifetime, in an attempt to secure the succession. It was in furtherance of this difference that Thomas was sent to Rome in 1151 to dissuade the Curia from sanctioning the coronation of Eustace. Thomas was already learning to be Henry's man. Two years later, with Eustace dead, Theobald reconciled Stephen and Henry.

In 1156 Theobald recommended Thomas to Henry, who was now king, for the office of chancellor, an office in which Thomas had control of the royal writs and the distribution of ecclesiastical patronage. Theobald hoped that Becket, so bright a star of his household, would, in his new position, favour the Church and support the various privileges conferred on it by Stephen. Theobald was the first to be disappointed by Thomas's switchable loyalty. As a member of the archbishop's household Thomas had been on the side of the archbishop and the Church. Now in the king's service he was the king's man *à outrance* and the interests of the Church now came second to those of the king. Under his administration the Church was heavily taxed to support Henry's foreign wars. To the archbishop and the priests it seemed that Becket had 'plunged his sword into the bowels of his mother'.

Becket even followed his king to the wars, and on one occasion accepted single combat against a French knight and unhorsed him—Becket, it should be remembered, was a big man, more than six feet tall, and no weakling.

As chancellor he maintained a large and lavish retinue, the magnificence of which was noted at home and abroad, and he was always on the best of terms with his royal patron. King and chancellor were fond of the chase and frequently hunted together and none could have been closer in friendship than Thomas and Henry. It seemed to Henry, when Archbishop Theobald died in 1161, that no man could be better qualified to succeed Theobald than was his faitful and competent chancellor: Theobald had also wished for this, despite Becket's exactions upon the Church.

The one person to doubt the wisdom of this appointment was Becket himself. He is said to have warned the king that nothing but trouble could follow. None the less, Becket, who had never been more than an archdeacon, now took full holy orders and in 1162 received the appointment of archbishop. Henry now had, he must have thought, his own man in the most powerful place in the English Church. Among the things the king hoped for was the coronation of his son as king during his, Henry's, lifetime, exactly what Stephen had wished for in the previous reign, and with the Church as dependent on the throne as it had been in the time of Henry I, nothing, it seemed, could go wrong.

In the light of this simple belief and expectation one cannot help feeling some sympathy for the king in the prompt disappointment of his hopes. Henry was all at once astonished, hurt, and outraged. How could Thomas so betray the demands of friendship and the duty of allegiance? Henry must have felt that he had *made* this man Becket, both as chancellor and archbishop, with his own hands and now his puppet was turning against its creator. Becket was simply following his new allegiance. Whatever he was, Becket was no one's puppet. Now, as he had once been the king's man entirely, he was the Church's man through and through, and where king and Church came into conflict, it was with the Church that he sided.

Becket was now a priest, and as in all things, *à outrance*. He took to wearing a long hair shirt and drawers to irritate the flesh, and to make this supplice more acute he allowed the garments to become filthy and verminous by seldom changing them. From time to time he had himself flogged, in furtherance of that curious belief of the middle ages that masochism and sanctity went together.

There were minor matters in which Becket, in his support of the Church, constantly inflamed the king, but the most important was the position of the ecclesiastical courts. Becket claimed that criminous clerics (which did not necessarily mean priests) should be tried and punished by the ecclesiastical courts, while Henry wanted all criminals to be subject to the secular courts.

It should be explained that almost all educated men at that time were members of the Church, in minor orders or as full priests. Consequently, churchmen of one kind or another were to be found in all offices, public or ecclesiastical, in which the ability to read and to write was necessary. In claiming jurisdiction over clerics, Becket was depriving the secular courts of the right to try men who, though in orders, did secular work outside the orbit of the Church (exactly as Becket himself had done as chancellor to the King), and had offended against the royal authority or the law of the land.

The argument involved the freedom of the Church, and somewhere in this freedom was the desire of the Church to appoint its own officers—in other words to abolish royal patronage, by which Becket himself had come to the see of Canterbury. In pursuit of and opposition to these principles both sides became embittered and sensitive, so that even minor matters, where they might touch upon the question, were blown up to gigantic proportions. From our standpoint eight centuries later it all seems complex, unnecessarily violent, and often petty. We look back from a time in which most of the things that Thomas Becket defended with such dogged persistence have long been lost to the Church and placed in the hands of the secular authority. We cannot easily comprehend how a man who assaulted a royal officer, as one Philip de Brois did in 1163, could claim to be tried by an ecclesiastical court for no better reason than that he was a clerk and could read. For de Brois and others like him the advantage was clear: the ecclesiastical courts dispensed lighter punishments. It was by means of the survival of part of this practice that Ben Jonson, four hundred years later, claiming 'benefit of clergy', was able to escape death for the killing in a fight of an actor called Gabriel Spencer.

Henry offered to compromise, to allow criminous clerics to be tried by the ecclesiastical courts if they were then handed over to the secular power for punishment. Becket could not agree to this. In 1164 Henry set up a council at his palace of Clarendon near Salisbury to draw up a code of 'constitutions', allegedly corresponding to the customs and prerogatives of the Crown in relation to the Church as they had been in the time of Henry I. Among them were provisions that all causes of advowsons or presentations to livings should be tried in the secular courts; that clerics should be tried by the king's justiciary; that no one should leave the country without the king's permission (which, Becket alleged, would stop pilgrimages); that no one holding in chief from the king, nor any of his household, should be excommunicated or subjected to interdict without the king's licence; that no appeal should be made to the Pope without the royal leave; and that all revenues of vacant bishoprics and religious houses should be paid to the king's treasury. One by one Becket objected to these constitutions, and at the close boldly refused to sign them. Asking for time for further consideration he took

DPW

his leave of a court now in uproar, with king and nobles incensed against him and even his own bishops, afraid of what the king might do, not steadfast in support. Others of Becket's party considered that he had been weak not to denounce the constitutions at once.

Becket now came to believe that his life might be in danger and he tried to flee. He took ship at Sandwich, but was twice driven back by contrary winds, difficulties that the sailors, terrified of what the king might inflict upon them for aiding the archbishop, were not too willing to overcome. Becket returned to Canterbury and sat quietly and sadly in a dark corner of his hall, where he was seen by a boy who came to shut the door, who, alarmed, believed that the figure must be a spirit.

Henry, with spies everywhere, was soon informed of Becket's attempt to escape. In the next meeting of the two Henry joked with him about it. The king could very well afford to be genial. His former love of Becket was now quite dissipated and he felt himself the master of the situation. He made little progress however, against Becket's resistance, and Henry now determined to overthrow him. A petty cause was fabricated by having a man lay claim to a piece of Church land. When this man, as was foreseen, lost his case in the ecclesiastical court, the matter was submitted to a secular court and Becket was called to attend in person. Becket, claiming to be ill, sent representatives. These were not accepted and a charge of contempt of the king's court was raised against Becket, who was peremptorily commanded to appear before a parliament in Northampton. This meeting resolved itself into a series of demands on the archbishop for money, one no sooner being dealt with than another was put forward. Henry was determined to humble Becket one way or another, and he raised the demands to a requirement of a statement of the expenditure of large sums received from vacant sees and abbeys. Becket, without warning, could not have been prepared for this. Henry even demanded an account of 500 marks he had given to Becket years before.

The trial dragged on, with Henry intent on humbling his adversary and perhaps hoping that he might be made to resign his see. Eventually, Becket asked for leave and safe conduct to visit the Pope, but this was refused by Henry until it should have been further considered on the morrow. Becket was now certain that violence and perhaps murder was intended and that night he left Northampton, travelling secretly by way of Lincoln and the Fenland monasteries to Sandwich in Kent, where he took to an open boat, the best that could be found for him in these circumstances. It was November and the sea was stormy and cold, but that evening he landed in France at Oie, a few miles from Gravelines. Secrecy was still necessary, for he was in the territory of an enemy, in this case Matthew, Earl of Boulogne, who held a grudge against the archbishop on account of his having opposed a marriage between Matthew and Mary (daughter of King Stephen), who was at that time Abbess of Romsey; such a marriage would have been sacrilegious. In Matthew's country Becket travelled as a lay brother, 'Brother Christian', in company with another monk, called Scailman. On at least two occasions they were in danger of being exposed, but eventually they arrived safely at Soissons, in the territory of the King of France.

In England, Henry, hearing of the flight of the archbishop, was furious and he at once sent off a group of bishops antagonistic to Becket, and including his old enemy Roger Pont l'Evêque, Archbishop of York, to visit the Pope and argue against the case that Becket would obviously present on his own behalf. In addition Henry sent off messengers to warn Louis, King of France, and the Earl of Flanders that the traitor, the '*late*' Archbishop of Canterbury, might pass through their territories and should be arrested.

Henry's delegations to Louis and to the Pope were designed to present his own case in the best light and also to compel Becket to return to Canterbury, where he would be in Henry's power, or to discredit him and so perhaps remove him from the scene. These moves had no success.

The Pope at that time dwelt in Sens, as a result of a schism that had driven him from Rome. There now came Becket to show the Pope a copy of the Constitutions of Clarendon, which Henry had desired him to sign, and to offer his resignation as archbishop. The Pope denounced the constitutions and would not accept Becket's resignation; instead he confirmed his appointment.

Becket could not in the climate of the time return to England, and he now retired to the Cistercian monastery of Pontigny in Burgundy. From this retreat he sent messengers back and forth to the Pope, to Louis, to Henry, and to others, and from here he excommunicated those who had taken part against him, or who occupied or pillaged Church lands. He also held in his hands, granted by the Pope, the right to impose an interdict on Henry; this would withdraw the services of the Church from the whole population of the kingdom and release the king's subjects from their allegiance to the Crown. Such a power could make the strongest of kings tremble and even the near-pagan Henry looked on the possibility with trepidation. He knew that it might come and spun out the time with appeals and arguments to the Pope (who returned to Rome in 1165). Henry also set guards at the English ports to prevent the entry of messengers bringing the documents of excommunication or interdict—as though it were enough to escape the sentence if by some means delivery of the papers could be prevented.

Henry could not directly reach Becket in the domains of the King of France, but he could do so indirectly. He informed the general chapter of the Cistercians, held at Cîteaux on the 14th of September 1166, that if they valued their monasteries and possessions in his lands they would cease to harbour his enemy Becket at Pontigny. The letter making this threat was shown to Becket, who chose not to embarrass his hosts and removed himself to the abbey of Saint Colombe near Sens.

From time to time attempts were made to reconcile Henry and Becket, and meetings were arranged at Montmirail and at Montmartre, but with no resolution of the problems. Thomas would obey the king, he promised, in all things where he should, but he always added 'saving my order' or 'saving the honour of God', and Henry, who saw that such reservations must negate any agreement, would fly into a rage and threaten and browbeat and swear wild oaths.

Becket in his exile is not altogether a figure of sympathy. The utmost he could do to punish Henry was to issue excommunications and threaten interdict, and he was altogether too liberal, too willing to excommunicate all who disagreed with him or harmed him or the Church or its property; probably at no other time were there so many excommunications in England as there were during Becket's exile. They included counsellors of the king, various priests, and even bishops. When Henry sought to annoy Becket by having his eldest son crowned by the Archbishop of York, he dealt Becket a double blow, first by usurping what was the privilege of Canterbury, the crowning of monarchs, and secondly by bringing Roger of York, Becket's old enemy, to conduct the ceremony. As a result Roger and other bishops who assisted were promptly excommunicated by Becket.

At last, in July 1170, a conference was arranged at Fréteval on the borders of Maine and Chartrain, that is between the territory of the King of France and that of Henry, where the two kings had agreed to meet to discuss other matters. Henry and Becket met in a meadow on the 22nd of July, Henry spurring his horse forward when he saw the archbishop approach, as though to be the first to greet him, and the two men shook hands. They then drew apart from their companions and seemed to onlookers as though talking familiarly as they had been used to do when Becket was chancellor. One observer noted that Becket kept shifting from side to side in his saddle, and this was supposed afterwards to be attributable to his hair shirt and drawers. 'Let us be friends again,' said Henry, 'as we were in the past. Let us forget our enmity.' The two men then returned each to his own party to discuss what had been said. Becket drew up a document of his demands and returned to deliver it to Henry, who received it graciously, promising to restore Becket to the see of Canterbury, to restore various properties of the Church and of those who had suffered exile on Becket's account, and indeed there was nothing that he should do that he did not now promise to do. Becket finally gave the king his blessing and the parties returned home.

The scene in that windy field, with the courtiers and soldiers of the kings of France and of England and the little group of churchmen, is easily visualized and the poignancy of it must have affected many of the onlookers as the two men seemed to be entering on a new and more promising episode of a friendship interrupted so long by obstinacy, pettiness, and the quarrel over rights and privileges. There were others in the king's train, however, who had no wish for such a rapprochement; these were men who had been given by the king, or had taken by simple theft, various properties belonging to the Church or to the archbishop himself; these people would lose their gains if Becket returned and claimed the restoration of his and the Church's rights. They might have comforted themselves with the knowledge that Henry was a deep man and what he showed on the surface might not be at all the same as he really intended. There were others who distrusted Henry, with good reason, and feared that the apparent reconciliation was false and would collapse as soon as it came up against the practicabilities of the case.

There was the rub. Representatives sent by Thomas to England to confer with the young king could get no satisfaction concerning the properties that had been alienated; and even while they were there a barbaric Norman called Randolph de Broc, who had insulted Becket at Northampton and had usurped Becket's castle at Saltwood, was, with his brother Robert, laying waste farms that belonged to Becket or the Church, swearing that when the archbishop returned he should find nothing but empty houses and vacant barns.

The state of things was reported to the Pope, who at once excommunicated all holders of Church property and threatened the whole country with an interdict. These powers he laid in the hands of Becket, to be implemented as he saw fit.

Nevertheless, Becket, urged by the Pope, decided to return to England, though he was well aware that he risked his life in going. He chose to go despite the fact that Henry at all their meetings had avoided giving the kiss of peace, which was believed in the middle ages to be equivalent to an oath and a safe conduct. Before his departure, Becket determined to visit Henry again, while the king was yet in France, and he pointedly asked for the kiss. 'Another time you shall have enough,' said Henry, refusing for that occasion, perhaps once more on the grounds that he had previously sworn not to kiss the archbishop again. Yet again Becket visited the king, at the castle of Chaumont, and this time was well received—Henry was for once in good humour. 'If only you would do my will,' said Henry, 'I would put everything into your hands', and Becket saw at once in these words the scene of the temptation of Christ by Satan—'All this will I give thee if thou wilt fall down and worship me.'

They met yet again and bade farewell. 'Go in peace,' the the king said, 'I shall follow and will see you in Rouen or in England.'

'My lord,' replied Becket, 'I fear that I part from you as one who will not see you in this life again.'

For a moment the king was incensed. 'Do you think me traitor?' he demanded.

'Let that be far from you,' said Becket.

Six years had passed since Becket was last in Canterbury, and now he had to wait on a French beach for several days because of contrary winds that prevented his ship from putting to sea. He might have taken it as a divine warning if he had been a more superstitious man and a less brave one. He embarked at last, with his fellow exiles, on the morning of the 1st of December. The year was 1170 and he had four weeks more to live. That he might die soon he was already convinced, and as the days passed he began to think of violent death in the service of the Church as welcome, as though he were determined to become a martyr.

The ship arrived at Sandwich with the cross of Canterbury at the prow and was welcomed by a crowd of excited people. Becket had been warned that there might be armed men waiting for him; in fact there were, but they were at Dover. Randolph de Broc, Reginald de Warenne, and Gervase de Cornhelle came galloping along the coast to intercept the exiles, and the blustering de Broc demanded to know why Becket had sent letters ahead, as he had, once more suspending and excommunicating the king's bishops and Roger, Archbishop of York. There might have been a battle there on the beach, but de Broc and his friends lacked courage to begin it and Becket and his party went on to Canterbury to a noisy and heart-warming welcome from the people of the town. De Broc was back again next morning, still demanding the release of the bishops and others from excommunication, but he met with no success.

Becket prepared to set the cathedral to rights and to reclaim those of his lands, houses, and castles that had been usurped by others. He sent a message to the young king at Woodstock that he would like to come to see him, and started off by way of London, but on the way Becket received a reply that he would not be welcome. He was also forbidden to make processions about the country and he was advised to return to Canterbury.

At Canterbury, Becket had to contend with the odious de Broc family. They held his castle at Saltwood and had appropriated the revenues of Church property, and now they would not give them up despite what the king had promised. From Saltwood the de Brocs made sorties at times to annoy the archbishop, seizing a ship laden with wine for the archbishop's palace, for example, killing some of the sailors and imprisoning the rest; they hunted in the archbishop's chase and killed both his deer and his dogs; and as an additional insult they captured a train of mules and horses carrying the archbishop's goods and cut off the tail of one of the sumpter horses. This cutting off of the tail may seem to be a small thing, a petty thing, but it was taken seriously by Becket as a deliberate insult not only to himself but also to his rank and order.

News had got quickly across to Henry in Normandy that Becket was excommunicating and suspending right and left and to this was added the information, brought by Roger of York and some of the excommunicated bishops, that Becket was marching about the country ejecting people from their homes and their lands where they had usurped his or Church property. Henry at once flew into a rage as terrible and as excessive as any and cried out some such phrase as: 'Will no one rid me of this low-born cleric?'

He was heard by four knights of his court, Reginald Fitz Urse, William de Tracy, Hugh de Morville, and Richard de Brito. Agreeing what they should do to carry the king's hint into effect, they set off by different routes to arrive at Saltwood Castle all on the same day. Henry is said to have repented his words when at last his anger subsided, and he sent other knights to prevent the first four from doing what it was feared they intended to do. The attempt seems not to have been vigorously prosecuted, however, and nothing hindered the four men at Saltwood. There they had been made welcome by de Broc.

It was Christmas. On Christmas night Becket celebrated midnight Mass and preached a sermon at the end of which he said to his congregation: 'You have had one martyr here, Saint Alphege, and it is possible that you may soon have another.' No one misunderstood what he meant. The dark, crushing tragedy seemed to be rolling on with no one having power to stop it, and indeed with its hero helping it along in a growing desire for a martyr's death. In the following two days Becket wrote and dispatched letters to King Louis in France, to his friend the Archbishop of Sens, and to the Pope. He also sent to a poor priest at Wrotham, who, like the soothsayer in *Julius Caesar*, had warned him of danger, a deed appointing him to the chapel of Penshurst, and excommunicating in advance anyone who should hinder this appointment.

Meanwhile, the intentions of the four knights at Saltwood had got about and messengers warned Becket that these men had come into the country and would kill him.

The four knights had arrived at Saltwood on the 28th of the month. They spent the night as guests of de Broc, and early in the morning they rode the fifteen miles to Canterbury and took shelter in the Abbey of Saint Augustine. From there they sent about for armed men to come and help them. Then with a dozen of these men they entered the city and gathered in the house of one Gilbert near the gate into the cathedral precincts.

Becket was told of their movements and had no doubt that his end was near. He assisted at Mass in the morning, confessed and did penance, and three times in the day received the discipline of the lash. After dinner at three in the afternoon he talked in a room in his palace with his clerics and monks, and it was here about four o'clock that the four knights found him. They entered with civilian clothes over their chain armour and without swords, but not in any spirit of humility—the pagan Norse from whom they were descended were never far from the surface in the Normans. Fitz Urse, who seems to have been the leader, demanded whether Becket would hear what they had to say in public or in private. He was answered that he would be heard in private and Becket ordered his companions to leave; but a moment later, after Fitz Urse had begun to speak about the absolution of the excommunicated bishops, Becket called his people back into the room, declaring that such things should be said before witnesses.

This action probably saved his life for that moment, for, as one of the knights afterwards confessed, they would have brained him there and then with the shaft of his own cross. There followed an altercation in which the knights demanded that Becket should swear fealty to the king and declared that Henry had ordered him to absolve the bishops. Becket pointed out that although the bishops had been excommunicated by the power the Pope had put into his hands, only the Pope could reinstate them. They demanded that he should own himself entirely the king's man but Becket replied that we are commanded to render unto Caesar the things that are Caesar's and unto God the things that are God's. One moment Becket was all dignity and courage, and the next, like a small boy, he was bringing forward trivial matters—the various insults and threats made against him, the wine that had been stolen, and then that miserable dock-tailed horse.

'If the king's men have injured you or yours why do you not complain to the king,' asked Hugh de Morville, 'instead of excommunicating them on your own authority?' Becket replied that in the case of any injury to the rights of the Church he need wait for no one's leave to do justice.

The knights, shouting that Becket was too free with his excommunications and waving their arms wildly, declared that he had spoken to the peril of his life. There was more that was said, but it only served to emphasize that whatever Becket declared the knights were determined that he should be regarded as a traitor to the king. They turned and ordered the appalled clerics and monks to seize the archbishop and to hold him. 'There is no need,' Becket told them. 'I shall not go away.'

The knights now left the building, calling out 'Arms, king's men, arms!' They stripped off their over-dress and girded on their swords and ran through the streets shouting 'The king's men, the king's men' back to Gilbert's house.

Becket had a moment of doubt and he asked if it would be possible to get to Sandwich before dark, but though he was told that it was, he made no move. As the time advanced he became more dignified and fearless, so that when a loud crashing and banging announced that the knights were returned he was ready for what might follow. Clerics and monks tried to drag Becket from his room into the cathedral, where they hoped that sanctuary would protect him even from these violent men, but he resisted. Nevertheless they *did* take him into the cathedral, entering from the cloister by the door into the north transept.

The knights found that one way the doors were closed against them, but they came by another, guided by Robert de Broc, through the ambulatory. Here they found a number of carpenters' tools and axes from some repair that was in hand and with these they broke down a partition, and then a door and a window, to gain access to the palace where they thought the archbishop would be. They then followed the way the monks had gone with the archbishop, and so entered the cathedral transept by the same door.

They now had their swords in their hands. 'This way to me, king's men!' called Fitz Urse, and the four were followed by three other knights and by a sub-deacon called Hugh Horsea or Mauclerc. The monks and clerics fled before them, leaving with Becket only Robert, Prior of Merton, William Fitzstephen, and a cleric called Edward Grim, who was on a visit to the cathedral. These attendants had tried to drag Becket from the well-like transept up the stairs to the choir and the high altar, but Becket had resisted them and they had been forced to cease their efforts. Now only Grim stayed with Becket.

Commentators remark that in the deepening gloom of the late afternoon of a December day Becket could easily have taken refuge by hiding in one or other of the dark corners of an intricate cathedral, but he did not take advantage of that. As the murderers entered the transept he stood behind a pillar. One of the men shouted: 'Where is Thomas, traitor to the king?' There was no answer. Fitz Urse then cried out 'Where is the archbishop?' Becket showed himself, saying, 'Here I am, no traitor, but archbishop. What do you want with me?'

'Your death,' said someone.

'I meet it gladly,' he replied. Some kindlier man among the knights struck him on the shoulder with the flat of his sword and said, 'Fly or you are a dead man.' The four knights and Hugh

Horsea faced him, with Horsea demanding, 'Absolve the bishops you have excommunicated.'

'I will do nothing more than I have already done,' he answered, and added to Fitz Urse: 'Reginald, I have done you many favours; do you now come against me with arms?'

'You shall know,' said Fitz Urse, 'for I will tear out your heart. Are you not a traitor?' and he knocked off Becket's cap with his sword and said, 'Come, you are my prisoner.'

As he pulled his cope from Fitz Urse's grasp Becket said, 'Do with me here what you will.'

Then the knights tried to lift Becket on to de Tracy's shoulders to carry him outside, some remnant of respect for sanctity rising in them, but Becket was a big man and a strong one and he pushed de Tracy away so that he staggered and nearly fell. Fitz Urse now came against him and Becket pushed him back, crying, 'Touch me not, Reginald; you are my man and owe me fealty and submission.'

'I owe you nothing contrary to my fealty to the king,' Fitz Urze cried, throwing down the carpenter's axe he still held in his hand and flourishing his sword above Becket's head. 'Strike, strike,' he shouted.

Becket bowed his head, clasped his hands, and said, 'I commend myself to God, to Holy Mary, blessed Denys, and Saint Alphege.'

De Tracy next aimed a blow at him, but Grim, who was still with the archbishop, raised his own arm and took the stroke, which bit deeply into his flesh and came near to severing the limb. With blood pouring down his sleeve Grim retreated to one of the altars. The stroke that wounded Grim also cut off part of Becket's crown or tonsure and glanced into his shoulder.

'Into thy hands, O Lord, I commend my spirit,' said Becket.

A second blow was struck by one of the men, but Becket did not fall until another stroke, this time from William de Tracy, brought him to his knees. A fourth and violent blow by Richard de Brito removed the whole of the top of Becket's skull and revealed his brain as the sword cut through and the point shattered on the pavement. Hugh Horsea, braver now that Becket was down, put his foot on the archbishop's neck and with the point of his sword flicked the brains out on to the pavement.

During all this action, the fourth knight, Hugh de Morville, had been keeping back people who had crowded into the cathedral and who saw this odious murder take place.

The knights and their followers, their work done, now rushed out of the church, crying again 'The king's men! the king's men!' and invaded the palace, looting, destroying, and attacking any who got in their way. They found a fortune to divide among themselves, and also came upon two hair shirts belonging to Becket, the discovery of which brought the first sobering doubts into the minds of some of the murderers. It had been in their opinion right to kill an enemy of the king, but now they wondered if they had killed a saint. It is marvellous what powerful symbolism a hair shirt presented to the medieval mind. The monks who laid out Becket's body were to be similarly affected on discovering the lice-inhabited shirt and drawers he wore. The four knights returned to Saltwood Castle for that night, laden with spoil, but not now so certain of themselves as they were.

The Golden Legend, printed by Pynson, says that the men, horrified by their own deed, went off on crusade to the Holy Land and each died a horrible death. In fact they seem to have suffered little for their crime and before long were on good terms again with the king, hunting with him and enjoying his favour. Some of them founded land-owning families in Devon, and another one in the north. Donald J. Hall points out in his *English Medieval Pilgrimages* that by Becket's own rule the murderers could not be punished: as the crime had taken place in a church it was a matter for the ecclesiastical courts and could not be tried by the secular court, and since the knights could not be arrested by the Church, they went free.

In the cathedral the monks and clerics crept from their retreats and took up the body, and also gathered from the pavement all the blood and brains they could, setting bowls to catch any more blood that might drip from the wounds. Some of the blood must have been Grim's, but it was no matter, it was now all holy, and before it was all taken up some of the townspeople crowding into the transept had dipped their fingers in it and drawn the sign of the cross on their foreheads. The body was placed on a bier before the high altar. Robert of Merton drew aside the dead man's clothing and showed the monks the hair shirt and the monk's habit that Becket wore beneath the magnificence of his outer vestments. It seems to have come as a surprise to the monks, who now perceived that he had been a true monk and was probably a saint. Such was the effect of the hair shirt! It is not easy to understand how the monks, who had had to flog Becket often, could have missed seeing that shirt before. As though in confirmation of their belief that Canterbury had a new saint, a miracle occurred—a blind man, led by some mysterious power to the cathedral, regained his sight.

But there were still enemies. Robert de Broc came with a message from his brother Randolph commanding the monks to 'remove the disloyal traitor as quickly as possible and to throw the body where none would know him' and threatened violence if this were not done. The frightened monks lifted the body and carried it down to the crypt, where it was laid in a coffin and strongly walled up, and then the crypt was closed. It was in vain. Wherever the archbishop's spiritual influence was invoked miracles took place, and eventually the monks opened the crypt, put the coffin into a rough shrine with holes round the base, and allowed the public to enter.

The news of the murder of the archbishop in his own cathedral caused a sensation throughout Europe. Henry heard the news at Argenton and burst at once into loud lamentation and for three days shut himself away, constantly crying, 'O that this should have happened!' Privately he did not deceive himself as to what the consequences of the murder must be: it meant the defeat of all his attempts to make the Church in England subject in law to the secular power, and the undermining of all the positions he had taken up to extend the pre-eminence of the Crown. It can be argued that here was the first limitation of the absolute powers of the monarchy, leading to the signing of Magna Carta by Henry's son John in 1215. Not until the time of Henry VIII was the Church again to be made subject to the Crown.

Excommunications and interdicts once more hovered about the head of Henry II as a result of the murder of Becket. In order to obtain favour with the Pope and to ward off these interdicts Henry had to surrender completely on the question of criminous clerks and the Constitutions of Clarendon were put away as now impossible. This was not enough, and in order to be out of the reach of the Pope's censures Henry took himself off to Ireland with an army of four thousand men, ostensibly to curb the ambitions of Strongbow, Earl of Pembroke, who had done so well in his invasion and occupation of that country that it seemed possible he might declare himself king there. Henry could not, however, altogether escape and he adopted various stratagems to avoid or delay the interdict in England, including once more guarding the ports, to intercept the Pope's legates. Nevertheless he had in the end to surrender and to receive the papal legates at Avranches, in the extensive and beautiful cathedral of which only one pillar survived the French Revolution: it bears the inscription: 'Sur cette pierre, ici, à la porte de la cathédrale d'Avranches, après le meurtre de Thomas Becket, Archevêque de Cantorbery, Henry II, Roi d'Angleterre et Duc de Normandie, reçut à genoux, des légats du Pape, l'absolution apostolique, le Dimanche, xxii Mai, MCLXXII'. The legates compelled Henry to swear on the Gospels that he had never sought or commanded the death of Becket, but he had to admit that it had taken place through his fault. He swore to undertake penance, to obey the Pope and his successors, and to admit papal legates to his dominions to root out bad customs. He had to swear to the same things again at Caen. What Henry's part in the murder really was no one will ever know; there is only slight evidence that he deliberately instructed the four knights to kill the archbishop. It seems, in the light of Henry's character and political astuteness, unlikely.

Henry undertook to do penance as his world seemed to be combining against him. In France his sons Henry (the young king) and Richard rose in rebellion, with Louis of France aiding them, and in the north of England, at the opposite and far end of the kingdom, William III of Scotland invaded over the border, captured Carlisle, and marched about the north unhindered. In these circumstances Henry took ship to Southampton, where he landed on the 8th of July 1174. It was a Monday. Living on bread and water only he set out for

Canterbury. By the following Friday he was at Harbledown, where
he descended from his horse and continued on foot. He paused at
Saint Dunstan's church, outside the walls of Canterbury, to
change into the sackcloth of pilgrims and to remove his shoes.
He walked barefoot over the stones and cobbles, which cut his
unaccustomed feet, so that he left a trail of blood. As he
entered the cathedral he knelt to pray, then in the transept
knelt again and wept to see the ground on which the murder
had taken place. Passing into the crypt he prayed for a long
time before the coffin of the archbishop. Henry's clothing was
then drawn down from about his shoulders and he received
five strokes of the lash from each of the prelates present and
three from each of more than eighty monks. Did these monks
enter into their task with relish, laying into the king with all
their might? Perhaps they did, but it seems more likely that out
of awe of the royal presence or out of their own charity they laid
the strokes on more lightly, for though Henry was undoubtedly
hurt and sickened, he does not appear to have suffered any dire
effect after so many strokes of the lash. After the flogging he
went the round of the martyr's altars and then returned to the
chill crypt to pass the whole night in prayer, ending with a Mass
at daybreak and the drinking of a cup of water in which a drop
of the saint's blood had been dissolved. He carried a phial of
the blood and water away with him to London.

He must have been a sore and morose man as he smarted
from the physical pain and contemplated the turbulence of his
dominions, with wars to be fought to the north and the south
and his tenure of the throne in jeopardy. But while he had been
undergoing his violent penance, his armies had been active, and
a few days later a messenger came to him to announce that the
Scots king had been defeated and captured. It seemed to Henry
a miracle, a miracle vouchsafed by his old friend and late
enemy. Within a short time afterwards the rebellion of his sons
was quelled and Henry's kingdom was once again secure and at
peace.

From the moment of his death and the first miracles it had
been apparent to many that Becket had been a holy man and
his sanctification was certain. He had died on the 29th of
December. Within a few days, in the New Year, pilgrims were

already coming to the cathedral, the first of many thousands who were to follow.

The possibility that a man may be a saint is not to be regarded lightly. Before he may be recognized as such the Church has to be satisfied, not so much as to the blamelessness, the innocence, or the goodness of the life he has led, as to the manner of his death and the power for good that might flow from that death. Papal legates were sent to England to examine the miracles that had issued from the tomb of Becket or were reported to have taken place through his intervention. The legates decided that miracles had indeed occurred and recommended therefore that Thomas Becket should be elected to the holy company of saints. On Ash Wednesday, the 21st of February 1173, Pope Alexander solemnly canonized Thomas Becket as saint and martyr, the day of his festival to be the anniversary of his murder, the 29th of December.

A condition of the Pope's instrument of beatification was that Becket's body should be removed from the crypt and placed on an altar or in a chest in the cathedral. Two months after the king's penance, however, the choir of the cathedral was destroyed by fire. This gave the monks the opportunity to rebuild in the new pointed gothic style. The work was a long time in hand and it was not until fifty years had passed, on the 7th of July 1220, that the new chapel was made ready to receive the saint's body. In a ceremony of great magnificence, the cost of which crippled the cathedral treasury for years afterwards, the saint's remains were removed from the crypt and placed in a new shrine east of the high altar.

Though the cathedral might have been poor for a time, the shrine of Saint Thomas grew richer and richer from the many gifts of gold and silver and of rare and precious stones brought by the faithful. Among these was a great ruby, the Régale of France, given by King Louis. Covering the whole shrine was a wooden box or cover suspended on a pulley. The box itself was lavishly painted, but when it was drawn up it was to reveal a shrine without parallel in brilliance and wealth.

The shrine itself remained so until 1538. By that time the numbers of pilgrims had sadly declined, not because of some fault at Canterbury but because everywhere throughout

EPW

Europe the ancient faith, deep and intense, was changing. Pilgrimage was a habit, a custom, a frame of mind of the middle ages, and the middle ages were passing away with the advance of thought and philosophy and a new and inspiring scholarship. Henry VIII did not create the Renaissance or the Reformation with his suppression of the monasteries, but took advantage of a changing climate of opinion. What he did could not have been done by Henry II or by any of the Angevins.

At the instance of Henry VIII the saint, dead some three hundred and fifty years, was tried as a traitor and when he did not appear in his own defence was found guilty in his absence of contumacy, treason, and rebellion. Becket's bones were to be publicly burned, offerings made at the shrine should be forfeited to the king, and the title of saint was no longer to be accorded to him. Further, all images and pictures of Becket, in books, in glass, and in paintings, were to be destroyed. This last order was obeyed with varying thoroughness, though there was severe punishment for those who did not comply. Though pictures and statues of Becket are comparatively rare in England, a number have survived Henry VIII's orders, and among these, supreme and splendid, are the Miracle windows of Canterbury cathedral. In the saint's own cathedral his followers somehow succeeded in hoodwinking and defeating Henry Tudor's intention (*plates* 30 and 31).

It is probable that the burning of Becket's remains was never carried out, but that they were secretly buried in a coffin in the crypt. In 1888 a stone coffin was discovered, containing bones and a damaged skull. These were replaced and quietly reburied, the last sad appearance, perhaps, of the man who in life had been the most magnificent and the most dedicated of archbishops, and who in death became the greatest saint of the English Church.

Becket remains a saint in the Roman Calendar to this day, but his story cannot be read without a lingering doubt of the appropriateness of the title. He fought and died for the political and secular rights and privileges of the Church rather than for the welfare of men, and if it was true that the rights of the Church could be synonymous with the protection and relief of the poor, that seems to have been not the primary element in

Becket's struggle with the king. As that struggle progressed Becket's motives became more and more bound up with the humiliation of his opponent, who appeared as the incarnation of injustice. William of Newburgh, one of Becket's contemporaries, summed him up as '*Zelo justitiae fervidus, utrum autem plene secondum um scientian novit Deus*'—'burning with zeal for the cause of justice, but whether altogether wisely, God knows'.

Becket's life and death are documented more fully than those of any other man of the middle ages. There are quantities of letters in Rome and elsewhere. Several persons who saw the murder, or who were present in the cathedral, wrote accounts of the crime. Among these was Edward Grim, perhaps the only literate man who actually saw the murder from beginning to end. A number of men who were Becket's contemporaries also wrote biographies of Becket. Since then many more books have appeared on the scene, all dealing or purporting to deal with fact; but among imaginative works few are concerned with this subject. I have already pointed out that the playwrights of the Tudor period could not have dared to write in praise of Becket any more than the poets could: if Henry VIII had not found them out and punished them his daughter Elizabeth would have done so. In less restricted times little has appeared of a literary character, despite the dramatic power of the tragedy of the life and death of Becket. The most notable works are T. S. Eliot's *Murder in the Cathedral* and Jean Anouilh's unsatisfactory play *Becket ou l'Honneur de Dieu*, in which, against all the evidence, Becket appears as a Saxon.

PART TWO

The Journey along the Pilgrims' Way

Preamble

The distance between Winchester and Canterbury by the Pilgrims' Way is some 112 miles. If you mean to walk the whole length of the Way you must necessarily take stock of your ability as a walker, or of that of the weakest member of your party, in order to plan your stages and accommodation for the night. Twenty miles in a day is as much as most walkers will want to do. At this pace, or anything faster, there will not be much time, especially in winter, for inquiry, for observation of the various plants, bushes, and trees that grow along the Way (which is rich ground for the botanist), or of the birds and animals and insects that inhabit the countryside, nor for inquiring into the attractions of villages, towns, and their churches.

The Way is not a continuous surfaced or certain path. In some places it is not easily made out, in others there appear to be alternatives running more or less parallel one with the other. This is as one should reasonably expect it to be, for if the Way is a prehistoric track, as no one doubts, then travellers by it in the early days would choose one line or another according to their inclination, the weather, or the state of the ground, so that it would not always have been a fixed and restricted line—some ancient tracks, in East Anglia, for example, were several hundreds of feet wide. In other places, and they are few, the Way disappears altogether, grown over from lack of use, lost in hop fields or orchards, or abolished by the plough. Some more serious interruptions are caused by the enclosure of lands over which the Way once ran unhindered. There are detours to overcome these difficulties, but they add some miles to the journey. If you do not expect to be too definite about treading where medieval pilgrims or ancient man once trod—and none can be certain of that—you may, over the greater part of the route, enjoy an attractive and not difficult or dangerous journey, with only occasional annoyances from modern traffic and its smells and hazards.

Over the greater part of the Way, I say, but not all. Long lengths of the Way, in Hampshire especially, are now motor roads and in parts dual carriageway, roaring with the row of tyres and engines, and offering no pleasure at all for walkers. In Surrey and in Kent there are lengths of country lanes between thick hedges and banks, lanes that are for miles only one car wide; these are delightful when no car is about, but productive of expletives from walkers who have to crush up into nettles or thorny hedges to allow a car to pass.

For the rest, the Way is footpath through fields and along the skirts of woods, with small doubt about its present line.

The best time to walk the Pilgrims' Way is undoubtedly in the spring, in such a spring as is only to be found in these islands, when the ground is dried by mild breezes and the air is washed with lucid light that seems all the more pervasive because the trees are skeletal and thin or only hazing over with green; and especially in the chalk lands the spring light seems to hover and to reflect from the slopes of the downs and from the ploughed fields in which chalk and greensand mingle. At this time, too, the air and the views for which the Pilgrims' Way should be celebrated are at their best.

The next best time is in the autumn, when the hedgerows and their trees and the frequent stands of chestnuts and beeches become lambent and bright, and many fruits and colourful berries abound. But in the summer there are many things to contend with, flies, and beetles, and inquisitive bees and wasps, and the flora of the Way doing its utmost to block every lane and path with looping brambles and wild roses and ragged armies of nettles. Sometimes these nettles are six feet high, leaning over the narrow path like the crossed swords of a military wedding. A man in trousers may be stung or scratched many times; a girl in shorts or short skirt and stockings or with bare legs will find the going painful.

If you choose to walk in the winter, in December, perhaps to do as Hilaire Belloc did, to arrive in Canterbury on the anniversary, the hour and the day of the murder of Becket, then you must go prepared for rain and for mud and in Kent especially for snow. Kent, the garden of England, has a surprising amount of snow in the cold season, certainly more than Hampshire and

Surrey have. The mud of the Pilgrims' Way over the chalk, where the lanes are cut up and pounded by farm tractors, is a thick, gooey, whitish, slippery stuff more than ankle deep in places. In such a time good walking-boots are the footwear to use. In a drier season, no special footwear or clothing is needed on the Pilgrims' Way.

Motorists may drive along a large part of the Pilgrims' Way, but they will have the worst of it, either on busy trunk roads or in lanes too deep for much to be seen from a car. Cyclists may ride far without having to dismount from their machines, over main roads and surfaced lanes; but for the rest, a cycle will have to be pushed and often carried and is a nuisance.

There is almost no refreshment along the Way, not even springs of fresh water—the springs run underground and come to the surface somewhere to the south. Wherever you mean to eat and drink, if you have not brought your subsistence with you, you must descend to one of the villages or towns to the south or occasionally to the north, and this may add two to six miles to your daily journey. Nor is there overnight accommodation wherever you might wish to find it. In Hilaire Belloc's day every village pub, it seems, was willing to put you up and the full-house sign was uncommon. Lack of labour, or the price of labour, and various sorts of taxes and other interferences have long ago convinced many pub-owners and householders that catering for accommodation is not worth the bother. In order to avoid having to sleep out on the hillside you must choose your caravanserais before you start and book rooms in advance.

Instead of walking the Way and settling in different accommodation each night, you may find it more convenient to put up in one place for two or three days and explore sections of the Way from there. Bus or coach services, both sparse, may then be used to reach each day's beginning in the morning and to return in the evening. In general these services cannot drop you nearer than a mile or two from the Way. If you have a car you may leave it at a convenient place to walk a stretch of the Way— but then you must come back to your vehicle and this means in fact walking the Way twice over. There is pleasure in that, and no one who has not done a journey in both directions can really claim to have seen the country, but it may take more time than you have to spare. The most convenient method, therefore, is to have a car with a patient driver who will not mind acting as chauffeur to drop you at one point and to collect you at another fifteen or twenty miles farther on. I have used all three of these methods, and in effect I have walked or driven over most of the Way at least twice or three times, and other parts more often than that.

In a week of fine weather, in any other than the winter season, a good walker may travel the Way from end to end in six to nine days. In 1174 Henry II, going to his penance and living on bread and water, covered the journey between Monday, when he landed at Southampton, and Friday when he entered Canterbury by the West Gate. It has been recorded that he went by cart, a thing I do not believe; I think he went on horseback. Whether he followed the Pilgrims' Way entirely is not known, but some parts of it he must have travelled. Farnham, with its fine bishops' palace, would have been a convenient place for him to stop, as would also have been the palaces at Otford and Charing.

Hilaire Belloc, walking the Way seven hundred and twenty-five years after Henry II, did it in eight brief winter days, so that he might arrive on the day and the hour of the murder. Belloc, travelling in 1899, was twenty-nine years old and a good walker. In his eight days from the 22nd to 29th of December, at the darkest time of the year, he had like a pioneer to search out what he supposed was the true line of the Way, where it was no longer clear or where it was blocked or had disappeared. His journey allowed altogether only about fifty-six hours of daylight, including stops and meals. It was certainly not enough. Belloc endows his chapters with an air of discovery and clear reasoning, and comes to several false or doubtful conclusions. Yet his book is the most interesting and readable of those written about the Old Road. However, though it seems quite practical from the viewpoint of the reader sitting comfortably before his hearth, in fact you cannot actually travel the Way with Belloc as your only guide: I have tried it.

Belloc's principal conclusions that are quickly dissipated by a journey along the Way are these three:

1. That the Way never turns a sharp corner without reason. It several times turns corners for reasons not apparent.

2. The line of the Way is marked by yew trees and when in doubt the true line may be perceived alongside these trees. There are plenty of yews along the downs but few, if any, are ancient (except for some in churchyards) and their connection with the Way is fortuitous. As I have already said, yews will flourish on any kind of soil where they are left alone, especially in the south of England. (The popular notion that yew trees along the Way mark the graves of pilgrims who died *en route* is not worth consideration.)

3. That when it passes a church the Way preferably goes by the south door, that is, past what was considered to be the more holy side of the church. It is true that some of the few churches that actually stand beside the Way do have it on the south side, but for no better reason than that the south side was the one preferably approached by the parishioners, and strangers, therefore, would gravitate into the plain paths. There are many more churches south of the Way, but not actually on it, in the lower land the path overlooks, and these, obviously, show their north sides to the Way. In any case, the Way is of neolithic origin and its course was trodden out two thousand years before the first Christian churches arose in these islands.

Belloc now and again speaks of trespassing over gardens and fields, but he says little of major interruptions such as the parks of Titsey Chevening, and Chilham Castle; he leaves it to his reader to discover that these are private land.

Julia Cartwright (Mrs Adie) wrote a different kind of book about the Pilgrims' Way, a book to which Belloc occasionally referred. She is less concerned with walking the footpaths and tracks than Belloc was, and I think it unlikely that she walked any great distance of the Way. Her book is interesting for her clear style of writing and for the work she did to elucidate the history of the path and of the towns and villages connected with it. The second edition of her book (1911) is the more useful.

Youth Hostels

Youth hostels, as is the case with inns, are neither near nor numerous along the Pilgrims' Way and there are not enough of them close to the Way to make them serve entirely for a walking holiday in this area. There is a charming hostel in the middle of Winchester, in the ancient, tile-hung City Mill, where you may sleep, or suffer insomnia, to the sound of water rushing through the sluice beneath the building. The next hostel that is anywhere near the Way is Holmbury, far too many miles distant, and in any case well off the route. The hostel at Tanners Hatch, on the edge of Ranmore Woods, is more conveniently placed.

Another eighteen miles, plus extra for approaches, brings you to Crockham Hill, and then ten miles farther on is Kemsing, beside the Way at last. It is then thirty-one miles to Doddington, which is well south of the Way, and eighteen miles from Canterbury. Finally Canterbury has its own hostel, in the New Dover Road.

Hostels close and others are opened. Consult the YHA handbook for up-to-date information.

Maps

The handiest map I know of that usefully shows the Pilgrims' Way from end to end on one sheet is the 'National' map for south-east England, sold by garages; but the scale is four miles to the inch, and this is too small for practical use by walkers. The one-inch Ordnance Survey map is also not really large enough in scale, though six sheets are required for the line from Winchester to Canterbury. These sheets are numbers 168 to 173. The best map for general detail is the $2\frac{1}{2}$-inch OS series, but unfortunately twenty-four sheets are necessary and this involves a sizeable outlay of money. The $2\frac{1}{2}$-inch map is the one I have principally used. Hilaire Belloc used the six-inch OS map; the present cost of the sheets of this map necessary to cover the Pilgrims' Way would leave some holiday-makers nothing with which to take a holiday. I have therefore avoided reference to this large-scale map.

Photographs

The photographs in this book have been made with Asahi Pentax cameras and Kodak Tri-X or Ilford FP4 films. I say so because there are keen photographers who like to know these things. They also like to know, if photographic magazines are correct, what apertures and shutter speeds were used, and whether or not a filter was employed and if so which and what value. I have no idea. I see no point in recording technical details resulting from light or weather conditions that may not be the same tomorrow or the next day.

Along the Pilgrims' Way and on the downs above there are many viewpoints enjoying wide panoramas southward over the greensand hills and the Weald to the South Downs. Except in spring, at almost any time of the year and especially so when the weather is warm, there is a light haze or aerial mist above the Weald that softens or conceals detail. Such mists may serve the purpose of photographers anxious to separate planes of the view. Others who would like to see the distance more clearly may get some help from using a red or orange filter (for monochrome films, of course).

A Footnote for the Future

New motorways and traffic roads are in course of construction or have been planned in the neighbourhood of the Pilgrims' Way. It does not appear that any of these will destroy the Way, but they will be very evident and audible from it.

The M3 will come south from Popham and through Micheldever Wood, parallel with the A33. It will cross the Itchen at Abbots Worthy to a junction at Easton and will join the existing Winchester by-pass below Saint Catherine's Hill. This development will seriously affect this part of the Itchen valley.

A proposed trunk road from Guildford to Petersfield must cross the Pilgrims' Way somewhere, but the precise line of the road has not yet been announced.

The M5 South Orbital Way is likely to have an important effect on the Pilgrims' Way. It includes a huge interchange system with the M23 at Merstham, from which the new road will run parallel with the Way and not far from it to join the new Ditton by-pass. This by-pass will run through Addington and Ryarsh to cross the A228 between two large ponds north of Leybourne Castle and then south-east to the Medway and a junction with the A20M.

Proposals have been announced for a high-standard traffic road from London to Folkestone and investigations are being made over a wide band of country north and south of the A20. The A20 and the Pilgrims' Way run parallel for many miles, and in places, as at Charing, are very close to each other. This proposal could have a very serious effect on the Way.

A by-pass is proposed to take traffic from the A2 at present passing through Harbledown, and a by-pass around Canterbury has also been proposed.

5 *Winchester*

The city of Winchester is built on the slopes of hillsides that drop down to the valley of the river Itchen, a clear chalk stream that rises south of Cheriton, turns a right angle near New Alresford (where it gathers the Alre), and another angle at King's Worthy, to flow south through Winchester. From the city it continues for twelve miles more to fall into Southampton Water. There was a town at Winchester before the advent of the Romans—indeed, if legend is to be believed, Winchester was founded ninety-nine years before the foundation of Rome itself. There is no reason to doubt that some kind of settlement may have existed here from prehistoric times. The site was attractive for its convenient crossing of the river by a ford, and would have gained importance by its being sufficiently far inland to escape the attentions of hit-and-grab coastal raiders, while yet sufficiently near to Southampton Water to be served by and to use that excellent harbour.

Hilaire Belloc stressed the role played by Southampton Water in the development of the town. Travellers coming from the Continent could cross from Cherbourg, or from Harfleur at the mouth of the Seine, without losing sight of land for more than a brief space of time between the sinking below the southern horizon of the modest heights of the Cotentin in Normandy and the rising to the north of the emphatic cliffs and the hill of Saint Catherine's Point on the Isle of Wight. That shore of the island, however, was dangerous for shipping, with cross currents and submerged reefs of rock, and it was necessary for the helmsman to steer to the west to round the island and then to enter the Solent, and so to come into the welcome calm of Southampton Water. All this had to be done before the light of day declined into dusk. A boat caught at sea by the fall of night was in peril. To assist sailors and their passengers the landfall on the Isle of Wight was furnished in the early fourteenth century with a lighthouse, built on the top of

Saint Catherine's Down. This lighthouse was put up at the cost and maintenance of a landowner called Walter de Godeton, as a fine and penance for his having illicitly received fifty-three casks of monastic wine plundered from a wrecked ship. De Godeton's lighthouse is still there on the down, though its light has not burned for centuries; in its shape it anticipates by six hundred years the design of interplanetary rockets. In the middle ages and earlier, the comfort of coming so soon from one land-fall to another must, for travellers too far west comfortably to make use of the shorter Dover crossing, have been strongly in favour of Contentin–Wight crossing of the Channel.

Whatever the origins of Winchester, there was certainly a sizeable settlement by the Itchen long before the birth of Christ. It was called by the Celtic name of Caer Gwent, which means the white town, and it was probably a fortified town. The Romans found it in flourishing condition and renamed it Venta Belgarum, the market town of the Belgae. They made it the focus of a system of highways connecting with Portchester, with Southampton (Bitterne), with Old Sarum and Dorchester, with Mildenhall and Cirencester, and with Silchester, another ancient walled town of the British. These communications centring on Winchester qualified the town as the obvious centre and capital for the Saxon kings who won control of the south of England after the Romans left, and who founded the kingdom of Wessex. In the seventh century Winchester became a cathedral city with the removal here of the see founded by Saint Birinus at Dorchester on Thames.

Two centuries later Winchester became the goal of a popular pilgrimage to the grave of its saintly bishop Swithun. Not much is known of Swithun, though his name comes at times to the lips of every Englishman concerned with the overmastering topic of these islands, the weather. Swithun enlarged his cathedral and built a defensive wall round the precinct, a wall that provided additional shelter and safety when the Danes came raiding, and it was perhaps partly for this security, which they shared, that the people of the town came to love Swithun, as well as for the humility of his character. The love and cheers of his people might raise him up and please his heart, but Swithun's essential humility made him ask that at his death he should be buried in some out-of-the-way grave on the north side of the church, the side always regarded as less desirable because it was cold and away from the warmth and light of the sun.

A hundred years later Swithun was still so well regarded, and indeed revered, as a saint, that his name was added to the dedication of the cathedral, and on the 15th of July 971 his body was transferred from the humble grave to a shrine behind the high altar. According to writers of that time, the translation of the body was accompanied by various miracles, including a rainstorm that went on for forty days. The showers, it seemed, were the tears of the saint in his dismay at being removed into so transcendent a place as the site of his new shrine. Despite the manifestation of the rain, no one thought of returning the body to the grave outside the cathedral, and the miracles that soon occurred at the new tomb suggested that the saint had become reconciled to the change. His shrine became the object of widespread national and even of international pilgrimage, the most popular pilgrimage in England until the shrine of Thomas of Canterbury came into vogue after 1170.

By that time, that is in the two centuries between the translation of Swithun and the death of Thomas Becket, pilgrim routes to Winchester from various parts of England and from the Continent had been firmly established, with pilgrims coming from all directions along the dry ridges and slopes of the hills that brought them conveniently to Winchester. Some of these pilgrims, as I have remarked, would have come from the east, by the Old Road, from which they diverged at Farnham. It is easy, then, to suppose that after 1170 devout pilgrims would achieve two pilgrimages in one by coming first to the shrine of Saint Swithun in Winchester and then going east to Canterbury. Those who came across the Channel from the Cotentin could recross the Channel from Sandwich or Dover. The convenience of this double crossing and the existence of miracle-working shrines at both Winchester and Canterbury is the reason why the Old Road from Winchester to Canterbury may, with all probability, be considered to have been trodden by pilgrims throughout the middle ages.

On the way the pilgrims, the poor and the rich, the pardoners and the palmers and the rest, would pass, and look into, many churches, some of which bore dedications to Saint Swithun or to Saint Thomas of Canterbury. In some churches they would see wall-paintings or pictures in stained glass of the life and deeds of the two saints, but rather more of Thomas than of Swithun, for the shrine of Thomas soon came to be the more renowned. For Thomas had lived so much more recently, had scarcely passed into history when the pilgrimage to his tomb was founded, and there were men who had actually known him and could personally testify to his human qualities, to his character and his courage, his obstinacy and his kindness, and to his atrocious death.

Pilgrims travelling from the south to Winchester would come up the valley of the Itchen, and a mile south of the city they would find the hospital of Saint Cross. Founded in 1136 by Bishop Henry of Blois, the active and vigorous brother of King Stephen, who became bishop at the age of twenty-nine, Saint Cross was not a hospital in the modern sense, but a hospice or almshouse for thirteen poor old men. This small hospital was provided by the bishop with a chapel as large and as ornate as the chancel of a vast cathedral. Built in the twelfth century and the thirteenth century, the chapel joins in one vessel the thickly ornamented style of the late Normans with the airy lightness of Early English, and does so in such a manner that one may see the transition as it were in action from the earlier east end (churches were usually begun at the east end) to the later west end. The masons, one may imagine, while the building was in train, pored over drawings of the new fashions, of this church or that, and as time went on they were joined by newcomers trained in different schools; piece by piece they amended the original plan, changing from the romanesque with which Thomas Becket was familiar at Canterbury to that pointed gothic he would have seen for the first time in his exile at Sens.

Travellers and pilgrims could knock at the hospital door and ask for a dole of bread and of ale, which was freely given. You may ask for it too, as you come by this ancient place, though in these days the dole has to be rationed and you must be prepared for the day's allowance having all been taken up. You may, too, as the pilgrims would have done, enter the great

FPW

chapel and kneel before an altar set in a blocked arch, on the wall of which, in the thirteenth century, an artist painted the scene of the murder of Becket. The picture is, unfortunately, now difficult to make out.

Refreshed by the dole, our pilgrims would have noticed, beyond the Itchen and its water-meadows, the welling hump of Saint Catherine's Hill, on top of which there stood a Norman chapel. Some of them would take time to climb to this lonely and elevated chapel for a service or a prayer. If they had come across the Channel they would, in this chapel of Saint Catherine, give thanks for their safe journey and the landfall of Saint Catherine's Hill on the Isle of Wight.

The chapel was destroyed at the Reformation, and in its place there now stands a grove of trees, at the centre of a much more ancient work than the Norman chapel, for this hill of Saint Catherine was fortified in the iron age. The earthworks thrown up then may be seen even from Saint Cross in the valley. There is also one of those strange mazes cut in the turf, called miz-mazes or Troy Towns, that have never been fully explained. Was this example a diversion of the iron-age dwellers in the fort, or was it cut for some medieval Christian symbol or lesson, or for some medieval game? What is certain is that in the middle ages such mazes were held in high regard, for similar patterns appear in mosaic or in tiles on the floors of many churches in this country and on the Continent.

Seen from the summit of Saint Catherine's Hill, the city of Winchester appeared in the middle ages rather like one of those tightly walled little towns shown in medieval illuminated manuscripts. Spread upon its hillside, with its walls switchbacking up and down, its crowded houses, and its great cathedral rising from the canyons of constricted streets, it promised the traveller rest, comfort and protection. Pilgrims entered by the various gates and, after having made sure of their bed for the night in one of the many inns or hostels or monastery guest-houses, made their way to the cathedral and its shrine of Saint Swithun.

There, before the rebuilding of the cathedral by the Normans, the pilgrim would have found an extraordinary thing. Two monasteries stood in close juxtaposition, with their churches so near one to the other—only a few feet apart—that the singing and the music in one was a nuisance in the other. The Old Minster, the earlier of the two, was the cathedral. The New Minster was the church of a monastery founded by King Alfred, who at his death was buried in this New Minster. What curious reason there might have been for this propinquity is not known, unless it was supposed that the new foundation might displace the old. It is not unknown for two churches to be built in the same churchyard, but in such instances the churchyard is on the boundary between two parishes, and each church stands just in its own parish. No such explanation seems to apply here at Winchester. In the end the monks of the New Minster grew tired of the disadvantages, though they had endured them for two hundred years, and in 1110 they moved to a new foundation, Hyde Abbey, which they built outside the north gate. They took the body of Alfred with them, together with the remains of an obscure saint called Josse.

Winchester, the capital of Wessex, became with Alfred the capital of England. Canute was crowned and was buried here. William I had himself crowned separately in Winchester and in London, and it was here in Winchester that he kept the Domesday Book, that key to the property of the kingdom that was the first record of the national wealth. His son Henry, after the doubtful accident in the New Forest that killed Rufus, neglected everything else to ride full tilt to Winchester to claim the crown that rightfully belonged to his elder brother Robert, who was then abroad. The body of Rufus, abandoned among the trees, was found later by a charcoal-burner called Purkis, who brought it in his humble grimy cart into Winchester. There, Rufus was buried in the chancel of the cathedral, among those Saxon kings whose bones now lie in painted mortuary chests on top of the parclose screens of the presbytery. It was not until more than a further century had passed that London became definitively the capital of England and Winchester was reduced to the rank of county town.

Walkelin, the first Norman bishop of Winchester, demolished the Saxon cathedral and rebuilt in splendid Norman style, preserving the shrine of Saint Swithun, which remained even after further rebuildings and alterations. These later changes culminated in the refashioning of the nave in the fourteenth century, a refashioning that lightened the massive Norman piers and made a branching roof of stone to grow from them as though it were the over-arching of an avenue of trees.

During these centuries of change, rebuilding, and enlargement that made Winchester's cathedral the longest in England, pilgrims flocking to the shrine of Saint Swithun must often have found the interior of the huge building in disarray, filled with the noise of the hammers and chisels of the masons and with the timbers of scaffolding. Nevertheless, the pilgrims could, with small interruption, worship at the shrine of Saint Swithun at the eastern end of the cathedral, in the beautiful retrochoir built in the first years of the thirteenth century by Bishop Godfrey de Lucy, whose modest coffin-lid of Purbeck marble you may see. They entered by a door in the north transept and, marshalled by monks, shuffled along in a queue, close now to the sanctity and holiness they sought, or to the cure of some persistent or loathsome malady. Anxious to spend as long as they might in the blessed and magic aura of the shrine, they knelt and prayed prayer after prayer.

No doubt, too, they lifted their heads upwards to the delicate vaulting above, where their attention would be caught by the scores of painted bosses in the roof. Among those bosses, as they wandered about the cathedral, their heads upturned and their mouths agape, the pilgrims would see things to move them to secular amusement—a bird on its nest, hanging upside down to feed its young, a cowled fox looking over the shoulders of two monks reading a book—what sly dig was there!—a man playing bagpipes and another baiting a bull with a dog, a labourer in a vineyard gathering grapes, and many others of the kind. Green men, with foliage about their heads and growing out of their mouths, would remind them of country pastimes, as they remind me of an old custom in Ireland when young men covered with leaves and boughs went about the villages chanting:

'The wren, the wren, the king of all birds,
On Saint Stephen's day was caught in the furze.'

A different series of bosses demanded the pilgrims' respect as symbols of their faith and as illustrations of the betrayal, the trial, and the death of Christ. These show an awesome God in Judgement and a charming Assumption of the Virgin, in which she stands crowned and wearing an ermine cloak, while six small winged angels bear her upwards and out of this world that had crucified her son. The symbols of the Passion clearly appear, tracing on the bosses the journey of Christ towards the cross. The pilgrims saw the money-bag of Judas, the head of the spitting Jew, the pillar of flagellation, with many-tailed scourges and the crown of thorns, the vernicle of Veronica, the cross with three nails (one nail for the feet in that position in which one foot is nailed over the other), a shield charged with the five wounds (the heart and hands and feet of Christ), the dice with which the Roman soldiers gambled, and so on. These biblical stories meant to be read by those who could not read letters, were reinforced by stained glass in the windows, glass similar to that still to be seen at Canterbury and in Continental cathedrals.

After so much staring upwards, the pilgrims would come with relief to the square, coal-black Tournai font, with its ornament of spiralling foliage on two of the sides and on the other two sides scenes from the life of Saint Nicholas of Myra, who by the transmogrification of centuries has become Santa Claus or Father Christmas. Here on the font Nicholas is seen performing some of his famous deeds—the saving of three young virgins from disgrace, the restoration of life to a drowned child, and then the revival of three youths murdered by a Sweeney Todd of a pork-butcher, caught in the act of pickling their bodies in a tub.

There was one part of the cathedral that the pilgrims of the common sort might not enter. The buildings of the Benedictine monastery lay to the south and the way the monks came into the cathedral, which was also their chapel, was through the south transept. To preserve the privacy of this transept they raised a wrought-iron screen, with a design of little curlicues of dark metal. Erected in the twelfth century it still stands today, perhaps the oldest of such things in this country, a little older than similar screens at Canterbury and at Lincoln. Today, with the monastery and the monks gone, you may climb the steps and pass through this Norman screen, through what in fact is a frontier between the solid romanesque of the Norman transept (*plate* 1) and the spiring gothic of the choir and the retrochoir, between the twelfth century and the very different world of the thirteenth and fourteenth centuries.

The pilgrims of later years might also have visited the various chantries in the church, chantries of richly ornate stone erected in memory of this bishop or that. In the nave they would have stopped to look into the chantry of Bishop William of Wykeham, whose painted image, mitred and in vestments, lies on his tomb with three little monkish men at his feet, the while, with hands together in prayer, he turns a blind face upwards to the ribbed canopy above him. It was this bishop who transformed the nave of the cathedral into the marvel of perpendicular design we see today, and it was this bishop also who built and endowed Winchester College, just outside the cathedral precincts, to educate boys who, he intended, should go on to his other foundation, New College in Oxford.

Winchester had to find accommodation for all these peripatetic people who came to the city throughout six hundred years to walk on ground where King Alfred of the Saxons and his tutor Saint Swithun had trod so long ago. Such a city must have had monastic hospices where poor pilgrims could stay free of cost. For those who had a little money there would be cheap inns or hostels where for a modest payment they might lie on a floor of rushes or straw over cold stone or stamped earth floors in draughty and smoky halls or dormitories. Some pilgrims may have been provided for by the monks of the New Minster, and later by the successors of these monks in the Abbey of Hyde outside the north gate. Women would find accommodation in Nunnaminster, a nunnery founded by King Alfred, on the site of which the blatant Guildhall now stands, built in a style of Victorian gothic neither sympathetic nor handsome. The betteroff pilgrims would have a choice among inns or monasteries, expecting better care and being charged for it. Important ecclesiastics would stay in a hall of the Bishop's Palace of Wolvesey in Winchester, built by Bishop Henry of Blois, who is said to have held the king's crown in safe-keeping here as a surety for money lent. In the days of the Conqueror there was a Norman palace by the High Street, of which only a few stones remain let into the chimney breast in an alley. Princes and great nobles who chose to make a pilgrimage might possibly expect to stay as guests in such a palace, or in the thirteenth-century royal palace at the top of the town, by the West Gate.

Not a great deal that is medieval remains to be seen in the pleasant streets of Winchester, but behind later frontages or restored façades there are older walls of timber frame. The house of Godbegot in the High Street is such a house. Godbegot once belonged to the Saxon Queen Emma, who must have had charm, for she became the wife in turn of the Saxon King Ethelred and of the Danish King Canute. Emma bequeathed Godbegot to the cathedral, in which her son, the most saintly of English kings, Edward the Confessor, was crowned in 1043. The house has been rebuilt more than once and the lavishly timbered façade is mostly restoration work, but the side along Royal Oak Passage is ancient enough to have sheltered beneath its overhang some of the last of the line of pilgrims. This passage, or alley, or ginnel, or pightle—there is a different name in almost every county for such narrow slots of streets—was once called Alwarene Street. In those days it was the boundary of the Jewish quarter, a quarter that flourished in Winchester until the general expulsion of the Jews from England in 1290. Alwarene Street I think it should be again, whatever the name may mean; it should be readopted because it has a fine and ancient look and because it is rare or unique, and because we have a number of streets (and pubs) named after the brief concealment of Charles II in an oak tree.

Opposite Godbegot, behind the fifteenth-century market cross, is a house called Heaven, now a restaurant, which also has ancient walls of timber frame and stud. These two houses, Godbegot and Heaven, are examples of many buildings in Winchester that are far older than their faces.

At the top of the town there stood a royal palace of which all that remains is a very beautiful Early English great hall, built for Henry III about 1235 to the design of a genius of a master mason known simply as Stephen. I hope that the affronted spirit of this Stephen may hover with all malevolence over the heads of those authorities who have allowed this beautiful hall to be sub-divided by an enormous concrete wall erected for 'temporary' purposes some thirty years ago. It was these same authorities, I suppose, who converted the larger part of the divided hall into a court-room and cluttered it with benches, dock, and tables and chairs for public, witnesses, lawyers, and justices. High on the gable wall above the bench and admirably placed to relieve the boredom of witnesses and accused, hangs a vast round table-top. This table, it is said, is the very table around which sat King Arthur and his knights. A figure of the king appears on it, and round the margin are the named places of all the knights. The table was painted, or repainted, in 1522 for the visit of the Emperor Charles V as the guest of Henry VIII, but it is certainly older than that. Hardynge in his Chronicle of c. 1436 declares it to be the very round table made by Joseph of Arimathea for the Brethren of the Grail. It is mentioned by Caxton in Malory's *Morte d'Arthur*, which he printed in 1485. The journeys of Gawain and Perceval and other knights of the Round Table were a pilgrimage of the holiest and most elusive kind, the search for the source of spiritual life, the Holy Grail. The Grail was the cup out of which Christ drank at the Last Supper, the dish out of which he ate, the vessel in which was caught the blood that issued from his wounds as he hung on the cross: it was all these and other things, and it was older than all Christian faith, trailing with it shadowy streamers of ancient beliefs. 'Twas not of wood, nor of any manner of metal, nor was it in any wise of stone, nor of horn nor of bone.' Nevertheless, it appears in imagination as a precious vessel of gold and of crystal, effulgent and beautiful. I do not think that the knights of the Round Table, despite their many adventures in search of the Grail, ever found it, but I and many others have seen a reputed Grail, and I have held it in my hand, a chewed fragment of a wooden mazer that used to be kept at a house called Nanteos near Llanbadarn Fawr in Wales. The house has been sold and the Grail removed, but that it was the true Grail, brought to England by Saint Joseph of Arimathea and long preserved in the monastery at Glastonbury and then at the Dissolution for a short space at Strata Florida, tradition asserts, and that it could and did perform miracles was popular belief until at least this century.

We cannot leave Winchester without reference to Saint

Giles's Fair, which was held on Saint Giles's Hill east of the city from the time of William the Conqueror throughout the middle ages. At the time of the fair whole streets of canvas booths and stalls sprang up within an enclosing fence, and business was done with merchants come from all parts of England and of Europe. The fair had no particular connection with the pilgrimage, but pilgrims passing through at the time would visit it, and if they did they would probably save themselves time by taking a different route down to the Itchen valley to begin their journey (see Appendix).

6 *Winchester to Alton*

18 MILES

This and the following chapters will guide the reader along the Pilgrims' Way so far as that Way has been established, but, as I have already said, the Way is not necessarily either a single line or a simple one. There are frequent places where there are alternative routes, and in fact the Way begins at Winchester with a choice of two routes—by road via Headbourne Worthy or by footpath along the Nuns' Walk. In this and the following chapters alternative routes will be marked *a* and *b*, with a blank line following alternative *b*, where the undivided Way is taken up again.

We leave Winchester by way of Jewry Street, once the main street of the Jewish quarter; it turns north from the High Street a little below the West Gate and the highest point of the old town. Jewry Street leads to the site of the vanished North Gate, at the junction with North Walls and the Andover Road. We continue over the crossing into Hyde Street, which comes shortly to the site of Hyde Abbey.

The abbey buildings stood to the east of the street. The monks coming from their cramped little monastery in the shadow of the cathedral had here the green fields and the streams of the valley of the Itchen, and here they raised their walls and built their new church, in which the bones of Alfred were laid with those of the little-known Saint Josse, for whom the monks erected a costly shrine. The abbey, or a large part of it, was burned down in 1141, but it was soon rebuilt. All that is left now is the parish church of Saint Bartholomew, which was built at the gate of the monastery, and that gate itself, leading into a maze of workshops and back gardens of cottages. The abbey was dissolved in 1538, when the keys were handed to Thomas Wriothesley, Henry VIII's commissioner, who later became Earl of Southampton; an unlovable character, he is remembered for his hounding of a 23-year-old girl, Anne Askew, to the rack

and the pyre. Wriothesley promptly set to work to strip everything of value from the buildings of the abbey—the gold of the
shrine of Saint Josse, and the lead from the roofs—and tumbled
down the walls. Some of the stone from the abbey went into the
building of a tower for the parish church at the gate, and more
was taken away to be used in the fabric of Wriothesley's new
house at Stratton. 'We intend,'Wriothesley reported to the king,
'to sweep away all the rotten bones that be called relics; which
we may not omit, lest it be thought that we came more for the
treasure than for the avoiding of the abomination of idolatry.'
It was a facile and self-deluding hypocrisy.

Despite the wreckage brought about by Wriothesley, considerable remains of the abbey were to be seen until late in the
eighteenth century, when the local authorities built a bridewell
on the site. During the work a labourer's spade turned up a
stone with the inscription 'Aelfred Rex DCCCLXXXI'. The stone
was allowed to be taken away by some stranger, and nothing
now exists, not a bone or a stone, to show where the body of
the greatest of Saxon kings lay in death. A brewery succeeded
the bridewell and for years the smell of hops and yeast prevailed
where the monks had sought to raise the odour of sanctity.

Saint Bartholomew's church, the chapel at the gate of the
abbey, keeps some of its Norman character, heavily emphasized
or overwhelmed in the nineteenth century by hearty neo-
Norman work in the north aisle. The church has some curiosities
and some charm. One of the handrails of the south doorway is the ironwork of a nineteenth-century inn sign upside
down, and the chancel rails of mahogany once swayed across
the Solent as the balustrade of the saloon stairway of an Isle of
Wight ferry. Far more important are a number of capitals
rescued from the wreck of the abbey, capitals of such beauty and
quality that they serve to arouse one's fury for what has been
lost in the destruction of Hyde Abbey.

Alternative 1a. By way of Headbourne Worthy
The straight road north from Hyde is a fragment of the
Roman road that led to Silchester. It would have been in
existence, though no doubt rutted and worn, in the earliest days
of the pilgrimage to the shrine of Saint Swithun. The pilgrims

to Canterbury, with the ordinary travellers and traders of the time, followed this road because it led directly out of the city and ran well above the marshes and water-meadows of the Itchen. The wear of their feet would have kept the road clear of grass and verdure, so that there could have been no doubt of its direction. I think that many of the pilgrims coming from Winchester and going to the north or to Canterbury would have come out by this road because it led past the isolated church of Headbourne Worthy. The word 'worthy' means an enclosure, and the element 'head' is the same as 'hyde', which denotes an area of land. The church is today on an island enclosed by small streams that flow around the church-yard and descend to the complex waterways of the Itchen. In spring the churchyard is full of small, wild daffodils, a great delight. Pilgrims did not, however, come here for the daffodils, no matter how charming they may have been. The interest of the church of Headbourne Worthy, this Saxon church, marked by long and short work and the typical shallow wall buttresses of the Saxon idiom, the thing about this church is the amazing rood that was sculptured at the west end, above the doorway. That great rood, with the figures of the crucified Christ and of his two companions, would be extraordinary in any context. Paralleled but not exceeded at Romsey and at Breamore, in this little church beside the ancient Roman road and the road the pilgrims trod such a rood cannot have had other than a special significance. It may be, of course, that it was carved simply and purely for the glorification of God, as the great cathedral-like churches of East Anglia, far too spacious for any possible congregation, were built to that same magnification of the Lord. I believe that that huge rood was carved there as a station of piety in the Saxon pilgrimage to the shrine of Saint Swithun, and this is confirmed by the dedication of this Saxon church to Swithun. After 1170 Headbourne Worthy would be important as a station in the pilgrimage to the shrine of the Norman Saint Thomas at Canterbury. It would heighten in the pilgrims their sense of devotion and worship, remind them that they had begun on a holy road and on a pilgrimage that too was holy, and they would come away with the image of that huge rood fixed in their minds, so that they would see it plainly in whatever circumstances they might encounter in the hundred and twelve miles they had yet to travel towards the east. The rood alone, it seems to me, is enough to provide the answer to the question which road out of Winchester the pilgrims would be most likely to take.

In the sixteenth century a kind of narthex was built at the west end of the church to shelter the rood from the elements. This narthex, or porch, was two-storeyed, with the whole of the rood in the upper room. In such a room the power of the sculptured figures cannot have been other than overwhelming. Alas, the narthex could not shelter the rood from those enemies of the Church who supposed all such images to be barbarous and idolatrous. In that same century some miserable zealot, at the order of the reforming Bishop Horn of Winchester, chiselled the figures off the wall. There remains a chipped silhouette, as it were a shadow that shows no more than the shape without the sculpture, with only the hand of God, pointing from above, still intact.

Three other 'worthies' follow. Kings Worthy has a restored Perpendicular church not far from the A33, which we have to cross in order to take the eastward road along the B3047. Then comes Abbots Worthy, obviously once the property of an abbot as Kings Worthy was that of the Crown, followed by Martyr Worthy, which owes its name not to some cruel martyrdom but to its having belonged in the early thirteenth century to a Norman Henricus de la Martre. 'Martyr' may alternatively come from the old French name for a weasel or marten. In that same century the church was held by the prior and convent of Saint Swithun's, and the dedication to Saint Swithun of this village church survives to this day.

The road above the Itchen was a lonely one in the middle ages, even though the villages are no more than a mile or two apart. To the north there stretched a vast area of empty country, rising no more than about two hundred feet above the road, but clothed with the woodlands of Micheldever Forest. Some parts of those woodlands are represented now by Itchen Wood, Shroner Wood, and Micheldever Wood and the woods of Northington. In this forest a Romano-British farmer had a villa on a site a mile north of Itchen Abbas, and through the hills and woods ran a Roman road as straight for seven or eight miles as a Roman ruler could draw it. Now the A33, it leads to Basingstoke.

Below the B3047 the Itchen flows peacefully, abrim with its levelbanks. We turn suddenly down towards it in the village of Itchen Abbas, whose neo-Norman church, rebuilt in this style in 1862, is near the water, with some genuine Norman fragments from the previous church on this site. The 'abbas' was the abbess of Saint Mary's convent in Winchester, who held land here.

East of Itchen Abbas the road and the river run side by side for a short time along a beautiful stretch, with a multiplicity of streams as we enter Itchen Stoke. This village has houses sloping down to the water, in company with a gothic church built in 1866 at a cost of £7,000, paid by the vicar of that time, Charles Conybeare. He got his brother Henry Conybeare to design the new church. The building has interest and some panache, and should not be dismissed out of hand as just another Victorian imitation.

Belloc considers that at this point the modern road into Alresford does not represent the Pilgrims' Way. East of Itchen Abbas, the Alre and other streams join the Itchen in a complex network of streams, channels, and rivulets, running through land that evidently was once marsh and swamp. It was probably impassable and any path or road, Belloc considers, would have had to loop too far to the north to get round this soft country and enter Old Alresford.

Alternative 1b. The route via Nuns' Walk, Easton, Avington, and Ovington

From Kings Worthy this route lies south of the Itchen and in lower country. Some part of it may not essentially belong to the Pilgrims' Way, but that the road is ancient the villages that lie upon it suggest, and in summer, when the ground was dry, it may have been preferred by pilgrims.

We begin at Hyde, passing down by Saint Bartholomew's church to turn left into a short street called Saxon Road. In a few yards this comes to an end at a bridge over an arm of the Itchen, and we continue on a distinct path beside the water. At a bridge below Abbot's Barton the path crosses the stream and continues along the far side, soon rising on a narrow causeway above the flat and marshy valley of the Itchen. A slight rise develops to the left, a gentle presage of the steep chalk scarps that are to come. It has been said by various authorities that the causeway and the path are evidently ancient, and I am willing to believe it with no obvious clue to any age greater than that of other footpaths. In places we found the path almost overgrown with grasses, brambles, roses, and nettles and this made it clear that the path is not today in frequent use.

The Itchen is a divisive river, flowing in all sorts of unexpected channels, and leaving a visitor puzzled to know when he is or is not by the main stream. It is likely, however, that in the middle ages there were fewer channels, some of those in existence now having been cut for irrigation or flood-relief purposes or for marsh reclamation. The valley hereabouts must have been much more marshy than it is today, but once he had passed Abbots Barton our pilgrim would have been above all but the deepest of floods and could make his way safely to Kings Worthy. Today we have to go under the railway and under the A33. A footpath through low-lying fields continues towards Martyr Worthy and comes into a lane that leads down to Easton, crossing the Itchen by a bridge at a point where, for a short distance, the river flows in a single main channel. Hang over the bridge to look into the clear water. You may see a trout or two, and with unusual luck you may sight a salmon, head to the current, returning to the haunts in which it was born.

Easton has some brick-built thatched cottages among modern houses. The church, built in 1150, has a showy Norman doorway and, what is not common, it retains the apsed chancel that the Normans gave it. The apse was a favourite of Norman church builders, but its attractions palled on the English, who in a few generations came to prefer the square east end. In most instances later builders or restorers did away with the apse of the Normans, and that is why the church at Easton is uncommon. Inside there is something else uncommon, a horseshoe Norman chancel arch that for a moment or two creates an illusion of Moorish influence; but it is more likely that the horseshoe shape has come about by subsidence. The Normans were never careful enough about their foundations, and sometimes they set their massive masonry direct on the earth, as they did, for instance, at Shalfleet in the Isle of Wight, where a tower with walls many feet thick rests directly on clay. No wonder the common story of Norman towers and churches is simply that they fell over, as did the great tower of Ely. Inevitably parts of the church were flattened in the fall. At Easton, however, all that happened was a deformation of the chancel arch.

See in this church, on the south wall of the chancel, a nicely if profusely lettered wall monument to Agatha Barlow, who died in 1595, having in her person bridged the eras between the middle ages and the Reformation, between the Catholic world of monastic faith, and that of Protestant dissent, between the cultivation of relics and the scepticism of the new age. She married the last prior of the suppressed monastery of Bromholm in Norfolk, which had been a famous place of pilgrimage because it had a piece of the True Cross. Transferring his loyalties with facility from Catholic to Protestant, the former prior became in succession bishop of Saint Asaph's, of Saint David's, of Bath and Wells, and then of Chichester. He had five daughters by Agatha, each of whom married a bishop, while a son, William, became rector of this parish of Easton.

A narrow, winding lane leads east to Avington, where, on the lowlands beside the river, stands Avington House. There may have been a house here in the time of King Edgar, that is in the tenth century, but the earliest masonry that can be dated in the present house is Elizabethan. The total effect now, however, is of the seventeenth century, for in that century the greater part of the house was rebuilt in red brick, to a simple design that, as in much Palladian architecture, hides its interior merit under a plain exterior. King Charles brought Nell Gwyn to stay at Avington when Thomas Ken, prebendary of Winchester cathedral, had refused to have her in his house in the cathedral precinct. Later, this stuffy, ugly little man, 'who wouldn't give poor Nelly a lodging', as Charles said, was appointed by the king to the bishopric of Bath and Wells. Charles did not hold grudges.

Later, the house belonged to the dukes of Chandos, and the wife of one of these, Margaret, set in train the rebuilding of the village church in the same red brick as the house. She died in

1. *The eleventh-century Norman south transept of Winchester cathedral*

2. *The Norman double chancel of Compton church*

3. *A hollow way: Sandy Lane in West Warren*

1768 before the church was completed. Avington church remains one of the least altered of Georgian churches in the country, and it should be seen. Sir John Shelley, brother of the poet Percy Bysshe Shelley, bought the house in 1848 and the Shelley family lived in it until 1952. The house is now divided into flats, but a suite of the grander rooms is open to the public.

South-east of Avington is Hampage Wood, which has a direct connection with Winchester, for from this wood came the timber used for the wooden roof of Bishop Walkelin's Norman cathedral. William I gave the bishop, his kinsman, permission to cut as much timber in this wood as he could manage in four days. The bishop, however, was an equivocator and he accepted the condition gratefully, even gleefully. Rapidly gathering an army of woodcutters he felled every tree in the wood but one. William was furious, but fury seems to have been the limit of his resentment. The single tree, known as the Gospel Oak, long survived as a rotten wreck and its name still appears on the map.

The road goes on through Avington Park along an attractive reach of the river and comes into the village of Ovington, whose houses, mostly modern, climb uphill to a Victorian gothic church. In the churchyard an ancient arch remains from the previous church on this site.

In the lower ground our route is joined by a footpath coming over the river and over watery land from Itchen Stoke. Belloc supposed that the pilgrims and earlier travellers on the Old Road would have come by this footpath down from Itchen Stoke to avoid the marshes of the Alre. If they did they would be exchanging marsh for marsh, but it is possible that they would have had at least less of soggy ground by this route. It joins the village road of Ovington just east of the Bush Inn.

Our two routes, now fused, run as a road beside the river, with a wet ditch on the other side, so that the road is between water and water, and so it comes to the dual carriageway of the A31. This has to be crossed—on a holiday week-end a feat in itself.

Here we come to two more alternatives.

Alternative 2a. The southern route from Ovington to Bishops' Sutton
In the present day it is possible to continue along the B road
Gpw

from Itchen Stoke to its junction with the A31. The southern route comes, as I have said above, from Ovington along the riverside road to the A31. East of the A31 the route follows a surfaced lane for a few yards and then turns off left into a rough little lane, which passes over the Tichborne road and comes to a ford, or, it would be more accurate to say, falls into a ford. And such a ford! It crosses a branch of the Itchen, and in a dry season I found it to be deep, with a soft bottom, and, moreover, it was seventy or eighty feet across. A Land-Rover could get through, but I doubt that any ordinary car would without a considerable dampening of all the people in it. Medieval travellers on horseback would manage very well, though in winter—and it should be remembered that for some fifty years the great day of the Canterbury pilgrimage was the 29th of December—it might have proved much more of a problem. Travellers on foot would not, I think, dare venture unless there was a ferry. Today pedestrians may get across dryshod along a wooden causeway.

Thereafter the lane soon becomes surfaced again, crosses the Cheriton road, and climbs Tichborne Down to a high point at 286 feet, near Tichborne Down Farm.

Tichborne itself, a mile and a half to the south-east, is a pleasant village with brick and timber thatched cottages and a church with the double-splayed windows that proclaim a Saxon origin, with other details, such as the buttresses, to show that the Normans, too, had a hand in its construction; while the tower of flint and brick is dated 1703. The Tichborne family have held the manor here since the twelfth century and can reasonably claim to be among the oldest families in the country. In 1969, for the first time for seven hundred years, the baronetcy descended on the distaff side. The Tichborne dole has achieved some fame from the circumstance of its origin in 1150 and from the fact that it is still in existence; it provides six pounds of flour to each adult each March, and three pounds for each child. The legend of the dole is that it is the product of twenty-three acres of land marked out by Isabel, Lady Tichborne, who on her death-bed had pleaded with her husband to institute this charity for Lady Day and had got from him a promise that he would devote as much land to it as she could crawl around before a blazing torch she carried burned out. She was farther from death than her unfeeling husband realized, for she managed, crawling and stumbling, to circumambulate these twenty-three acres. The same story, with the same characters, is told of a dole at Brighstone in the Isle of Wight.

Tichborne for a time became known to all England because of the notorious Tichborne claimant case, in 1871, in which the fat and froward Arthur Orton attempted to prove that he was the long-lost heir to the family estates and fortune; he got a long spell in jail for his temerity and his perjury.

Members of the Tichborne family lie in the vault beneath the north aisle of the Norman nave of the church, and in that aisle, protected by solid Victorian iron bars, are several monuments of the family, including a fine alabaster set-piece with effigies of Sir Benjamin Tichborne, who died in 1621, and his wife, Amphillis, with a row of children along the front of the tomb-chest. An effigy of another child, Michael Tichborne, who died at eighteen months, recalls the story of a gipsy who, annoyed at not receiving charity at the house, prophesied that on a certain day the child would die by drowning. On that day the cautious parents sent the child for safety up on to the downs, and there, while attention was lax for a moment, he fell into a water-filled hollow or rut and drowned, as the gipsy had foretold.

The Tichborne family remained Catholic even through the dangerous days of the Reformation. Today their private chapel in the church is one of those uncommon but ecumenical oddities, of which I have seen only a few, a Catholic chapel in an Anglican church.

We have wandered a little, as we shall again hereafter. On the summit of Tichborne Down Belloc and his companion paused to look westwards along the Itchen valley, the way they had come, and saw the river fiery and gleaming under the light. They then turned to look eastward over the rising ground towards Chawton. The Old Road has followed up the valley of the Itchen, rising slowly and keeping to dry ground wherever possible, but at the deep ford it finally leaves the trout-inhabited river and heads for the water-divide between the watersheds of the Itchen and those of the river Wey, and for a while the Old Road runs through bleaker upland country.

We descend White Hill to Bishop's Sutton.

Alternative 2b. The route by way of Alresford

The B3047 from Itchen Stoke and the lane from Ovington join the A31 within a short distance one of the other, and from either exit we turn left on this busy road to follow it into the crowded main street of New Alresford.

Before you come any further with us, you need to know how to pronounce the name of these two villages of Old and New Alresford and of the river Alre from which they take their name —or, it may be, the river has been named after the villages. I plump for the first of these alternatives because 'Alresford' means 'the ford of alders', and that has primarily to do with water. The name has at times in the past been written with the *r* and the *l* transposed, and here is the clue. The pronunciation is 'ahlsford' or 'awlsford'; the *r* disappears in this lazy-tongued country, in which this liquid consonant is seldom trilled and is often no more than a silence, an hiatus between one vowel and the next. It is not that English tongues cannot vibrate to sound an *r*. Where the sound is not needed it is too often put in with vigour, as for example when television news-readers talk about 'lawr and order'.

Old Alresford is the original village of Alresford. It lies north of the river and has little now to suggest that it preceded New Alresford in time. The houses are mostly of the eighteenth and nineteenth centuries, and the church is of the eighteenth century, with a nineteenth-century gothic interior, put in at a time when this was the only fashion for churches, especially in the opinion of those who knew least about it.

New Alresford was new about the year 1200—you may be sure that if anything in English topography is called 'new' it is at least several centuries old. Bishop Godfrey de Lucy of Winchester laid out the village in relation to his scheme to make the Itchen navigable from Alresford through Winchester and into Southampton Water. It was a time when the wool industry was growing to importance and many families were founding fortunes on the backs of their sheep. The bishop succeeded in his intention of making Winchester prosperous, for it became the staple, that is to say, the official market, for wool.

In order to control the river the bishop built a long dam across the course of the Alre and impounded a huge quantity of water in a lake two hundred acres in extent, with the necessary sluices and locks. But in 1353 the wool staple was removed from Winchester to Calais. Together with Winchester, New Alresford and its waterworks fell on evil times and were neglected. The great pond is still there, reduced to about sixty acres, and crowded with reeds, among which coots and moorhens chuckle and move, while swans slide gracefully over the clearer surface. The long dam now carries the road that goes past Old Alresford to the Candovers. Below the dam a watercress farmer has formed a broad expanse of shallow lagoons, which in season are thick with green plants.

The centre of the village is a broad street, perhaps better called a 'long square', which must have been planned with the expectation that it should be the scene of fairs and a market, and in fact a charter for a market was granted by King John. Along the top of the square the A31 funnels its eroding traffic between eighteenth-century inns and other buildings of a happy colour of brick. The church of Saint John hides behind shops, but its fourteenth-century tower, with a top stage of brick put on a hundred years later, peers over the roofs and down into the broad descending square. At the bottom of that square the B3046 has to do such a jiggle to the right and to the left to cross over the dam that it seems evident that it was not in the original plan to have a road on the dam at all. Despite its traffic, New Alresford remains a pleasant and attractive village, and in the days of the pilgrimages it would surely have had inns to attract pilgrims and travellers, many of whom would want to pause here in order to see Bishop de Lucy's famous waterworks. Belloc, who would put New Alresford aside from the Old Road, descended into the village to spend his first night here.

The A31 continues through New Alresford to Bishop's Sutton, at the beginning of a length of the Way that is single and undoubted.

The Alresfords and much of the land around belonged, before the Conquest and afterwards, to the priory at Winchester, and at Bishop's Sutton the bishops had a manor-house, often called

a palace. Nothing remains of this building except some foundations said to be those of the kennels. The manor-house may well
have been a port of call for indigent pilgrims, who could, or
would like to, count on the charity of a bishop. In the Norman
church there is a small, pleasant, but incomplete brass of an
armoured knight, with his lady standing beside him in a gable
head-dress.

There is general agreement that for at least a mile east of the
village the Old Road, the Pilgrims' Way, and the A31 coincide,
and may in fact coincide all the way to Chawton. But I would
not wish on anyone the duty of walking along this busy main
road, with its noise, dust, and fumes. For half a mile from
Bishop's Sutton you may find pleasanter going along Water
Lane, which runs a little to the north of the main road. But at
Ropley we come to another pair of alternative routes.

Alternative 3a. Along the main road to Four Marks

These three miles should be done by car rather than on foot,
the latter mode of progress giving no pleasure. We have
arrived in the technological seventies at a state of civilization
and technical triumph in which cars and people have become
uncomfortable companions except when one is inside the other.
The road, in places dual carriageway and undoubtedly
destined to be dual all along its length, passes through good
upland landscapes to a point just beyond Ropley Soke after
which there are more and more houses on one or both sides to
interrupt the view, for the last mile to Four Marks and beyond.

Alternative 3b. The route from Ropley Dean to Four Marks

Belloc counts the beginning of this alternative, which he considered to be the true course of the Old Road, from Ropley
cross-roads east of the hamlet of Ropley Dean. He accepted as
evidence of this a straight embankment diverging from the
main road across a field and passing through the garden of the
Chequers Inn. The evidence seems to me slight, and to follow
it means trespassing on private land. Belloc, on his own admission, trespassed frequently without meeting objection, but I
suspect that in his day there might have been less opposition to
harmless strangers on private land than there is now, when a

great many more strangers, not all of them innocent or harmless, have to be kept at arm's length. I think it better to continue for another mile to take the right turn at North Street. This leads very soon to a road junction, where we take our way along Brisland Lane, on the line recommended by Belloc, continuing the direction of the non-existent path projected from the Chequers. Brisland Lane is long and lonely and not too much affected by cars. It rises through farming country, passing at a cross-roads a hamlet called Pilgrims' Way, a name that, I hasten to explain, means nothing at all other than that some modern man or some modern committee chose it as appropriate.

Belloc considered it significant that Brisland Lane and its continuation, Blackberry Lane, the latter now a modern street, rise directly to the water-divide (or 'watershed', as he insists on calling such terrain). This, he thought, was what one should expect a primitive road to do, to overcome the hill with the least possible loss of distance. At Four Marks, if the theory is correct, Blackberry Lane ought to go straight ahead; instead it veers to the north and joins the A31 opposite the trees of Fourteen Acre Plantation, which is an extension of Chawton Park Wood or Alton Forest.

The next length of the Way is along the main road, the A31. Some writers would have the Pilgrims' Way diverge from the main road three miles before Alton. If this was so, then the route has been usurped by the railway line, and I would not recommend that you should walk along that, no matter what the evidence may suggest, even though the alternative means braving the traffic of the A31.

The main road is joined at Chawton by the A32 coming up from the Meon valley, a valley and a stream that keep the name of a Jutish tribe that settled hereabouts in the fifth or sixth century. The durability of many place-names is such that, as in this case, they descend through an unknown number of generations and survive even conquest and change of language.

At the junction of the two main roads in Chawton stands an unpretentious house of red brick, at one time—and excellently placed for the purpose—a posting-house and an alehouse. Here lived Jane Austen, one of seven children, the tall, slim, baby-faced Jane whose calm hazel eyes were so unusually observant and who knew how to manage words so that they became limpid and clear to describe a world in which it seemed to be nearly always Sunday morning. In this house she wrote, in the intervals of genteel house work, and her sewing and embroidery, the last three of her six novels, *Mansfield Park, Emma* and *Persuasion*, and revised the previous ones, which had suffered refusal by purblind publishers, for yet another attempt at publication. The Austen family—Mrs Austen, Jane, her sister Cassandra (who was named after her mother), and Cassandra's friend Martha Lloyd (who married Jane's brother Captain, later Admiral, Francis Austen)—moved here in 1809. The house had been provided for them by Jane's brother Edward, bailiff of the estate of Chawton House, whose owner Thomas Knight had adopted Edward as his heir on condition that he changed his name to Knight. Jane was born in Steventon, a few miles to the north-west, where her father George Austen was rector. In 1801 the family moved to Bath, where George Austen died, and then in 1805 to Southampton, and finally to Chawton. At the time of this last move, in 1809, Jane was thirty-four years of age. In 1817, on Saint Swithun's Day, feeling ill, she went to Winchester to consult a physician, and there, a few weeks later, she died. She lies buried beneath a lettered ledger stone in the north aisle of the cathedral and is commemorated also by a mediocre stained-glass window. The house is open to visitors and in it there may be seen a number of objects that Jane owned or used.

We shall meet the Austens again towards the end of our journey, at Godmersham.

A mile and a half to the south is Farringdon, where Gilbert White was curate for twenty-four years from 1761 before returning, still as curate, to Selborne, his birthplace, which he made famous by his gentle accounts of the natural history and antiquities of the district. At Farringdon a later incumbent, between 1870 and 1930, built with his own hands and a minimum of help the most horrid piece of architecture you may expect to see, as a school and village hall. Of liver-red brick and terracotta, the building has a powerful impact on this otherwise unremarkable village. I am not sure whether it should be blown up as a horror or maintained as an awful example.

The greater part of the village of Chawton flanks the main road. Even in Jane Austen's time it was deemed necessary, because of the noise and the dust, to block up their sitting-room window, which gave on to the road, and to open another on to the garden. The noise and the dust and the fumes are worse now, but the simple brick and timber houses, some thatched, of the village that Jane Austen knew are still there along the margin of the main road, resisting the traffic.

The road continues north-east towards Alton, passing beneath a railway bridge and alongside a triangular green called the Butts, where archery was once practised in a time when it was ordered that all able-bodied men should be able to use a bow.

The road through Alton passes between the shops and houses of a town that retains much of the eighteenth century and earlier. It boasts an interesting museum of bygones and other objects, founded by Dr William Curtis, son of a doctor who treated Jane Austen and her family. The church of Saint Lawrence, west of the main street, is largely of the fifteenth century, but it retains a Norman tower that was the central tower of a cruciform Norman church and now rises strangely above the south aisle of the present building. There are some extraordinary capitals, including a cock and a pair of asses upside down and waving their legs in the air. The fine seventeenth-century pulpit was no more than a few years old when the Royalist Colonel Boles, on the 13th of December 1643, retreated into the cold church with the remnants of his force of five hundred half-trained Irishmen who had attempted to hold the town against ten times as many Roundheads. Boles, fighting from the pulpit, is said to have accounted for half a dozen opponents before he was himself cut down. Various holes in the entrance door to the church and in the wood of the pulpit are attributed to bullets fired in this uneven battle.

The small village of East Worldham, two miles south-east of Alton, preserves a tenuous connection with the pilgrimage to Canterbury. In the modest thirteenth-century church, the nave of which was rebuilt in the previous style in 1865, lies the recumbent figure of a lady, the surface of the stone a little worn and the sculpture of less than moderate quality. It was found during the rebuilding, set face down in the floor. This wimpled lady has on her bosom a wheel-like symbol, from which it is deduced that she was a member of the family of Rouet (French *roue*, a wheel). Geoffrey Chaucer married a Philippa Rouet. The effigy at East Worldham may represent Philippa Chaucer, and this seems more likely against the fact that it is known that Thomas, a son of Geoffrey and Philippa was lord of the manor here. The simple, naïve sculpture of Philippa Chaucer is in sharp contrast with the elaborate, costly, and aesthetically fine tomb and effigy of her grand-daughter, Alice, which you may see in the chancel of the Perpendicular church of Ewelme just north of the Thames in Oxfordshire. Philippa's monument is that of modest bourgeois: Alice was a great lady, a countess, and duchess of the Duke of Suffolk.

7 *Alton to Guildford*

18 MILES

This length of the Pilgrims' Way, shared between Hampshire and Surrey, is for the greater part modern road, including as such the whole of the nine miles between Alton and Farnham. If you, as a modern pilgrim, think it important to keep to the line the medieval pilgrims are believed to have followed, then I counsel you to take a bus from Alton to Farnham rather than to walk all this distance in the wuther and the fumes of a copious flow of traffic. If, however, you are willing to depart from the reputed Pilgrims' Way, you may choose a different and pleasanter line along the minor roads and lanes of the ancient Hoar Way. You may reach the Hoar Way by taking any road running northwards east of Alton. It will add two or three miles to your journey, but you will consider this a small price to pay for avoiding the Alton–Farnham length of the A31. In certain circumstances the Hoar Way diversion might have been chosen for preference by ancient man and by medieval pilgrims also.

Alternative 4a. The Hoar Way

From Alton to Farnham the Pilgrims' Way runs along the valley of the north branch of the river Wey, for the greater part on the gault and the greensand. Wish away the hard surface and the definite line of the A31 and see in its place a trodden path winding in and out among trees. In places in this low land the path would sometimes be muddy and sticky, sometimes awash with water. Belloc points out that this length of the Old Road, off the chalk and approaching the river, is peculiar and uncharacteristic of the Old Road in general. He reasons that a study of the contours of the area on the map will show why the road goes where it does. The higher land immediately to the north, along which one might expect the Old Road would have gone if it could, is uneven, with an alternation of hilly capes and hollow bays. Any road over these hills and hollows would have to switchback continually up and down and would have been

tiresome. Belloc argued that primitive man, who usually preferred to travel along dry hillsides or ridges, would choose to
paddle a straight and more level line in the mud and slush of
the valley rather than cope with those repeated ups and downs.

I wonder if this could really have been so. It would not have
been difficult for our ancient traveller to get out of the watery
valley if he wished to. He had only to make his way to the north-
east from the position of Alton by a route we can follow, let us
say by way of the ridge that rises to 738 feet above Yarnham's
Farm (OS 73.44), where later, a Roman road crossed over the
summit, over Sutton Common, and then by Frog Lane, to come
to Well on the Hoar Way. On that ancient way he could travel
along a dry ridge some 500 feet up, and from this he could have
conveniently dropped down into Farnham to recover the
original line, the line that is in fact the true projection of the
Hoar Way all along to Canterbury.

I do not say that this is what ancient man, coming from the
region of Winchester, did do, for there is no evidence to back
such an assertion; it is what he could have done and might well
have done when the lower road was at its worst. It would be a
sensible thing to do—and it may be remarked of the Old Road,
the Pilgrims' Way, that its siting along most of its length is
characterized by a free employment of practical common sense.

Primitive travellers could, and no doubt did, choose their
time for travelling. The matter was not so free for Christian
pilgrims going to Canterbury. Thomas Becket died on the 29th
of December and consequently the principal festival of the saint
and of his shrine, from 1170 to the time of the translation of the
body into the upper church, was in that month. Until that
translation many pilgrims would choose to travel in December
in order to come to the shrine in Canterbury on the saint's day,
and even after the translation the anniversary of the murder
would be considered by many to have more potency than the
anniversary of the translation. In most years these winter
pilgrims would have had a cold, damp journey, for in that
month not even the southern face of the downs could have
given much shelter from the winds, the rain, and the frost. The
pilgrims would not have relished in addition the sticky mud and
the slush of a lower road, and they too, it may be imagined,

would have preferred the higher route along the Hoar Way, along which they would turn to the east, past the site of a Roman villa, past the motte and bailey of Barley Pound, past Powderham Castle (an earthwork), and so by Dippenhall down into Farnham. Between Powderham Castle and Dippenhall they would pass over the line of the modern county boundary between Hampshire and Surrey.

Alternative 4b. The main road

The main road goes by way of the villages of Holybourne, Froyle, just to the north of the road, Binsted a mile to the south of it, and Bentley.

The main road to Holybourne has some pleasant old houses. Off the road, a quarter of a mile to the north, church, pond, and cottages make a picturesque group. The church has Norman fragments and Early English details, but it has been severely restored. What is of more interest is the village name, which was 'Haliborne' in Domesday Book and 'Haliburna' in the Pipe Rolls of 1167. The sanctity of the place therefore antedates the Canterbury pilgrimage, but what might have been holy about the little stream that flows from the village pond southwards towards the river Wey I do not think anyone can now tell. Some ancient water-deity, perhaps.

Froyle has a name from Old English, that is to say, Saxon 'Freohyll', which means 'the hill of the goddess Frig'. That, clearly, is pagan and comes from a time before the Christianization of the district in the seventh century. The hill on which the goddess Frig was worshipped must be the low knoll on which the red-brick Georgian church now stands in place of earlier churches. It was not uncommon for early missionaries to adopt pagan sites for their churches, for by doing this they demonstrated that the new religion had overcome the old and so cancelled it.

A mile farther on, and south of the main road, Saxon Elesa's people had a *tun* or settlement where now stands Isington Mill on the river Wey, a brick-built water-mill with two square oasthouses, the points of which may be seen from the road. Field-Marshal Lord Montgomery found the mill derelict after the war and turned it into a very attractive house, with a special building to shelter his famous wartime caravan. The road south past the mill leads into Binsted, whose church of Holy Cross, built of a whitish stone called malm, dates from the twelfth and thirteenth centuries. It contains the worn figure of a knight in armour with his legs crossed, and with angels by his head; he was Richard de Westcote, who is said on the score of the crossed legs of his effigy to have been a crusader—but scholars have long ago denounced as false the popular notion that cross-legged effigies mark the tombs of crusaders. If this Richard was the one who founded a chantry here in 1332 he was too late to have gone on any crusade. His Norman-French inscription, however, suggests an earlier date, early enough for him to have gone on the eighth or ninth crusade, or even on the seventh in 1239. The inscription sempiternally prays:

> Richard de Westcote gist ici
> deu de sa alme eit merci
> amen

In the Norman tower is a peal of bells, with an inscription on the tenor:

> In 1695
> Nicholas Wheeler did contrive
> out of four bells to make five.

Bentley is one of the few places in which the Pilgrims' Way is identical with the main street, and it is of interest to remark that of these few two others, Alton and Farnham, are on this same stretch of road. Bentley's seventeenth-century and eighteenth-century houses, mostly on one side of the street, shelter demurely behind walls and trees. The church is half a mile away to the north, on high ground that affords broad and distant views over a countryside of rolling fields and woods and to the south of the dark mass of Alice Holt.

Saint Mary's church at Bentley, approached through a churchyard with two distinct avenues of trees, one of limes and the other of yews, is Norman and Early English, with a nave rebuilt in neo-Norman style in 1890; the Norman tower has an eighteenth-century brick top. There is some old glass in the church—a little—the best of which is a small fifteenth-century censing angel in the tracery of the east window.

The extensive woodland of Alice Holt, once continuous with Woolmer Forest farther south, stands as a remnant of the great forest of Andredesweald, which in the middle ages covered and made impassable much of the country south of the Pilgrims' Way from here to Canterbury. 'Alice' has changed sex; the name was 'Alfsi' in 1169, and earlier than that was 'Aelfsige', who must have been a Saxon owning land here. Alice Holt is now a State forest with interesting nature walks and informatively labelled seed-plots and stands of young trees. A large area is planted with conifers, but there are still many acres of hardwoods to the south, where Alice Holt extends towards the river Slea and the southern branch of the Wey. The two branches of the river Wey join at Tilford in Surrey, a pretty village with two old bridges recently spoiled, and with a large green bordering the water, where in summer it is a delight to watch local teams play cricket. But we on the Pilgrims' Way have lost the river Wey by then, for the north branch turns southwards after Farnham and we do not see the river again until we have to cross it below Saint Catherine's chapel south of Guildford. That is, if we do not choose to go to Waverley Abbey.

The greater part of the road between Bentley and Farnham is dual carriageway. It comes, south-west of Farnham, to a roundabout, from which the Farnham by-pass veers off to the right and the road into the town to the left.

Farnham is of unknown antiquity, though its name is Saxon and needs only a change of vowel—'Fernham'—to show what it means, a village or settlement among the ferns or bracken that grew on the commons in which it was set. But we can go a long way farther back than that: mesolithic pit-dwellings have been found on a site east of the town, dating from approximately the sixth millennium BC, while to the north at Caesar's Camp there is an iron-age fort. And then, of course, there is the neolithic Hoar Way, coming directly from the west to join one of Farnham's main streets, West Street. In 688 AD Caedwalla, king of the West Saxons, gave land at Farnham for a Christian church or minster and then departed for Rome, where he was baptized by the Pope and shortly afterwards died. In 803 the manor of Farnham was in the possession of the Bishop of Winchester, for Farnham then and for long afterwards was part of a vast see covering a large part of the south of England. From the twelfth century Farnham castle, built by Henry of Blois, was a palace of the bishops of Winchester, and then, but briefly, after the division of the see, was the home of the Bishop of Guildford.

From the roundabout we come into Farnham by West Street, which in turn becomes the Borough, and then East Street before it becomes once more the Guildford Road. Farnham is an agreeable town that has striven to preserve its architectural heritage. Its general flavour is Georgian, but the sophisticated frontages are in many instances simply new faces to much older buildings of timber and brick, some of which go back to the fifteenth century. The pleasing red brick made from the gault clay of the district and the red tiles of the roofs are what give Farnham its present character. One of the best classical houses, Willmer House, on the south side of West Street, was built in 1718 by one John Thorpe, but it takes its name from Miss Willmer's boarding-school for girls, which flourished c. 1823. Today the house is the town's museum, with, among other things, exhibits concerning the geology of the district. The front of Willmer House is built of rubbed and gauged brick so beautifully done that it would not be easy to find anything to compare with it. Vernon house, a few yards farther along West Street, is visually dull Georgian of a few years later than Willmer House, but the exterior hides a sixteenth-century house that has undergone various alterations; it is now the public library.

There is a great deal more of charming domestic architecture to be seen in the main streets of Farnham, and in particular one should not pass by Castle Street, a broad street designed for a market, rising to the castle in such a manner that from the foot of the street one has an excellent view of the consonance, the neighbourliness that architects of the seventeenth and eighteenth centuries were able to achieve. This agreeableness is in sharp contrast with the work of many modern architects in other towns, who conceive that their duty and perhaps their ideal is to make a building to dominate those around it. At Farnham not even the castle at the head of the street can be

4. *Saint Martha's church*

5. *Stepping-stones over the Mole at Burford*

6. *Stile at Burford, below Box Hill*

7. *Continental pulpit and woodwork in Gatton church*

said to be domineering. Castle Street has no planned unity; rather it is a mixture of houses of different periods and different styles, that cohabit happily. Nor is this street as yet too much spoiled by the vacuous stare of inserted plate-glass shop windows. Along it are some buildings of timber frame, such as the Spinning-Wheel, the Seven Stars, and the Lion and Lamb, the last dated 1537. That there is a lot of timber-frame behind the urbane frontages of Farnham generally you may see by poking into any of the narrow alleys leading off from the streets, and here too you may find a favourite device of the south-east counties, the tile-hanging of walls and gables.

In the middle ages there were many inns in Farnham, and in these our pilgrims, yeomen and poor men, the gentle and the rough-hewn, the palmers and the pardoners would have found shelter and food. The poorest would climb up to the episcopal palace to seek charity from prelates for whom the eye of the needle must sometimes have been a cause of desperate dreams.

Farnham Castle was built by Henry of Blois, Bishop of Winchester, about 1138 rather as a castle than as a palace. Its accent was military and perhaps it was a little old-fashioned for its time, some seventy years after the Conquest. For what Henry of Blois built was the usual inverted pudding-basin motte topped by a tower with walls of immense thickness, in the middle of which was a well, that indispensable element in a castle, dug to prevent the defenders in time of siege from dying of thirst. It was a tumultuous time, with the Empress Matilda marching about the country claiming the throne for her son, and King Stephen also marching about, so that the two factions occasionally met and fought. In that undisciplined time many castles were built without licence from the king—the so-called 'adulterine' castles. When Matilda's son Henry became king as Henry II (Becket's friend and enemy), and authority lay once more with the Crown, these adulterine castles were knocked down one by one on the king's orders. The king took advantage of the absence of Henry of Blois in France to demolish the bishop's castle in Farnham.

The castle was soon rebuilt, but not in the same form. The motte was now ringed by a defensive wall like a crown around a bald pate, and the space between the motte and the wall was

HPW

filled in, so that what had been a pudding-basin now became a solid drum bordered by cliffs of masonry. This drum was contained in an outer bailey, in which a more habitable house was erected with a great hall, a courtyard, a kitchen and a chapel. The connection with the surface of the drum was by steps.

Louis, Dauphin of France, captured the castle in 1216 in the French invasion invited by English barons disaffected with the rule of King John. Louis taking this as an invitation to claim the English crown, landed at Stonor, near Sandwich, and he was in fact actually crowned in London before his defeat in the battle called the 'Fair of Lincoln'. He had, however, in the meantime, captured several castles, Guildford, Odiham, and Farnham among them. Farnham castle was retaken for the king in 1217. It was taken again by Sir William Waller for Parliament in the Civil War, when Cromwell ordered it to be slighted so that it should not any further imperil the peace of the land. With such interruptions Farnham castle or palace continued to be a residence of the bishops of Winchester from the time of its building until 1927, when the new dioceses of Guildford and Portsmouth were created out of the former extensive diocese of Winchester.

The medieval bishops held it a duty to provide hostels for the poorer class of pilgrims—such provision was surely a deed that would be remembered in Heaven. One such hostel remains in the shape of the Old Vicarage in Church Lane, where a medieval house is concealed by later alterations.

Near by is the parish church, partly Norman and Early English, but largely of the fourteenth and fifteenth centuries, done over in 1855 by Ferrey and in 1865 by Ewan Christian. The most notable thing in this church is the suite of three sedilia and piscina, which dates from the fifteenth century and is in the Perpendicular style, but has the ogees and something of the gusto of a century earlier.

In the churchyard, surrounded by iron railings, is the grave of William Cobbett and of his wife Anne. I wonder what sort of life Anne Cobbett had with that self-appointed prophet and critic of all political and agricultural causes, this bumptious, vociferous, obstinate, energetic, violent, and intensely hardworking fellow who supposed himself the last authority on almost any subject. He did not hesitate, for example, to tell the bonnet-makers of Tring how to do the job that was their speciality. 'If these people of Tring', he wrote, 'choose to grow the straw instead of importing it from Leghorn and if they choose to make plat and to make bonnets just as beautiful and as lasting as those which come from Leghorn they have nothing to do but read my *Cottage Economy* (paragraph 224 to paragraph 234 inclusive) where they will find as plain as words can make it the whole mass of directions for taking the seed of wheat and converting the produce into bonnets.' Forthright, downright, argumentative, dictatorial, this very model of a John Bull was fortunately for his country an original, *sui generis*, unique. Having set the world to rights several times over, served a term in jail (for sedition), and at other times having found it urgently necessary to remove himself abroad, Cobbett died in 1835. He was born in 1762 at the Jolly Farmer, which still stands at the end of Longbridge to the south of the river Wey in Farnham; its name has been changed to the 'William Cobbett'. It faces, across the street and across a corseted stream, a complex of early nineteenth-century industrial buildings called the Maltings, which more than once has been threatened with demolition, but appears for the present to have been saved for community use.

Cobbett left a prodigious amount of printed and published matter, but is remembered most for one work, the *Rural Rides*, in which he recounts his observations in travelling about the south of England. He should be remembered also as the founder of the Parliamentary reports that go by the name of the printer Cobbett chose for them, Luke Hansard.

After Farnham, some pilgrims would choose to leave the Pilgrims' Way for a while to follow the river southwards to Saint Mary's Well and Waverley Abbey. Following in their steps we pass Moor Park, now a college. It appears as a somewhat bald Georgian mansion of no great intrinsic interest, but it has been shown to be a redressing and replanning of a Carolean house built about 1630. The alteration was done for Sir William Temple, a notable diplomat who forged the Triple Alliance against the aggression of France. At Moor Park, which he bought in 1680 as Compton Hall and renamed after the more famous Moor Park in Hertfordshire, he indulged himself in redesigning the house and in laying out a formal garden beside the river Wey. He employed as secretary a bright young man, taking his first job, called Jonathan Swift, and it was here that Swift met and became unofficial tutor to Miss Esther Johnson, whom he immortalized as Stella. If the heart of Swift ever held love, then it was for Stella, but he never married her. His regard for her outlived the more passionate siege of Vanessa (Esther Vanhomrigh), and it was with Stella that Swift was buried in Saint Patrick's cathedral in Dublin, the cathedral of which he had been made dean.

Saint Mary's Well, nearly a mile to the south-east, at the far end of the park, was no doubt Saint Mary's Well long before the time of Temple and of Swift. Here in a shallow cave a small stream rises to flow down to join the river. The cave was reputedly the home of Mother Ludlam, a witch, who brewed her potions and her magic in a great cauldron that you may see to this day in Frensham church. She was an amiable lady who made it her business to lend whatever vessels were required for local weddings and other festivities, and the cauldron stands in the church only because someone, for ever offending Mother Ludlam, borrowed it and neglected to take it back on time.

Saint Mary's Well may have got its name from its nearness to the abbey of Waverley, which stands on low-lying land in a curve of the river below the wooded slopes of Crooksbury Hill. It seems to me that the abbey is on the wettest of sites, more likely to be flooded by the river than any other abbey I can think of, though many (Fountains and Bolton Abbey, for example) stand on similar grass plats by a river. The extensive floods of the Wey in 1233 (which resulted in the building of the charming little bridge still standing at Eashing) must have sadly affected Waverley Abbey.

Waverley, the first Cistercian house in England, was founded about 1128 by William Giffard, Bishop of Winchester, who brought a small group of monks from the abbey of Aumone in Normandy as a nucleus. Fifty years later, it is recorded, the abbey had seventy monks and a hundred and twenty lay brothers, so in numbers it may be counted as a major foundation. Between these dates the domestic quarters of the monks, with the ancillary domestic buildings, the cloister, and the church, were completed. The church was rebuilt in the thirteenth century in a far more ambitious size and style, to a cruciform plan, with aisled nave and chancel and with transepts, along the east walls of which were chapels with altars, a plan followed in many other English abbeys and in the numerous monasteries of Ireland.

In summer when the quick river flowed lucent and smooth over the stones and the weeds in its course, sidling against its curving cliff, the monks, shuffling around in their monastery, must have found the situation pleasant and grateful; but in winter, when the frosts came and the river ran high and sullen, the cold was damp and piercing, and life in the long monastic day scarcely endurable. Even the heavy gowns and hoods of the monkish habit could not have kept out the searching chill. The monks would have entered eagerly into the calefactory, the warming-room, where they were allowed for short periods to warm themselves at the only fire kept in the monastery apart from that in the kitchen. The Canterbury pilgrims on their winter journeys would have found shelter and refreshment at Waverley, but not much warmth to relax their stiffened limbs.

The monastery was surrendered to the commissioners of Henry VIII in 1536 and its lands were granted to the king's treasurer, Sir W. Fitzwilliam. The ruins are in the hands of the Department of the Environment and they will one day be open to the public; but there is very little to be seen that is informative, and only the most knowledgeable and imaginative of antiquaries will be able to construct a mental picture of what stood here—a noble gatehouse in the walls of a precinct enclosing a huddle of claustral buildings out of which rose the great church with tall lancet windows and soaring central tower.

East of Farnham the Way goes a mile along the main road to an enormous roundabout, where the Farnham by-pass joins. We go nearly all the way round this and take the Guildford road out, the A31, for another mile, when, a little beyond the hamlet of Runfold, we come to another pair of alternatives, one route going over the high chalk down called the Hog's Back and the other taking the lower line through the villages of Seale, Puttenham, and Compton. These two miles from Farnham offer little pleasure to walkers, and those who have visited Waverley Abbey may avoid them by returning along the leafy Sands road from Saint Mary's Well to a cross-roads, and turning to the left there to follow the Runfold road through woods. You come to the Pilgrims' Way on the main road a little west of the point where the alternative routes begin.

Alternative 5a. The Hog's Back to Guildford

The Hog's Back is the main road into Guildford from the west. It takes its name from the long and narrow ridge of chalk rising to 504 feet at Greyfriars, a house built by Voysey in 1896 and accounted one of his best works. Along the summit of the ridge the A31 runs a straight and breezy course. The road is in parts dual carriageway and is always busy. For long stretches there are no sidewalks and walkers must go either along the edge of the carriageway or along a hummocky strip of grass. By the roadside are one or two areas of grassy common where motoring families like to come and picnic or simply to lie in the sun. The great pleasure of the Hog's Back is the splendid, extensive, and very remarkable view it has over the countryside, especially to the north, a countryside of hedged fields of meadow, pasture, and arable, tree-inhabited, spangled with villages and painted with colours throughout the revolving year that never clash, but soften into the haze of the far distance, where, unseen but on the clearest of days, the lights and houses of the London conurbation begin. This is a landscape derived from the Tertiary strata of the London clay and the Barton and Bracklesham Beds of gravel and sand; far away the chalk begins again in north Hampshire and Hertfordshire. There are many villages and towns in that airy champaign, but, and it is remarkable too, only one small village is close at hand, sheltering under the slopes of the Hog's Back. Wanborough is one of the tiniest of villages, with so few houses it seems no more than a hamlet, but it has a manor-house and a church as well and so is claimant to the larger denomination. The manor-house is of brick of the sixteenth century, with a front perhaps a little later, rustically aping, in brick, the fashionable string-courses and ornament of its time. It mothers the black barns and the silos for which it was or is the farmhouse, and nuzzles up against the church. The little church of Saint Bartholomew, built mostly of flint, is older, more than old enough to have invited a pilgrim or two down from the windy hill. It was built in the thirteenth century by the monks of Waverley and was restored, after long disuse, in the nineteenth century.

From various points on the summit of the Hog's Back, you may see over to Guildford's new cathedral, which stands within a litter of undistinguished modern buildings about the skirts of the hill on which it is set. The litter represents the new University of Surrey (which, when it moved down here, changed its name and character from that of the Battersea Technical College). The university buildings are not complete, but the promise is depressing. Depressing too is the tall brick cathedral, over which floats a gilt rag that is nominally an angel, too far away and perhaps too abstract in design to make any useful impression. The cathedral from many points of view looks rather like a power station, like those at Battersea or Kingston—and perhaps the bishop will take that as a compliment and a true statement of what it *should* look like. But come inside. The interior of whitish stone is chaste and clear of impediments; it speaks with a lucid and gentle voice and invites visitors to prayer more insidiously than does the fine complexity of older, high-gothic cathedrals such as Winchester and Canterbury. The architect is Sir Edward Maufe.

From the Hog's Back there are also views to the south, but they are interrupted for most of the length of the ridge by bands of trees. The views, through gaps in the trees, are less broad, less distant than those to the north, and there are subsidiary ranges of hills in the greensand to diversify the scene.

Towards the end of the Hog's Back the main road comes to a junction, and we keep straight on and then right up a rough lane, passing at 453 feet the disused Henley Grove fort, and descend the Mount, a steep street dropping down into Guildford and the town bridge over the river Wey, at the bottom of Guildford's deservedly famous High Street.

Alternative 5b. The Pilgrims' Way by Seale and Puttenham
Hilaire Belloc believed, the Ordnance Survey believes, and I believe that the Pilgrims' Way ran not along the Hog's Back but

along the parallel road less than half a mile to the south, over the greensand, and passing through Seale and Puttenham. There is a little clay around Puttenham, but for the most part the going was over soft sand. There is nothing in the ground to deter the pilgrim on this route, and therefore nothing to cause him to climb the hill to the summit of the Hog's Back, which is decidedly cold and windy at any time other than in summer. For nearly four miles, as far as Puttenham, the Way, a grassy lane in Julia Cartwright's day, is now surfaced, widening slightly through pleasant farmland country with frequent woods and stands of trees. The woods in fact, set a puzzle that conflicts with Belloc's theory of the Pilgrims' Way. He supposed that the line of the Way was often decided by the need to avoid woodlands and any surprises they might hold. This lower land around Seale and Puttenham is rich in trees today; in the middle ages it must have been more thickly wooded. Why then did the Way pass along this low land? I do not know, but what I can say is that this is only the first of many occasions that conflict with the theory that the Way kept clear of woodlands.

Seale was originally a small village, but in modern times it has become a residential district with a number of larger and more expensive houses. Some of the old cottages have been restored and converted at greater cost than their original inhabitants could have afforded. The most attractive is East End Farm, which is of sixteenth-century timber frame on a plinth of clunch. The church, dedicated to Saint Lawrence, may have been founded by Waverley Abbey, and in confirmation of this some of the details are believed to be of the twelfth or thirteenth century. The greater part, however, dates from no earlier than the fifteenth century and this is overlaid by a considerable amount of imaginative work and rebuilding by Victorian restorers, whose work includes the upper part of the sandstone tower, with its too-quaint pyramid roof. The body of the church is largely of clunch, the clear hard chalk that is so easily worked. Inside there are a plain Norman font, some minor brasses, and an interesting monument to Ensign Long, who died in 1809 in a collision of two naval ships in which several men were killed. The accident is shown in bas-relief on the monument. Ensign Long was a school friend of Byron and the memorial verse is attributed to that poet.

East of Seale the road passes on the north side a footpath sign pointing directly into the garden of a large, restored seventeenth-century timber and brick house. This path is not our way, unless you choose to make a diversion here to the Hog's Back, to which the path leads, but it is a matter of interest. Although you might feel self-conscious and intrusive as you walk across a stranger's lawn in full view of the windows of his house, you will not be a trespasser. Beyond the far corner of the house you will find another sign pointing into a nettle-infested path between barbed wire and a hedge and confirming that you are indeed on a public right of way. It may be that the house once had a smaller garden and that the path then ran outside and perhaps out of sight behind a hedge; the extension of the garden has abolished any such shelter and has left the walker naked to the view. Whatever was the reason, the interruption of the path by a garden and its lawns must derive from a past owner of the house rather than the cussedness of footpaths.

No part of the Pilgrims' Way is quite like this, but there are places where stiles from the Way lead straight into cornfields in which a farmer, for his own advantage, has ploughed through the path and has seeded over it. You may suppose it kinder to walk around the margins of his field, but if you do so you could be charged with trespass, despite your good intentions; you have no right to such a course. But you *have* a right to follow the path, to take a sight of the opposite stile or place to which the path should go, and to tread through the corn in a bee-line for that point. In fact, this is what you *should* do, for by this action you are affirming your right and the right of the public to use the path.

There are limits, of course. A farmer would be rightly incensed if half a dozen persons charged through his corn in line abreast, but those same persons in Indian file reasonably exercise a privilege to which they are entitled. What happens if the farther stile or outlet is not visible? You should consult the OS map. I do not think that you could be forgiven for thrashing about over crops to discover the true line.

Hereabouts the narrow, tree-lined road that is the Pilgrims'

Way runs in a valley bordered by sloping, convex and concave fields with frequent small woods. It is delightful country, if a little claustrophobic. A small disused sandpit shows by the yellow and orange sand what the chameleon greensand can do to belie its name. Shortly, the road passes over an infant stream, of interest because to the south it soon falls into a series of ponds or dams, the earliest of which was made probably in the thirteenth century to provide a head of water for Cutt Mill. That mill, after six or seven hundred years, is still there, but nobody these days wants water-powered mills and Cutt Mill, with additions of various periods, is now a house.

East of the bridge over the stream, beside the Pilgrims' Way, stands an irregular house of brick and plaster, built about 1618. It rises from the remains of moats that suggest a much earlier house on this site. Its name is Shoelands. Julia Cartwright remarks that 'to shool' is an old dialect word for 'to beg' and seems to equate the name of Shoelands with opportuning pilgrims, or with the mendicant rascals who attached themselves to pilgrim groups.

East of Shoelands, it is a mile and a half to Puttenham along Dark Lane. The modest cottages of the village come along the road to meet you, showing in their walls the contrast between chalk, which, commonly cut in neat rectangular blocks, produces whitish walls of clunch, and clay, which makes the mellow brick of this district. Of this brick is a pub, the Good Intent, whose name at least is a banner for the pilgrim. The church is set strategically on a rise where the street curves to the left, so that its west tower looks down through the village with a dominance that Farnham castle avoids over Castle Street. It must have been even more impressive before it lost its spire by fire in 1736. The church, dedicated to Saint John the Baptist, has a twelfth-century south doorway and north arcade and some other details of the thirteenth century, while the prominent tower, patched with brick, dates mainly from the fifteenth century. The interior has a lot of restoration work done in 1861, furnishings of 1936, and some art-nouveau chandeliers. There is a small brass of Edward Cranford, who was rector here in the early 1400s and may have seen the tower raised. The tarred and weather-boarded barns and oast-houses opposite the church belong to Greys Home Farm, and date largely from the eighteenth century. Close to the church, but not easily seen because of trees, is Puttenham Priory, a good Palladian country-style house, built in 1762. It may stand on the site of and owe its name to a small monastic settlement or grange.

Puttenham is of interest to our subject because of its winter fair, which was held in the churchyard. The fair took place conveniently at the time when pilgrims would be passing on their way to the December festival of Saint Thomas and perhaps depended in part on their custom. If it did, then pilgrims took the roads in larger numbers than has been supposed. This question has to be considered in relation to other fairs the timing of which seems to have a connection with the winter or summer festivals of Saint Thomas, taking place some days before or after these festivals so as to catch the pilgrims either going or return- ing. Such fairs could be established only by royal licence—as, for example, the great fair of Saint Bartholomew in London was established by the monk Rahere by licence of Henry II. Fairs were primarily periodical markets and meeting-places, in which the exchange of goods and of information were both important. Shalford Fair took place on the Feast of the Assump- tion, the 15th of August, in time to catch pilgrims returning from the festival of the anniversary of the translation of Becket's body, while Guildford's fair originally took place in December, conveniently for pilgrims going to Canterbury for the anniver- sary of the murder.

Belloc supposed the Pilgrims' Way went by the south door of Puttenham Church and over the site of Puttenham Priory, clambering over the knoll called Bury Hill. In this manner the Way would have maintained a straight line, whereas the modern road describes an arc round the north side of the church. Where the two lines join is an inn in which Belloc pre- sumably suffered some discomfort, since he says that it was mis- called the Jolly Farmer. See for yourself if the name is apt these eighty years later.

Opposite the inn is a piece of rough green from the far side of which a double-headed lane goes eastwards, beside some nineteenth-century and twentieth-century cottages; this is the Pilgrims' Way once more. It runs to Clear Barn, opposite which is a bowl barrow on a golf-course, decorated by a modern flagstaff. The lane bears off to the left with a 'do not trespass' notice, and our way lies straight ahead alongside the golf-course and later beside a cricket field. The path, crossing Puttenham Heath and Wanborough Common, is now loose sand, covered in places with thin grass. It sometimes goes among hawthorn and blackthorn bushes, and occasionally there are junctions of paths where the use of a compass will confirm the eastwards direction and settle doubts. There is not much likelihood of getting lost, however. The path runs along the northern margin of the wooded Hurt Hills and passes under the A3 through a tunnel-bridge built of rock-faced stones cut to the dimensions of bricks—an unusual effect. On each of the two parapets of the bridge rises a large wooden cross, set there to remind motorists that they are passing over the Pilgrims' Way. On the last occasion on which I saw this bridge, some driver, perhaps distracted by the crosses, had demolished the parapet.

East of the bridge the path falls into Down Lane. This lane descends from the A3, crosses the Pilgrims' Way, and passes a cemetery with an eye-catching chapel on a hill (to which we shall return presently). The lane joins the B3000 and a few yards down from the junction we find the village of Compton.

There are several things that are surprising about this Surrey village of Compton. Not the least is the neat antique atmosphere of a village street whose houses turn out on examination to be as much of the nineteenth and twentieth centuries as of anything older. Some of the older cottages, of brick and red tile, are pleasant to see, and it is amusing to know that many have extensive cellars that served for contraband when smuggling was a common occupation—we shall find the same sort of thing at Shere. Near the church there is in addition an eye-catching timber-framed and jettied cottage attributed to the year 1530 and so appropriately and inevitably called Tudor Cottage; it was once an inn. The church of Saint Nicholas stands on a hillside just off the street in a churchyard rising on ten centuries of burials. The church is of venerable antiquity, with a Saxon tower and some other Saxon parts built perhaps fifty years before the Conquest. Here, for once, the triumphant Normans respected the work of their predecessors and incorporated it into a church of their own romanesque fashion, with aisles whose piers have a variety of leaf capitals, some of which show the way to Early English stiff-leaf. In the Saxon north walls of the chancel is a small rectangular window of no apparent use if it did not open into the cell of an anchorite, one of those strange people who preferred to live walled up in a small chamber attached to a church. They depended on the charity of the priest and his congregation for their food and drink, took no exercise, and disposed of their excretory wastes in some manner I have never seen explained. A small window in the church with a fragment of stained glass of the Virgin and Child may be Norman.

But it is in the sanctuary that the most astonishing feature is to be seen, a feature unique in England and perhaps in Europe. Inside the eleventh-century chancel the Normans of a century later built a low quadripartite vault with thick ribs (*plate* 2). It opens to the choir through a decorative round-headed arch in which occurs an early use of dog-tooth ornament, a motif more typical of the Early English style of the thirteenth century. The building of the vault made the sanctuary into two storeys. The upper storey or upper chapel is reached by a wooden staircase occupying a tower on the south side of the chancel, which is now accessible only from within the church; a blocked doorway shows that there was formerly access directly from outside. The upper chamber was provided with an altar, as the presence of a piscina shows, and the open edge above the sanctuary arch was protected by a balustrade or screen of wood. This balustrade miraculously survives from *c.* 1180 and it is probably the oldest piece of ecclesiastical woodwork in this country.

What was the purpose of the upper chapel? And why was it supported on a stone vault when it would have been cheaper and easier to have built the floor on wooden joists, as the Normans were perfectly capable of doing—the balustrade itself shows that they were no mean workers in wood. The more costly stone vault must have been built partly for the glory of the sanctuary, partly for the permanence it was desired to have. So what was there in that upper chapel that merited the honour of the east end of the church, the holiest of places? There has been much racking of brains, much scratching of heads and of pens on paper, and many wild ideas aimed at explaining this thing without parallel. The most likely explanation, in my opinion, is that this upper chapel was formed as a shrine for the housing, display, and veneration of some precious relic. If that is so, then Compton church comes prominently into the picture of pilgrims and pilgrimages—so much so that one must ask why the Pilgrims' Way did not loop off from Puttenham and come through Compton, returning to the original line in Sandy Lane east of the village. A glance at the map will show that this loop was possible, represented now by the B3000 south-east from Puttenham to the A3, then by footpath and lane past Eastbury Manor (a nineteenth-century house) into Compton, and then by paths no longer in existence to the lane that leads to Polsted Manor, and so by path to Sandy Lane on the accepted lower route of the Pilgrims' Way.

We, however, return northwards through the village and turn again into Down Lane. From a point near the corner there is a plain view of the strange, red-brick and terracotta chapel near the head of a steeply sloping cemetery. It looks as though it might somehow have been brought from Italy, perhaps from Florence, by those same removers who so easily handled the Holy House of Loretto. A closer acquaintance dispels the impression. The chapel is certainly romanesque, but of an original kind. It was designed by the wife of the painter G. F. Watts, with a separate cloister higher up for the grave of her husband. The interior is astounding: Celtic twilight and art nouveau married and merged with the two distinct cultures of the nineteenth-century sinuous line and the La Tène spiral making uneasy bedfellows. The whole of the walls of the circular interior is covered with larger-than-life angel figures, medallions, and broad spaces of ornament all in relief and managed through the medium of some kind of gesso or plaster, painted and gilt. Even the ornateness of the exterior and the elaboration of the doorway in sharp terra-cotta cannot prepare one for this interior display. Exterior and interior are meant to impress, to display, to lay claim to high art. The failure of that claim is absolute, yet the chapel still attracts and is still impressive for the scale of its achievement. Look at it and perhaps like it, and return to see it again with double advantage for its gusty energy allied to attention to detail—but you will find nothing here that is seminal.

A little distance farther north is the house in which Watts and his wife lived. Hidden among trees on a height, it was called by the painter by the likely but not admirable name of 'Limnerslease'. Below it and directly beside the Pilgrims' Way Mrs Watts built a large low gallery to house her husband's works.

George Frederic Watts was a stage artist if ever there was one, prototype of the Victorian notion of artist and originator of many stereotypes long since gone out of fashion; but he was no bohemian. He was tall and spare, with a good brow and head and a sharply pointed beard, and had a penetrating gaze. He worked at painting—and how he worked! From the first days of his taking up a pencil or brush to his death in 1904 at the age of eighty-seven, he never ceased to work. He had exhibited in the Academy before he was twenty and was soon famous and fêted and honoured, and eventually he was given the Order of Merit. He loved symbolism and allegory and painted pictures with such titles as 'How should I your true-love know?', 'Saint George overcomes the dragon', and 'Love Triumphant'. Without effort he attracted prizes and wealthy patrons, and also beautiful women. His first wife was Ellen Terry, who was thirty years younger than Watts; the marriage was brief and was dissolved. In 1886 he was cajoled or persuaded by friends, who thought they acted for his own good, to marry again, and his second wife was Mary Fraser-Tytler, a wealthy young woman who thereafter devoted her life to him. She it was who built the gallery below the house as a kind of shrine for Watts's work, and founded there a pottery in which the terra-cotta of the cemetery chapel was made. The gallery is freely open and there you may see notebooks full of charming pencil drawings and illustrative memoranda made as easily and as unselfconsciously as you or I write a word; a few vivacious portraits; and a mass of Watts's symbolic or allegorical pictures some of which are huge and nearly all of which are incredibly bad. Watts was also a sculptor working in bronze, and here in the gallery, but hidden away, there stands a giant plaster figure of Tennyson in cloak and broad hat, brooding as he might have brooded along the downs and the cliffs of the Isle of Wight; a bronze cast from this model stands beside the cathedral in Lincoln. Another giant figure shows a nude man astride a vigorous horse. This latter work, called 'Physical Energy', may be seen in bronze in Kensington Gardens in London and up in the Matoppo Hills of South Africa. Especially interesting are the small maquettes Watts made for his sculptures; one of Tennyson, only about a foot high, has the same intensity and feeling for mass as has the ten-foot plaster figure.

The Pilgrims' Way at this point is the sunken, tree-shaded, sandy lane that runs beside the gallery. 'Sandy Lane' is in fact the name of this path, and it is appropriate, though the first few yards beneath the trees may be muddy. It runs partly beside arable fields, in which the plough turns over pastel furrows of sand mixed with chalk, and occasionally climbs a little and occasionally descends, sometimes sunk as a hollow way (*plate* 3).

It passes at a distance, and to the south of, Conduit Farm, an attractive eighteenth-century farmhouse seen against the backdrop of the Hog's Back, and has occasionally the slightest glimpse of Loseley House to the south. Loseley was built in 1561–9 largely with stones from Waverley Abbey, by Sir William More, whose descendants still live in it. Any old house is eclectic in its structure, its furnishings, and its fittings, and Loseley follows suit, but with many things of special interest. For example, within these walls of Waverley Abbey that are now Loseley are furniture and fittings from Henry VIII's ephemeral Palace of Nonsuch, which itself was a mass of undigested borrowings and gatherings from various sources. Loseley, the admirable, many-gabled main front of which faces away from the Pilgrims' Way, is open to the public on certain days in summer.

Half a mile farther east the Pilgrims' Way descends under trees to three wooden posts set up to prevent cars from driving in off the surfaced road we now enter, which comes up from Littleton to the south and turns sharply east. This eastwards stretch, a mile long, is still Sandy Lane, and it is the way we take, but whether it is the Pilgrims' Way is another matter. The OS 2½-inch sheet shows the Way as a track through trees parallel with and only a few yards north of Sandy Lane, but this track now leads only to a house. For all practical purposes Sandy Lane is the lane we must take. It passes an entrance to

Brabœuf Manor, a late sixteenth-century house cocooned in Victorian Tudor, and now a college of law.

Sandy Lane joins the Godalming road opposite a pub, the Ship, which may be a welcome sight after more than two miles of sandy track.

Turn right on the Godalming road, up the slope, and in a few yards on the left you will find a grassy hill, on the summit of which rises the grey ruin of Saint Catherine's chapel. This is the second of the chapels to pose problems peculiarly associated with the Pilgrims' Way.

According to some authorities, the first chapel on this emphatic little hill above the river Wey was built by Henry II, but the present building is later, Early English rather than Norman. The north and south sides are divided into three bays by prominent buttresses of white sandstone or of malm, on which there must have been pinnacles. The chapel as the masons left it in 1317 was a dignified and delicate construction with pointed windows and doorways of good proportions; but a change soon occurred, something unusual and special, something that can only be explained on the assumption that this chapel held an object that brought crowds or queues of people. The original west doorway was not sufficient and two more doorways were made, one in each of the north and south walls, the south doorway being given a foiled head. Even more remarkable, the window above each of these north and south doorways was partly blocked to provide two more doorways; these two doorways could have been reached only by outer stairways. The hood moulds of the former windows remain and show clearly what was done. The total was therefore five doorways in a chapel of modest size. The two opposing doorways on the upper level led into an upper chamber, or, as someone has suggested, to a bridge across the interior of the chapel. But why a bridge? For that matter why an upper floor? One can only suppose that here, as at Compton, there was some venerated relic that drew people in large numbers, people who shuffled along in queues to enter by the various doorways, knelt to say a prayer or to beseech aid or cure, and then moved out by other doors. Nothing else along the Pilgrims' Way is quite so convincing in the supposition that the Old Road did indeed

IPW

become a Pilgrims' Way, and that here at Saint Catherine's was one of the features of the pilgrimage to Canterbury.

The hill of Saint Catherine is of sand, a bright orange sand that is one of the unlikely colours of the greensand. The hill falls in places precipitately and is nowhere shallow. On the east side it is astonishing to find some iron railings and to discover that they are there not merely to protect incautious visitors from rolling down the hillside, but to stop them from falling down a cut cliff on to the railway; for the main railway line burrows under the hill and emerges in a deep cutting.

There are good views in most directions from the hill-top. The most interesting for us, travelling east in the steps of the pilgrims, and looking where their eyes looked, is the view in the eastern quarter. Down below the cliffs of sand runs the river Wey, lost and found among trees whose tops do not reach to our elevated station. The far shore is rough marshy ground, across which the Way lies, and then over firmer ground, now a sports field, to the Horsham road. This land used to be part of Shalford Park, whose Georgian house, beside Shalford church, has given place to a modern water-purification plant. Beyond the Horsham road the Way is continued by a road, ascending towards another hill covered with trees, among which are many yews. This is Saint Martha's Hill.

To the north-east there are the streets and houses of Guildford, with the Saxon tower of Saint Mary's church rising below a hill on which stands the great square keep of Guildford castle. In front of this a white gash marks a chalk quarry, from which stone, flints, and clunch were mined for building parts of the castle; the quarry-men hewed their way into the cliff face like rabbits digging burrows. The galleries they made used to be one of the sights of Guildford, until they were found to be unsafe and were closed.

There are two ways down to the river from Saint Catherine's chapel. One is a scramble down the steep, soft slopes and fissures of orange sand to the riverside path. An easier way is to descend over grass to the little lane below the north slope of the hill, a lane with a pretty row of terraced but varied cottages of local brick and tile, charming in their doll's house appearance. They have been recently restored, and while this work was in hand we wandered about their tiny rooms and found in one of them a brick-built fireplace with a haunched, four-centred arch that does not appear to be later than the sixteenth century. The lane comes down to the riverside tow-path beside a tumbling little tributary stream.

Here we come to a problem. For centuries there was a ferry here, in my remembrance no more than a punt quickly pulled across for a charge of a penny or two. Like most ferries of the kind it has been closed since the war and is never likely to be resumed, and now there is no way over other than by swimming. Belloc and his companion came here late in the evening and found the ferry closed for the night. They discovered and stole a boat from the bank and paddled it across with a walking-stick for an oar, followed by the agitated imprecations of a woman who rushed out of a house. Belloc, landing on the far bank, apologised for his theft, pleaded 'grave necessity', and putting some coppers on the seat of the boat he and his friend hastily departed, with what dignity they could muster, under a hail of well-deserved insults from the furious woman.

No such boat is likely to be so conveniently available to you, whether legitimately or illegitimately. No doubt the riverside houses do have boats of their own, but they are kept away from borrowers and purloiners. A footbridge is planned to cross the river as part of the High Downs Way, which hereabouts is identical with the Pilgrims' Way, but the footbridge is not there yet, and nothing can be done but turn along the path down-stream to Guildford three-quarters of a mile distant, or up-stream to a lock at Shalford—the river is canalized as part of the Wey Navigation.

Before we leave the river, however, the question of Shalford must be considered. Shalford is a scattered village less than a mile to the south of the defunct ferry and on the east bank of the river. 'Shalford', which was 'Scaldefor' at Domesday, obviously implies a shallow ford in the river. There is no shallow ford anywhere along these reaches of the river today, but the name clearly shows that there once was, and it is evident from the topography that the Wey formerly flowed in a wide channel of no great depth through marshy ground. Was this a place where the pilgrims and their ancient predecessors crossed the river?

It does not seem so, for it was not conveniently on the direct line of the Old Road, and the continuation of the Old Road on the east side from Shalford is not convenient either. One has to suppose a diversion upstream along the bank and downstream on the far side, and this seems plainly not to have been undertaken. We are compelled then to suppose that in ancient times the river by Saint Catherine's Hill was fordable. The topography is much the same as at Shalford, with a broad flat lowland on the east bank, a lowland that is at times marshy even today, and through which the now disused path from the ferry runs straight towards Saint Martha's Hill.

Shalford, none the less, is not to be dismissed as of no account. I have spoken of fairs in relation to the Canterbury pilgrimage, and Shalford had a famous fair in August, originally held in the churchyard, but later held along the street and on the green some distance from the church. The date, you will see, would be in time to attract pilgrims returning from the July festival of the translation of Saint Thomas's body. It is by details such as this that we may believe that the Old Road was in fact used by pilgrims in large numbers, despite the absence of more direct evidence or record.

John Bunyan is believed to have lived in a cottage facing the green, a cottage, called Horn Hatch, demolished long ago. There is a local tradition that the marshes of the Wey provided him with the original of the Slough of Despond and that the August fair of Shalford was the pattern from which he derived Vanity Fair. One could go on to say that he must have known of the Pilgrims' Way and that this Way gave him the idea for his allegory. Alas, the theories are mere speculations with no basis in ascertained fact.

The church that Bunyan would have known at Shalford was rebuilt in classical style in 1790 and this in turn was knocked down and rebuilt in 1846 to a gothic design by Benjamin Ferrey. From the church a street of old and modern houses runs down to a bridge over the railway, beyond which is the green that was the later site of the fair. Today cricket is played on the green during summer week-ends, cricket sometimes vigorous and surprising, sometimes bubbling and inept, but often more enjoyable on a summer day than a game of finer class.

8 Guildford to Dorking

12 MILES

Guildford is an ancient and delightful town. It was once the county town of Surrey and it still retains that air of social stability and importance that belongs to a capital, which it has not surrendered to the usurper Kingston upon Thames. (Kingston, since the expansion of the London metropolitan boundaries in 1965, is no longer in Surrey, but retains the Surrey county offices simply because of the money invested in bricks and mortar.)

The name 'Guildford', declares the *Oxford Dictionary of Place-Names*, means the 'ford where golden flowers grow'—the flowers would have been marsh-marigolds or yellow flags. From its earliest occurrence as 'Gyldeford' in the *Cartularium Saxonicum* about 880 and as 'Geldeford' in Domesday Book, the name has changed little, and it was not until comparatively modern times that the misleading conjunction of the vowels *u* and *i* were adopted and seemed to connect the name with the powerful merchant guild that certainly existed here in the middle ages and prospered in the wool trade.

There is no ford in the river Wey now, there are no marsh-marigolds or flags. The river, cribbed and deepened for navigation, passes under a nondescript modern bridge at the foot of the High Street. Whether you arrive at this bridge by descending the Mount from the Hog's Back or by coming along the river path from Saint Catherine's, you will at once be aware that Guildford is not a valley town. It is rather a hillside town set on steep slopes either side of the river. The oldest part is to the east, where the cobbled High Street (paved with setts rather than cobbles) is one of the great pleasures of Surrey. It is at once a busy shopping street, as a High Street should be, and a varied display of antique buildings with only a few modern intrusions other than the inevitable inserted plate-glass shop windows. The corresponding hillside rising from the west bank, the Mount, was not colonized until much later, and although it has some old houses, it has never had the commercial importance of the High Street. Its continuation of the line of the High Street, of the road through the town, suggests that it must be an ancient way, a conclusion confirmed by the fact that it leads to the site of an Anglo-Saxon cemetery in use from the sixth century onwards. Here in 1036 were buried the Norman victims of what has become known as the Guildown massacre.

Guildford was for long a royal town. It was part of the property of King Alfred the Great and is mentioned in his will —he died in the year 900, leaving in the last words of the last of his several books a motto that would have served alike for the pilgrims of the middle ages and for the sceptics of the Renaissance: 'Therefore he seems to me a very foolish man, and a very wretched, who will not increase his understanding while he is in the world and ever wish and long to reach that endless life where all shall be made clear.'

The Saxon kings may have had a castle in Guildford. If they did it was one of few such buildings in the country, for the Saxons were not a castle-building people until they came under the influence of Norman military ideas in the eleventh century. There were Normans in this country before the Conquest, however, and it was a party of six hundred Normans who suffered in the Guildown massacre in 1036. This would have taken place in the castle, if any castle then existed; that it took place in Guildford and not on Guildown is likely. The Normans, led by Alfred the Aetheling, that is to say, the heir to the throne, had landed on the Kent coast and were on their way to Winchester, where Alfred's mother, Queen Emma, lived as widow of King Canute. It is likely that the party came by the Pilgrims' Way, which at that time would have been in use by pilgrims going to the shrine of Saint Swithun. At Guildford, Alfred and his followers were received with courtesy by Count Godwin, Earl of Wessex, who set them down to a feast. Godwin, however, was a supporter of a rival claimant to the throne, Harold Harefoot, and while his guests ate at their ease the count and his followers set upon them with swords and spears and killed most of them. The aetheling himself was taken prisoner and sent to Ely, where he was first blinded and then murdered. The bodies of two hundred and twenty of his followers were carried up the

Mount in carts and were tumbled into shallow graves dug in the old Saxon cemetery. The searches of archaeologists in 1929 brought to light the skeletons of these persons who had died such violent deaths. Fifteen of them had been buried with their hands tied behind their backs. The Saxons, whose graceful art seems to put them culturally far above the Normans, were on occasions as cruel and as vicious as could be the men who conquered them in 1066.

All that remains of Saxon Guildford is the strong tower of Saint Mary's church in Quarry Street. Whether this was built as a strongpoint to guard the ford in the river is doubtful; it seems probable that it was attached to a church from the beginning. That church, however, must have been smaller than the present Norman and Early English building. The Normans rebuilt the church with three apses at the east end, around which Quarry Street curved as no more than a narrow lane. George IV, who used to come this way *en route* to Brighton, complained of the difficulty of passing in his carriage through this restriction, and the town authorities had the church's central apse removed to widen the street. Thus was lost one of the few examples of a Norman triple apse in this country. The church of Saint Mary had probably served as a chapel royal to the castle on the hill above, but that would have meant nothing to the thick-headed Georges.

The interior of Saint Mary's church is spacious, echoing, and cool with the air of nine centuries of enclosure, and it is well worth while to go into it and to study its architecture of half a dozen periods; but what is of more interest for our subject is a curious low-side window. Now, such windows, of unknown purpose, are more usually found in the walls of chancels. They have been called leper windows, by means of which lepers, who were not allowed inside, could see and hear the mass, but this explanation has long been scouted. It was then suggested that these windows were made to allow a bell to be rung at the elevation of the Host to inform people in the churchyard, which suggests an overflow of worshippers into the open air of which we have no confirmatory evidence. The low-side window of Saint Mary's, however, is not in the chancel but in the west wall of the north aisle, immediately below the great gothic west window of that aisle. It has been suggested that in this case the low-side window was for a light to guide travellers to the ford in the river, a beacon to keep them from tumbling head over heels where the water was not safely passable. If you imagine uninterrupted space instead of the present old cottages lining the little street round the churchyard, you will see that this is a reasonable assumption.

The castle, higher up on the hill, set on a mound now landscaped as a colourful garden, was built or rebuilt by Henry II not long after the death of Becket. The strong square keep is described as grim, and so it is, for it was meant to be; but it is also handsome and impressive, in its light-coloured Burgate stone, with its flat corner buttresses not quite meeting and leaving a channel between them that adds to the impression of height. The Angevin kings often came to Guildford and stayed in this castle. Henry III, according to records in the Pipe and Liberate Rolls, whitewashed the interior walls of the hall and of the great chamber and had marble patterns painted on the pillars and arches, while the ceiling was divided into squares flecked with gold and silver. The military atmosphere, at least inside, was thus alleviated.

The only other ornament was in the castle chapel; there, years later, when the castle had become a jail, prisoners carved their initials. The castle is today a hollow shell, with a stairway by which visitors may climb to the top for a view of the town, and to the south, of the valley across which the Pilgrims' Way takes its course from Saint Catherine's chapel to the dark, yew-wooded slopes of Saint Martha's Hill. Not much else remains of the castle. There are traces of an earlier shell keep near the square keep, and of some of the bailey buildings, and down in Quarry Street, near Saint Mary's church, is a tall, thirteenth-century arched gateway gently crumbling away.

Along Guildford High Street the shop fronts have for the greater part been let into façades of diverse dates and styles, all jogging and nudging each other in enduring amity. Some of the few modern buildings pay tribute to the character of the street, if only in symbolic manner. The lion sported by Woolworth's, for instance, comes from the roof of the old Lion Hotel that stood on the site until 1957. Harvey's department store is mostly a modern building, but it hides its modernity along narrow passages while to the street it shows Georgian façades.

But let us start at the bottom of the street. Saint Nicholas's church, by the bridge but west of the river, is Victorian gothic, the latest of a series of churches that have stood on this site since the twelfth century; its theatrical baldaquin over the font is worth seeing, but the principal interest in this church is the fifteenth-century south chapel of the Mores and the Molyneuxs of Loseley. In it stands a large Jacobean monument of Sir William More and his wife; Sir William, the builder of Loseley, died in 1600. A rector, Arnold Brocas, who died in 1395, is represented by a damaged effigy under a canopy. A few other monuments are to be seen, but most of the long line of the owners of Loseley are not represented here.

Beyond the bridge on the left is a narrow street, Friary Street, recalling by its name the Dominican friary founded by Queen Eleanor; nothing remains of the friary, but the memory of it has been carried far and wide by the brewery (Friary Meux) that took its name. Nothing is left, I have said, and as far as I am aware, nothing has been found in the extensive building work now going on in Friary Street, but in George Abbot's Hospital at the top of the High Street two fine windows of the fifteenth century, with their Flemish glass, may have come from the Dominican friary. The friary remains were finally destroyed about the time the hospital was built.

Higher up the hill, beyond Woolworth's, the Angel Hotel is facially Georgian but shows in its tiny courtyard timber-framing of the seventeenth century. The hotel stands on thirteenth-century stone-vaulted cellars (now a bar), which suggests that the Angel may have been an inn, and a resort of pilgrims, for two hundred years or more before the pilgrimage was stopped by the Reformation. In those days, the days of the pilgrims, the inn would have borne a different name; it would have been the Salutation of the Virgin, in other words the Annunciation. In the middle ages such pious names for inns were not uncommon. They are uncommon now because the symbolism was too much for the reformers of the Reformation or of the Commonwealth, who were never more dire than on the subject of mariolatry. The name and the sign of the Virgin had to be removed if the owners of the house were to avoid fine or imprisonment. The announcing angel remained, and so inns that were once called the Salutation of the Virgin became simply either the Angel or the Salutation.

As you climb the steep High Street of Guildford you cannot have missed noticing the domination of the street by the over-hanging Guildhall clock on its scrolly beam and iron brackets. Made by John Aylward, the clock was erected in 1683, when the Guildhall was refronted in the extravagant and joyous manner that is described in the Surrey volume of the *Buildings of England* series as resembling the carved and windowed poop of a ship, a ship of the time of Nelson or earlier. It would, clearly, have been a ship that had come from the South Sea islands, for the carved figure brackets beneath the first overhang have a great deal of the savage and pagan in their form and look like Polynesian rather than English work, Architecturally the frontage of the Guildhall is all wrong, so critics say, but I would be loth to be one of the critics who thought so, for it would deprive me of the pleasure of seeing something that is admirable, something that, technically and aesthetically wrong or not, is in fact a considerable triumph in the nature of buildings that are loved rather than coolly admired. You may go inside at times to see a good iron gate, a plaster ceiling, and perhaps a few uncertain and apprehensive individuals waiting for their turn in the court on the ground floor; but this I have to say, the interior has neither the charm nor the quality of the exterior.

Nearly opposite is the Tunsgate, which leads to the castle grounds and must once have led to a gateway to the castle or in the meagre defences of the town. The large brick Tuscan portico through which you pass has been there since 1818, when it was built as a grand frontispiece to the corn exchange; no corn exchange stands there now.

Higher up the street and on the same side as the Guildhall, is another house of decorative character, though not so emphatic as the Guildhall. Guildford House was built in 1660 as a dwelling for a wealthy merchant, called John Child. Now an exhibition centre, it has been wisely restored. It contains a good staircase and has a rear elevation to North Street that is different but also of interest. North Street runs parallel with the High Street and is not at all remarkable except that it is extraordinary that so poor a street should exist in a town with such a High Street. North Street is built along the line of the town defences on this side, and for centuries it was known as the Lower Backside. A weekly market, survivor of ancient markets, takes place in North Street.

In the High Street again and a few steps towards the top of the hill you will find the Hospital of the Holy Trinity, a hospice, that is, or almshouse, rather than a hospital in the modern sense. It was built in 1619–22 by George Abbot, Archbishop of Canterbury, one of the greatest of the sons of Guildford. To see the building most satisfactorily you should stand on the terrace of Holy Trinity church across the street. The great gatehouse, of dark reddish-brown brick dressed with stone, is late of its kind, but it is one of the finest in England, with four splendid corner turrets topped by cupolas. The low brick-built almshouses within the gate gather round a courtyard that is surprisingly peaceful and relaxed so near to the noise of traffic rattling over the setts outside. In one corner there is a little chapel where the eleven brothers and eleven sisters (originally twelve and eight) gather for prayers. Here are the two windows of which the stained glass and the tracery are reputed to have come from the friary; they are certainly large for this little chapel.

George Abbot, born in Guildford in 1562, who became Archbishop of Canterbury in 1611, was the son of a cloth-worker. He was educated in the grammar school a little higher up the High Street, a school that still exists and teaches, with its gabled buildings, dating from 1557 to 1586, gathered round a paved courtyard. Abbot was an ambitious man, and not always a lovable one, but he was capable of good works such as his hospital in Guildford. When he accidentally killed a keeper during a stag hunt at Bramshill, he gave way to remorse for something that was clearly and admittedly not his fault, and he lived out the rest of his life feeling that he was a murderer. His enemies asserted that murder was indeed his crime, and designate but unsympathetic bishops refused to be sanctified by him, by hands that had shed blood. When he died Abbot was buried in Holy Trinity church, opposite the hospital, where his body still lies, though the church, destroyed by the fall of the spire in 1740, was rebuilt in brick in classical style in the mid 1700s. His monument, with his effigy under a canopy, stands south of the altar, with a tomb-chest formed of carved books flanking openings with iron grilles through which you see the skulls and bones of a charnel house. It was designed by Gerard Christmas and cut by his sons Matthew and John, whose signatures attest their work. A brass to Maurice Abbot and his wife, who both died in 1606, commemorates George Abbot's parents.

There is much more in Guildford for the visitor to see, many happy discoveries to be made by those who have time and leisure. We, however, have stayed no longer than a pilgrim might before resuming his journey, and as, like him, we are on our way to Canterbury we must regain the Pilgrims' Way.

In order to do this we turn near the foot of the High Street into Quarry Street, which takes its name from those white-faced cliffs we saw from the top of Saint Catherine's Hill. We pass the shorn end of the chancel of Saint Mary's church, which still seems to constrict the street, and come again to the thir-teenth-century gateway into the castle precinct; beside it is the town museum, with a very good collection. Here I would like you to interrupt your progress for a moment or two to look at Quarry Street and at Rosemary Alley. The Georgian façades of the houses nearly opposite the castle gate are very good, if not as purely classical as they might be; their faults and their charm come from their having been tacked on to more ancient houses, as you will see in Rosemary Alley. The alley, constricted and abrupt, is really a slot with a series of flights of steps down between the bulging and leaning timber-framed and brick-nogged walls of the apparently Georgian houses. The alley drops down to Mill Brook, a modern road on the line of an earlier street running parallel with the River Wey. Here is the modern building of the Yvonne Arnaud theatre, with its work-shops in a large, brick-built water-mill. Yvonne Arnaud, an actress with a lilting French accent that did all kinds of enjoy-able things to English pronunciation, made herself beloved of the people of Guildford, and took great interest in this theatre, and that is why it has her name.

Millbrook and Quarry Street fuse a little farther to the south, and the road thenceforth runs parallel but some distance from the river Wey. It runs, in fact, along the outer edge of the flat land of the former Shalford Park, land that was in some earlier time part of the river bed and comes to that state again whenever the river floods. On our left-hand rise the abrupt slopes of the former river banks or cliffs. Saint Catherine's chapel is seen on the far shore, and opposite this we turn east on to a modern residential road called the 'Pilgrims' Way', which climbs directly up the hillside. We follow this line and maintain an easterly course, as it becomes a footpath sheltered by and just within the trees of Chantries Wood. The name of this wood has led some people to suppose that it has some connection with the Pilgrims' Way, but what that connection might be is not clear. What is clear, and what disturbed Hilaire Belloc, is that here, for the first time, the Pilgrims' Way takes its course on the *north* slope of a hill, whereas elsewhere it chooses for preference the drier southern slopes. Certainly the Chantries stretch is a contrast. It is dank and cold and dark and was probably always so while the trees grew, but the path is the straightest possible line projected from the Saint Catherine's crossing of the river.

As the wood comes to an end, the way divides.

Alternative 6a. *By Tyting Farm*

Below Whinny Hill we take the lane bearing to the left and shortly cross a surfaced road on to another lane that passes by Tyting Farm. There used to be a chapel or oratory near this farm, which is still marked on the maps, though the last bits of it were cleared away some years ago. Tyting Farm and Saint Martha's church belonged to the Priory of Newark, which stood a few miles to the north; the priest serving the church is believed to have lived at Tyting. I cannot believe that the oratory could have been much visited by pilgrims who had seen from Saint Catherine's the answering hill of Saint Martha's and who knew of the church on the summit of that hill. There is nothing else of moment in the pleasant walk through fields to the surfaced Guildford Lane, which we meet just south of Whitelane Cottage, and on which we turn to the right to join

within a few yards the alternative path coming down from
Saint Martha's.

Alternative 6b. The route by Saint Martha's

At the division of ways below Whinny Hill and on the edge of
Chantries Wood we keep to the right, cross the Chilworth road,
and climb on loose sand up through a wood. The trees are of
several kinds, but yews are dominant in the generally sombre
effect. You may see a deer or two here, as we have, though these
large animals are adept at keeping cover and remaining
invisible. This sandy track leads directly to the west gable of
Saint Martha's church, a church that stands 720 feet above the
sea, alone on its hill of dark greensand and ferruginous sandstone or carstone.

Saint Martha's was the parish church of the village of Chilworth, which lies some 500 feet below in the Tillingbourne
valley. Chilworth today is a sad strip-development of modern
houses and bungalows with an architecturally unusual church
of brick that was originally the Greshambury Institute. The
village was castigated by Cobbett on account of two evils that
were in his view one as wicked as the other. The first was a factory producing gunpowder, founded before 1589, and the
second a paper-mill making paper for treasury-notes and bank-
notes. These industries gave the village, according to writers of
the time, the appearance of an industrial town, as though here
in the south of England was something equivalent to Blake's
dark satanic mills. Both industries have long since disappeared
and the village is purged of these wickednesses. The paper-mill
was burnt down in 1896. As for the gunpowder, it was evidently
potent stuff, since the collapse of the tower of the old church of
Saint Martha, far above on its hill-top, was attributed to the
effect of an explosion in the factory in the valley below, but the
mill did not cease working until after 1911.

Saint Martha's has the appearance of a simple, venerable,
Norman church somehow cast up on the hill summit. The
Norman appearance is misleading. The style is certainly Norman,
and there certainly was a Norman church on this site, but by
the 1840s, as a picture in the church shows clearly enough,
Saint Martha's was almost a total wreck, with small

evidence of its original appearance. The church, as it stands today, is the work of Woodyer, who rebuilt it in 1848–50 (*plate* 4). Demolishing what was left of the west tower he built another tower over the crossing. He worked with the irregular old stones gathered from the ruins, the dark hard carstone of the district—you may pick up odd-looking lumps of it almost any-where on the hill, lumps that have the colour of wet rusty iron and seem to owe their shape to the action of a human hand, like shards of pottery. In the church are a Norman font brought from elsewhere, genuine, but reworked, some old carved stones, pieces of white clunch incised with the small knob-ended crosses said to have been cut by passing crusaders (which might equally well have been cut by passing pilgrims), and a likeable figure of Saint Martha carved in pine-wood grown on the hill, sculpted by Miss Audrey Rose-Casemore in 1942. A modern window showing Saint Thomas of Canterbury recalls the existence in the middle ages of a chapel in the church dedicated to Saint Thomas.

The dedication to Saint Martha is rare and is probably a mistake. Saint Martha had no known connection with this hill in Surrey. French tradition says that she arrived in a boat as one of the three Maries who came to Les Saintes-Maries-de-la-Mer about the year 40. She was called to Tarascon to deal with a fierce monster, which she tamed by sprinkling holy water on it and putting her crucifix on a chain round its neck. She then led the bemused beast into the town and handed it over to be stoned to death by the people. A dirty trick, you might suppose. The Tarasconnais remember it to this day in a pageant in which eight persons caper about in the guise of a dragon.

There is nothing in this story to suggest any connection with the church on the hill above Chilworth. The dedication to Saint Martha may result from confusion with 'Saint Martyrs', the hill of martyrs, a name coming from an old tradition that some six hundred Christians suffered martyrdom on this hill about the year 600. That must have been not long before the district became converted to Christianity, and soon afterwards a church may have been built on this prominent hill of martyrs. Before that, what? Perhaps a pagan temple or a shrine or some other kind of pagan holy place the site of which was taken over for a Christian church. On the south side of the hill are some vestigial earthworks tentatively assigned to the iron age and perhaps part of a hill fort. Antiquity is in the air. Saint Martha's Hill is a place where the ancientness of the Pilgrims' Way, of the Old Road, may be sensed, light as threads of silk or as gossamer hanging in the air.

The churchyard is bordered by a low wall of stone. By the wall east of the church is a headstone to the actress Yvonne Arnaud, whose ashes, following her desire, were scattered here on the hill.

East of the church there is a broad panorama of rolling hills with dark tracts of woodland. Somewhere in that tumbled country goes the Old Road, but exactly where is not always certain. Some writers would have you leave Saint Martha's to cross the valley to the north and to ascend to Newlands Corner. There you would find another notable viewpoint so well known that a vast car park has had to be made to accommodate those who come to enjoy it. Here you will see each week that amazing gregariousness and non-gregariousness of the British people, who like the consolation of crowds while still preserving the family unit, each family securely shut up in its own inviolable private cocoon. Newland's Corner is the way the North Downs Path goes, continuing from there in among the woods, following an old trackway towards West Hanger and Netley Heath. But this is not, I think, the line of the Pilgrims' Way.

The sandy path down Saint Martha's Hill, leading almost directly east, comes into Guildford Lane, on to which we emerge from a clearing decorated with signs about parking cars. This is where our alternatives 6a and 6b fuse.

On the far side of Guildford Lane is a fence, with a wooden barred gate. You may find no evidence of a path here, especially if you come when the fields have been ploughed, but in fact a path does exist, still going directly east. If you consider Guildford Lane running south-east as twelve o'clock, then the path diverges in the direction of eleven. It drives across the field to a stile into another field, and thenceforwards the direction is clear until you come down a lane to join the road that leads to New Barn Farm. The farm itself lies to the north, in a shallow valley against the background of the Albury Downs. Cross over this lane to an iron field-gate, where you may find once more that the plough has obliterated the path. There is right of way, nevertheless, and you must cross at an angle in a direction canted to your right until in the southern boundary of the field you come to a small wooden gate leading into a wood. This path in the wood ought to go directly east, and surely once did, but now it bears a little to the right and drops down to Water Lane Farm. Nothing more than a yard or two is lost. In the lane you must sidestep to the left for a short distance, and enter another lane, leading along the north side of Weston Wood, with the wooded height of the hill between you and the warm south.

Belloc was deeply puzzled by this eccentricity of the Old Road, by the fact that it should run, as it so rarely does, on the north side, the colder, damper side of a hill when everywhere else it chooses the drier and warmer southern slopes—but not quite everywhere, for we have just come by such a very path, the path along the north side of Chantries Wood. That the problems are exactly the same you may see by a moment's reference to the map. The map also shows why the path takes the line it does. To avoid the north side of these wooded hills the Way would have to loop to the south into the valley of the Tillingbourne, and by doing this it would lose a mile or two of distance and more of time and energy wasted in toiling up and down a succession of slopes. I believe that the line of the Way lies to the north of these two woods because that was in the circumstances the reasonable line for it to take, *faute de mieux*.

That the path within the north margin of Weston Wood is ancient is shown by the fact that it is a hollow way, and not only a hollow way but also a way on a shelf or terrace such as we shall expect to find along the slopes of the chalk downs.

Deep in Weston Wood we come to a cottage and a junction of paths. The direction to follow is ahead and slightly right round the cottage into a lane descending in the shade of trees. The next junction requires some care. The lane splits and the two arms diverge: neither of these lanes is the one to take. At the point of divergence, another path, hidden among bushes, takes off exactly between the two more obvious ones. This is the line, leading without further difficulty out of the wood and alongside a field or two

KPW

to the Albury road, which is reached by crossing a footbridge over a stream. This clear, racing little stream comes from the Silent Pool just to the north and shortly joins the Tillingbourne.

The Silent Pool, or the Shireburn Ponds, is actually two pools, set among trees, formed by dams of ancient origin. The upper is encircled by a public path, from which you may look down into transparent green depths typical of deep water on chalk, to see majestic trout taking their ease or idly feeding along green forests of weed. They are used to admiration, these fellows, and bask in it and in the sun all at once. And they are tame enough sometimes to nuzzle up against an enquiring finger.

Martin Tupper, that sentimental novelist and poet of the mid years of the nineteenth century (who is buried at Albury), set a scene here in his fanciful 'historical' novel *Stephen Langton*: a beautiful girl, surprised while bathing in the pool by King John, refused to come out and drowned before the wicked king's eyes rather than sacrifice her modesty.

We come back to the Albury road at the point at which we have arrived from Weston Wood. Near the road stands an ornate stone-built Victorian gothic church. Erected in 1840, it belongs to a strange sect called the Catholic Apostolic Church, or Irvingites, the latter title from one of its leading members, a Scottish divine. Edward Irving was a member of a circle of friends who met for conferences, or as 'a little prophetic parliament', in Albury House, the home of Edward Drummond, who paid for the church you now see.

Before we go any further we need to examine Albury House and its gardens in more detail, so I leave you standing before the Irvingite church (which you are sure to find locked), while I carry you off spiritually where physically we may not be allowed to go.

The entrance to Albury Park lies a little to the south of the church. I feel sure, and other writers have felt sure, that the Pilgrims' Way went directly through the park, past Albury old church and Albury House, to come out at the other side into the village of Shere. How long there has been a house here in the deep and narrow valley of the Tillingbourne is not precisely known, but one Azor, a Saxon subject of Edward the Confessor, is recorded in Domesday Book as having possessions here. That he had a house seems likely from the fact that the neighbouring church is of Saxon origin and may be credited to him. Beside the church, certainly not long afterwards and probably in that time too, there was a village with a village green. Azor was deprived of his property by the Conqueror, who gave it to Robert de Tonbridge; from him or his successors it passed to the family of d'Abernon, one of whom, Sir John, is represented in Stoke d'Abernon church by a magnificent brass of 1277, the oldest brass in this country. The property at Albury next came into the hands of the Westons, whose name we have already encountered in Weston Wood. Thenceforward there was a succession of owners, ending with Helen, Duchess of Northumberland, who opened the house to the public. After her death the house was acquired by a housing association to be converted into flats for retired people. Whether the house and its grounds will again be open to the public is not yet certain. I think it probable.

The gardens are worth seeing. They were laid out in the seventeenth century for Henry Howard, sixth Duke of Norfolk, by John Evelyn, the diarist, who lived not far away at Wotton; Evelyn planted fine avenues of various kinds of trees and built a curious cavern or grotto. On the 23rd of September 1670 Evelyn came to see the results of his work: 'To Alburie', he wrote, 'to see how that garden proceedeth, which I found exactly done to the designe and plot I had made, with the crypte thro' the mountaine in the park, 30 perches in length. Such a Pausilippe is no where in England besides.' The 'Pausilippe' was inspired by the grotto of Sejanus at Posilippe near Naples. It cannot be expected that the garden should survive exactly as Evelyn left it, but his work can be traced and there are rare and beautiful trees from his time and later. Cobbett found it entirely to his satisfaction and solved the problem of entry into private land by riding through it and up to the front door and asking permission to carry on and out the other side; cheek was the last thing Cobbett lacked.

The gardens Evelyn designed began, indeed, to deteriorate in his own lifetime, especially when the house was acquired by Heneage Finch, a son of the Duke of Nottingham; he was M.P. for Guildford, became Solicitor-General, and was created Earl of Aylesford; we shall meet him again. In 1687 Evelyn wrote that he 'found the gardens which I design'd for the Duke of Norfolk nothing improved'. Finch's boorish brother, Captain Finch, who had made a fortune in freebooting, next took over the house and started a campaign against the villagers, enclosing their green and shutting off roads. This work was continued by the next owner but one, Henry Drummond, who in 1842 succeeded in moving the villagers half a mile to the west, to Weston Street, a hamlet that now took the name of Albury. It has some old houses, but is distinguished by the tall carved brick chimneys of the houses Drummond built for some of the villagers of old Albury.

Albury House has been considerably altered during its long history, mostly by Sloane inside and by Pugin outside, who turned the place into a sham and unlikely Tudor mansion with no less than sixty tall carved chimneys, of the same kind as those at Weston Street.

The Saxon church remains, now seldom used but still accessible (1970). The original church comprised a nave and chancel only. The Normans thickened the walls of the chancel and set a tower upon it, and built a new chancel east of the tower. This second chancel was rebuilt in the thirteenth century, but it now stands roofless and excluded from the church. Forty or fifty years later a south chapel and south aisle were added, and about 1750 a wildly anachronistic dome or cupola was put on the tower in place of a spire, with an effect altogether endearing. Drummond turned the south chapel into a private mortuary chapel with the walls and practically everything else decorated by Pugin and in violent contrast with the calm of the rest of the church. There are two monuments of the Westons, one a marble slab of the late thirteenth century and the other a brass of 1440, and over the south doorway is a mural painting of Saint Christopher, patron saint of travellers. Note also the very fine and unaltered north porch of about 1500, and the enormous key you may have to borrow to get into the church—the timbered cottage north of the drive from which you get it was, in the days of the village, the Little George Inn.

Though you may be allowed to visit Albury old church, there is no right of way through Albury Park, where the Pilgrims' Way possibly ran along the line of a yew avenue in the grounds, planted by Evelyn. If you do not have the impudence of Cobbett, an alternative route must be found, and there is one to hand. It begins on the Albury road, where a lane runs east a little to the north of the Irvingite church. We follow this lane through a stile into a field, cross this field towards some thin trees a little to the left, where there is another stile, keep right at a junction, and go through woodland or beside woods until we come to another narrow, surfaced, and sunken lane. There are now two possible ways into the village of Shere. Neither of them, it may be, is on the line of the Pilgrims' Way, for after leaving Weston Wood the line of the Way is uncertain or lost. One path into the village is found by crossing over the sunken lane and following a path that soon meets with houses, among which you turn to the right down to the Tillingbourne on the western edge of the village. The second way, and the more interesting, is to turn down the sunken lane to the right to a ford in the Tillingbourne and to take a stile to the left just beyond the ford. This brings us into a field alongside the tree-shaded little river. The path enters a noble avenue of tall lime trees, and comes to another ford, beside which begins the first street of Shere, parallel with the river but hidden from it by walls, gardens, and houses. A little way along this street is the Prison House, a seventeenth-century jail—it is too big to be called a mere lock-up—with its windows still barred beneath a thrusting jetty; it is now a dwelling. The street comes out by a green bank beside the Tillingbourne again, with a low bridge that marks the centre of the village of Shere.

Shere, once a centre of smugglers (some of the old houses have large cellars to store the contraband, as at Compton), has the reputation of being one of the prettiest villages in Surrey and consequently at week-ends it is choked with visitors in search of the pretty and picturesque. Certainly the shallow stream over-hung by willows, the flotillas of ducks, the old black and white houses, and the White Horse Inn—part of which is as old as the fourteenth century and consequently contemporary with the Canterbury pilgrimages—all these have their charm and are delightful, but they do not form a coherent whole. There is, too, a good deal of nineteenth-century building of no admirable character. The church of St James, at the head of a short, broad street, is well placed on a rise, but it plays little part in the villagescape.

The church may stand on the site of a church of the eighth century, when the name of Shere was Schir or Essira and was understood to mean 'the bright one', presumably a reference to the clear and rippling river that is now in the same Saxon tongue the Tillingbourne. The Normans rebuilt the church late in the twelfth century, when their architectural style had developed from plain mass to ornament designed to leaven the rigidity of that mass. The south door shows the strong late Norman penchant for thick pattern dominated by one prominent motif, in this case the popular zig-zag. The time was that of Henry II and the first years of the Canterbury pilgrimage. Some sixty or seventy years later the low Norman tower was heightened. Another century and a considerable amount of building and rebuilding was done, including the replacement of some of the Norman arches of the tower, which had probably begun to founder under the weight of the additional upper stage and now had to bear the further load of the octagonal broached timber spire. Inside the church there are a strange Norman font of Purbeck marble and a crusader chest of the type ordered to be put in churches by Pope Innocent III to collect money for the crusades to the Holy Land.

In the north wall of the chancel a quatrefoil aperture and a squint formerly opened into the cell of an anchoress called Christine, the daughter of a carpenter. Letters between the Bishop of Winchester, whose diocese at that time included Shere, and the Archdeacon of Surrey concerning the enclosure of this girl survive among the Egerton MSS. in the British Museum. They make disturbing reading. One sees between the lines that it was desirable and an advantage for a church to be able to boast of an anchorite or anchoress, but nonetheless careful inquiry was made concerning the character, virtue, and piety of Christine Carpenter before permission was finally given to wall her up in a cell. Whether she was truly devout, or a religious fanatic, or a simple and half-demented woman seeking escape from a world that tortured her one cannot tell. After a couple of years of her horrible imprisonment she got out, but, according to the correspondence, she was soon begging to be enclosed again, perhaps not altogether willingly but because people had worked upon her mind. In the words of the correspondence, she was 'thrust back' into her cell and there was a hint of excommunication if she escaped again.

From the moment the route leaves Weston Wood and comes to the Irvingite church south of the Silent Pool the known line of the Pilgrims' Way, as I have remarked, is uncertain or lost, and it is not recovered until a point north of Westcott is reached. If Belloc's theory concerning the tendency of the Way to pass by the south doors of churches were to be trusted, then from Shere the Way ought to go up the short but broad street to the church and take the path around the south side of the churchyard; but the path there goes nowhere that is useful to us. To regain the known line of the Way above Westcott we have at some point to cross the A25. The OS one-inch map names a short length of the Way north of Shere, and this may be reached from the village by a path that goes through a tunnel under the main road. This length, however, is a disjointed piece of only about half a mile, running into the grounds of Netley House and beside the house itself. If this length is to be regarded as part of the Pilgrims' Way it raises more problems than it solves. It would be nothing uncommon for the Way to pass thus to the north of and to ignore the village of Shere, but how the lost sections connected Weston Wood with the Netley piece, and how the Way is continued eastwards thereafter are not apparent either on the map or on the ground.

We must go for a time along the road. The way out of Shere is to the north. At the junction of the street with what, before the building of the by-pass, was the main road, there is a well that dates in its present form from 1886. It is in an arched stone recess in a wall, with inglenook seats as though it were a fireplace, and it is railed in by ornamental ironwork that is an early and unexpected example of the art-nouveau style, a style that may be traced back to William Blake through the Pre-Raphaelites, but in the form we are considering is more commonly attributed to the early 1890s. How much older than its present dress the well may be, I cannot say, but if it is ancient, as is probable, it may reasonably have drawn pilgrims down from the thirsty hill slopes to refresh themselves.

At this junction in Shere, where the well is, we turn to the right along the road and into the next village, Gomshall, about one mile distant. Gomshall is an old village with its cottages shouldering in upon a street now far too busy with motor traffic for its width. At a junction stands an interesting seventeenth-century house of brick. Called King John's House, it stands on the site of an older building in which King John is said to have punished an erring servant by locking him up in a room and leaving him to die. If only a tithe of the crimes and cruelties attributed to that unamiable monarch were true, he must now be roasting irretrievably.

South of the road and extending for more than a mile and a half towards Abinger Hammer, is a series of old hammer-ponds, some of which have been turned into water-cress beds. They were built to work the hammers of bloomeries, that is of iron-foundries, in which, it is believed, some of the guns were made that defeated the Spanish Armada. The foundries worked with the local ironstone and heated their furnaces with charcoal made in the surrounding forests. From these hammer-mills comes the name of Abinger Hammer, the hamlet distinguished by the Clock House (built in 1891); it has a jack dressed as a smith, who sounds the hours by beating on a bell with his hammer.

Just before we enter the hamlet of Abinger Hammer we have a choice of routes.

Alternative 7a. By Hackhurst Downs and White Downs

About three-quarters of a mile after the railway bridge at Gomshall is passed, and just before Abinger Hammer, turn left into Hackhurst Lane and climb the hillside to pass again under the railway. Turn off to the east along a track about the 700-foot contour. This is excellent walking country, raised high above the Tillingbourne valley, with fine panoramas to the south over the greensand country and the clay country of the Weald. There is a profusion of plants and insects. Blackthorns and hawthorns, their white blossoms one following the other in spring, mingle their branches in close thickets, and here and there are cool caverns beneath the interlocking branches of yew trees. If Belloc's conclusions concerning the relation of yew trees to the Old Road are accepted, then this high path, although its yews are not old, might be identified with the road; this, I think, cannot be proved. But some of the many paths that criss-cross in confusion do lead eventually eastwards towards the accepted line of the Old Road. You may easily be lost, but the thing to remember is not to allow yourself to be diverted to the summit of the hill and not to take any path that descends too directly down towards the valley of the Tillingbourne.

Along these downs a variety of insects flourish. On a fine day grasshoppers in the tough grass beneath the furze fiddle their persistent calls, more like a dry vibration of the air than a musical note. Wasps and striped flies that imitate wasps take turns to enter the mouths of a variety of flowers, and a dance of variegated butterflies takes place under the sun—dark blue, nearly black butterflies, brown spotted fritillaries, gay peacocks with their staring coloured concentric roundels like the markings of RAF planes, noble red admirals, and many others some of which I have not seen elsewhere. Interrupting this peaceful country atmosphere with grimmer thoughts of quarrels not so very far off or very long ago are half-hidden wartime strong-points, so many that you will conclude that in these hills there must have been concealed some high direction of the war; in fact, what was here in the woods was vast quantities of ammunition. I once wandered into these areas with a camera and was politely asked to leave after satisfying an army officer that I was not a German agent.

The path gradually descends along the hillside towards the Effingham road, a road deeply sunk and turned into a tunnel by the overhanging branches of trees—limes, elms, yews, and others —whose roots half-exposed on the sandy banks are tormented, twisted, and interlocked.

We need to cross this road and to find an opening with a central concrete pillar bearing the letter E. This gap, a little way above a sharp hairpin of the road, leads at once to an open path running alongside a wood on the left hand. Just within this wood is an overgrown path on a shelf, partly sunk and now abandoned and impassable. It is the type of the Pilgrims' Way in many places, and the discovery of this old path suggests that we may be on the true line. The path we follow remains outside the wood and shows the blanched surface of the chalk, like a trickle of milk. It is narrow but clear, and it leads along the south shoulder of White Downs, which rise in the wood to 723 feet. Suddenly our thin track dives straight into closely growing blackthorn bushes and yews, with brambles and briars looping across the gap. There is nothing to do but lower your head and push bravely through. Thereafter the path enters woodland and begins to climb among many yews and other trees, rising distinctively on a terrace along a steep hillside, with occasional downward views through the leaves of the long straight line of the railway and sometimes of the tower of Wotton church across the valley.

We are coming up to Pickett's Hole, and here we join the alternative path coming up from Wotton.

Alternative 7b. The route by Wotton

Abinger Hammer is no more than an outlying hamlet of the village of Abinger a mile to the south, a village that has been called, not very intelligently, the oldest in England, on the strength of a pit-dwelling inhabited by Mesolithic hunters some seven thousand years ago, which was excavated in 1950 west of the church. The church, dedicated to Saint James, a saint popular with pilgrims on account of Compostella, was seriously damaged by a bomb in 1944 and again by lightning and fire in 1964, and consequently much of the present structure is restoration work—but its origins are Norman. A notable survival is a fifteenth-century alabaster relief of the Crucifixion, in Nottingham style, now in the porch. A fair held annually in the churchyard is claimed to be a revival of a medieval fair that attracted pilgrims. East of the church is a Norman motte, surrounded by a wet moat fed by a spring, and Abinger Manor, an altered Jacobean house believed to have been built by John Evelyn, but apparently earlier than his time. The Evelyn family have held the advowson of the church for the last three hundred and fifty years.

We can return to the A25 by Abinger Lane and Raikes Lane. Where Raikes Lane meets the main road there stands an excellent seventeenth-century farmhouse, Crossways, of reddish brick, in design like a little manor-house; it can be seen only by peering through a barred wicket in a door set centrally in a high wall; inquiring faces, are, I fear, one of the penalties of living in so lovely a house. It figures in George Meredith's novel, *Diana of the Crossways*.

North of the house and of the main road there stood a Roman villa, and farther north still, in Evershed's Rough, there is, or was, for I have never been able to find it among the trees, a pillar in memory of Samuel Wilberforce, Bishop of Winchester, who in 1873 fell off his horse here and was killed. He has a white, elaborately gothic, shrine-like monument in the Norman south transept of Winchester cathedral.

Wotton, a mile to the east of Crossways, is marked on the map as though it were a village. In fact it comprises little more than a manor-house, an inn—the Wotton Hatch—on the main road, and a church, so spaced one from the other that each is individual and distinct and not part of a village group. Of houses there are only a few, of the nineteenth century, hidden in a valley. It is supposed that there was somewhere here a Saxon village, for the name is Saxon, but that this village was destroyed by the Danes and never rebuilt. The Danish raids and the Black Death of the fourteenth century are often quoted as causes for the disappearance of villages or for their being sited some distance from their churches.

The manor, or Wotton House, a building of several periods, was the home of the Evelyn family from the late sixteenth century until the twentieth. In this house John Evelyn, the diarist and authority on trees, was born in 1620 and here he died in 1706. His passion for trees is perhaps reflected still in the wooded nature of this parish, as we also found it to be in the gardens of Albury Park. He planted pines for their 'odiferous and balsamical emissions', and because he thought these trees, as evergreens, created a perpetual spring. He was considerably upset when on the 26th of November 1703 a hurricane destroyed many of his trees and made Wotton, he lamented, 'no more Woodtown, stripped and naked and almost ashamed to own its name'. A friend of Charles I, Evelyn preserved at Wotton the blood-stained prayer-book used by the king on the scaffold on that day, the 30th of January 1649, when he was beheaded in

Whitehall. The house has been so sadly altered since the eighteenth century, and bereft of its contents, that little of the spirit of John Evelyn can remain in it. It is now a fire-service college and is not accessible to the public; nor, as far as I know, can it be seen from any public way, for it hides deep in the valley of the Tillingbourne away from public paths.

The church stands to the north, all alone on a ridge, but it is visible from the main road—a road hereabouts more like a country lane than a busy main artery, but having to carry the traffic of such an artery. A modest little lane turning off north opposite the Wotton Hatch inn leads to the church, which is nicely set in a leafy churchyard and is not seen at first to be standing, as it is, on the edge of a slope. Beyond it is a broad valley and then the wooded slopes of the downs. A brief avenue of paired lime trees and chestnut trees brings us to the porch against the base of the tower, a porch the successor of one in which John Evelyn records that he received his first lessons. Wotton church is singular in many ways, but it is attractive from first glance, with its broad and dumpy west tower on which is set a small square belfry with a pyramid roof. The effect is homely and not in a common English idiom, but it has been achieved, I feel, by accident rather than by intent. The porch leads directly into the tower on the south side, and that too is singular. It has been proposed that the tower was originally central and a blocked arch visible in the tower west wall may be taken as confirmation of that. But the arch is pointed and early English, while the tower is indubitably Norman, and even Saxon in the sense that it was built under Norman direction by Saxon masons in the first years after the Conquest. A lot of work was done in this church in the thirteenth century and it appears to me that some kind of forebuilding or narthex was raised against the west wall of the tower at that time. I think this a more likely theory than is the notion that the tower was originally central or that the forebuilding too was Norman; either of these arguments would require a reason for the alteration of the west tower arch from the Norman round to the Early English pointed style.

Inside the church a good deal of Victorian and twentieth-century restoration work is evident—an obvious bit is the lush

Victorian gothic tracery filling the north chancel arch. Not-withstanding the modern work, Wotton remains a church of great charm, a charm that enchants people who come here principally on account of the Evelyns. The Evelyns worshipped in Wotton church for nearly four centuries after George Evelyn bought the manor-house. All that time they held, as they still hold, the presentation of the living. The Evelyn chapel leads off the north aisle, an aisle of thirteenth-century build small enough to be more like a transept than an aisle. We pass through an arch in the east wall of this transeptual aisle, and through a simple screen dated 1632. This is the gate into the Evelyn chapel which occupies the thirteenth-century north chancel chapel of the church.

Here the Evelyns are all around us. On the south wall hangs a large monument to the first of the Evelyns of Wotton, George Evelyn, who died in 1603. He is shown between his two wives Rose and Joan, and with his twenty-five children ranged below, sixteen from Rose and nine from Joan. Some of the children appear as babies in swaddling-clothes, showing that they died at birth or in early childhood, and above the heads of some of the older ones skulls are seen, marking those children who died before their parents or before they became adult. Also on the south wall hangs a monument to one of George's sons, Richard, who died in 1640 after begetting five children from one wife only; the interesting thing about this monument is the survival through the Puritan times of the little carving of the Virgin and Child at the top.

There are other monuments and memorials of the Evelyns in this chapel and in the adjoining chapel built of brick about 1680, but the Evelyns for whom most visitors come lie in simple coffin-shaped, separate sarcophagi on the floor of the old chapel, one for John Evelyn's wife and the other, below the east window, for John 'Sylva' Evelyn himself—'Sylva' because that was the title of the book he wrote about his consuming interest. An old font near his tomb is very likely that in which John Evelyn was baptised; it was once thrown out of the church as superseded and was recovered years later in a builder's yard.

As you come out of the church turn in the porch to look at the series of small heads carved around the arch. Too small to have great effect, they date from the thirteenth century and the troubled reign of King John, and especially relate to the papal interdict John brought upon the nation, with excommunication for himself, because of threats he had made against the appointment of Stephen Langton in 1206 to the see of Canterbury, instead of a worthless courtier whom John proposed. Like his father, Henry II, John wished to control the appointments of prelates in his country. As a result the people of England were shut out of their churches and Langton, like Becket before him, whose example no doubt stiffened Langton's will, was shut out of his archdiocese. Also like Becket, Langton resided during his exile in the abbey of Pontigny. The table below shows what each of the small heads at Wotton represents and what it was meant to stand for:

A cardinal	papal legate
A pilgrim or a peasant	the common people
A queen in a wimple	Queen Isabella, wife of King John
A nobleman	Ralph de Camoys, patron of the church
A priest	the rector of Wotton
A king	King John
A mitred priest	Pope Innocent III
An archbishop	Stephen Langton

At the western end of the churchyard a stile leads into an arable field full of stones and irregular flints. The path goes down to and into a wood, and before you get half-way there you should turn to look again at the church; bright in the western sun, with laburnums golden in the churchyard, the little church with its comfortable west tower looks very well indeed.

The wood is nicely called Deer Leap Wood, and you may see a deer or two hereabouts. Among the trees there are at least two tumuli, one of which is believed to be an example showing the continuance of the mesolithic peoples into the neolithic period. The path goes by Park Farm in the valley, and farther on crosses a small stream and then over the railway by a bridge, after which it climbs aslant the breathless slope to the head of

Pickett's Hole. There we meet with the path of our alternative 7a, on the thickly wooded White Downs.

Pickett's Hole is a surprising feature, or it would be if it were not solidly choked with trees. It is the head of a dry valley that long ago lost its stream in the underlying caverns of the chalk. The large, deep chasm with rounded sides instead of scarped cliffs, is really more like a combe than a 'hole'.

The land around and above the head of Pickett's Hole is Forestry Commission property, and there are nature walks among trees of many kinds. Leaflets that may be obtained at the upper borders of the wood, by the Ranmore road, explain what may be seen and guide visitors round the paths. Among rare plants you may see here is the bee orchis, which likes to grow in the shade and has a flower in appearance very like a feeding bumble-bee.

There is not yet any assurance that we have arrived on the true Pilgrims' Way, but wherever we may be on these hills we cannot be far out, for the Way is marked again on the map a little ahead of us on the slopes of the downs and its connection must be somewhere near Pickett's Hole. That it did not go straight through the hole is certain, for no one would choose to descend that dangerous steep only to be faced with the climbing of another such slope on the far side. Hereabouts the contours on the 2½-inch map are so close together that they look like combed wavy hair. A traveller, prehistoric or Christian, would rather choose to go along the valley or along the downs above Pickett's Hole than to waste his energies uselessly.

Here I should add that if you wish to avoid Pickett's Hole altogether and to climb the downs by a less energetic route, you should continue along the main road past Wotton to Westcott. You will see Westcott church set high above a green, a church designed in 1852 by Sir George Gilbert Scott. The hill on which the church is set is greensand and the village lies in such convenient relation to quarries of chalk and sandstone that its houses are built of one stone or the other, or of the two mixed, as the builder pleased. A little beyond the church, at a triangular 'island', turn left into a street and right when this street turns left, immediately after a stream, to go along a path leading to and passing under the railway to meet the Pilgrims' Way above Landbarn Farm.

What we are now on is a sombre drive running along the 400-foot contour and rising from it. The drive was originally made as a carriageway for Denbies, an expensive Italianate house put up by Thomas Cubitt for himself and his heirs in 1850. Cubitt was a famous builder and contractor and a wealthy man, and nothing was too good for his house. Alas for such vainglory! The house declined after Thomas Cubitt's death in 1855, and in 1954, in a time in which great houses have become rather a liability than an asset, it was demolished; only the stables remain and are still in use.

The drive is clearly marked on the OS map as the Pilgrims' Way, but this attribution is not unchallenged. A higher route, on the road coming along Ranmore Common and descending to West Humble, has been suggested in whole or in part, and we now examine these two ways.

Alternative 8a. The lower route to Pixham

This route follows the path through Ranmore Wood marked by the Ordnance Survey as the Pilgrims' Way. It is easily traced, though modern developments have put hindrances in the way. The Denbies drive goes along a terrace on the hillside. It is a sombre, claustrophobic path, not much used and full of that still silence that trees and especially yew trees gather about themselves. There are occasional openings in the leafy curtains, through which the valley is seen, with the sprawling town of Dorking. We continue along the drive until it divides, and there take the right-hand way. This drops down to and emerges on to the Ranmore road, just above a modern development of streets and houses that effectually covers over any trace of the old Way.

We have to make for the valley of the Mole and a suitable crossing over the river, a river that is the first of three that cut so surprisingly through the massif of the chalk; the river passes by Mickleham and Leatherhead on its way to the Thames at Molesey. The place of crossing, the place where primitive man crossed over this little river and pilgrims crossed it many centuries later, is as uncertain as is the true line of approach to

8. *Abandoned chalk quarry in Dawcombe Wood*

9. *Widening of the Way in Pilgrims' Lane, north of Bletchingley*

10. *Sweeping contours of the greensand north of Godstone*

11. *Charing church, with remains of the bishops' palace on the left*

the river from the west. Belloc, too, was puzzled by these problems, but having reached Box Hill, he had only to look back and see a line of yews growing in a field to be satisfied that there, along by the yews, was the true line of the Old Road. Julia Cartwright follows him in this conclusion. Poppycock! I admire Belloc for his liveliness of writing, and respect him for his pioneer work on the Old Road, but he is frequently incautious and sometimes mistaken.

We make our way among the houses, going slightly north of east, and crossing the invisible course of the Roman road called Stane Street to arrive shortly on the A24.

The A24 is today a dual carriageway, and because it is dual, with a central strip, it is not difficult to cross even on a busy day. We cross where we can and turn along the pavement on the far side until we come to an unmade, tree-shaded lane turning off to the right and marked 'Stepping-Stones'. It brings us in a few yards to the river Mole, which is said to have its name from its habit of disappearing into the ground. Perhaps it does burrow, but not here, where the stepping-stones cross. The stones are a series of polygonal concrete blocks with flat tops, spread on a curved line across a tree-shaded pool (*plate* 5). That pool has quite sufficient water for a ducking if you miss your step on the stones. If the water is deeper than usual, or the river is in flood, curling and swirling over the stones, we have only to follow downstream, that is by turning along the left bank in among the trees, to come to an iron footbridge that takes us safely across.

This footbridge shall be our meeting-place for the alternative route coming down from Ranmore.

Alternative 8b. The Ranmore route

Any footpath leading north from the Denbies drive will bring us past a woodland called the Spains on to the Ranmore road, which runs like a spine along the lengthy Ranmore Common. This common used to be the site of an annual Scout jamboree and on those occasions there would be hundreds of tents with thousands of boys moving about. The Scouts have not been for some years now. Instead, there are large car parks where car-borne families come on fine week-ends to wander in the

LPW

woods, to play games or to picnic, or simply to lie and sunbathe.

Ranmore church, at the east end of the common, raises a tall sharp spire above the trees. The church was built in 1859 to the design of Sir George Gilbert Scott, who, it has been said, could turn out a gothic church in an hour or two. Ranmore, however, is no run-of-the-mill job. Built at the considerable expense of Thomas Cubitt's son, it is not so much a copy of gothic as an original essay within that style. Interesting and fresh, it is at the same time hard and unsympathetic. Nothing seems to have been too good for the Cubitts in their church at Ranmore and money was not spared for the work or for the material. Pillars and other details of coloured marble, competently carved ornament, and colourful frescoes (of uncertain quality) may be noticed. Nothing, however, so much underlines the lavishness of this church and of the funds available as does the font: a lush, pretentious, and in every way remarkable piece of work, it is expensive enough and sufficiently large for a cathedral—if any cathedral would have it. It is staggering in this small church. In company with the church and built of flints, as the church is, there are also a school and a vicarage, probably also by Scott.

The road divides around the church. The right hand branch goes down to the point where we emerged from the Denbies drive on the previous alternative route. The road to the left of the church goes along the level top of the ridge and then turns left to drop suddenly down a hill, which it negotiates by a tight hairpin bend; it then goes along one of those dry downland valleys typical of the chalk, valleys once the courses of streams and rivers in some past distant beyond knowledge. We come to a T junction and turn right into a slender hedged lane. This is Chapel Lane and in a third of a mile we find on our right, opposite Chapel Farm, the inconsiderable and valueless remains of the twelfth-century flint-built Norman chapel of West Humble. The ruin is in the hands of the National Trust and one cannot help wondering why they collected it in the first place or bother now to preserve this featureless little wreck, except that they suppose it to be on the Pilgrims' Way and to have served pilgrims on their journey to or from Canterbury. More prosaically and more accurately it was built as a chapel of ease to Mickleham, to serve parishioners who could not cross a river Mole frequently in flood. The ruin comprises little more than east and west gables, with no details that can be recognized as Norman.

Paternoster Lane and Pray Meadows are names in this area that have been held to owe their origin to the passing of the pilgrims through West Humble. The connection is thin.

Farther east we come to the hamlet of Camilla Lacey. Fanny Burney lived in the house of this name, deriving the name 'Camilla' from her successful novel of that title; the present house is modern Tudor. Fanny became acquainted with a number of French exiles, including Talleyrand, then living at Juniper Hall, a mile to the north-west, and in 1793 she married one of them, Alexandre d'Arblay, in Mickleham's Norman church.

The name of Lacey shows that the Norman family of Lacey held land here. It occurs again over the hill to the west, at Polesden Lacey, where it stands for one of the National Trust's most desirable country houses. According to Sheridan, who lived in the preceding house on this site, this was 'the nicest place, within a prudent distance of town', and visitors who walk in the thousand acres of the magnificent park will find it hard to disagree. Sheridan's house was demolished and rebuilt by Thomas Cubitt for Joseph Bonsor in 1824. Cubitt's house was altered in 1906, when the clock cupola was added to give the place a distinctive charm and unusual character. The house, with superlative contents of furniture and pictures, was bequeathed to the National Trust by the Honourable Mrs Greville, together with 910 acres and an endowment. Nothing could more forcefully underline the diversity of the properties of the National Trust than these neighbours, the vestigial chapel at West Humble and the affluent Polesden Lacey, neighbours close in space but six hundred years apart in time.

Polesden Lacey has little to do with the Pilgrims' Way, but among the old paintings there are several done at a time when the atmosphere of the middle ages still hung like mist in the air. Look especially at a portrait painted in the late fifteenth century by the Master of Saint Severin. It shows an old woman, in a wimple, with a rosary in her hands. With her sad eyes and firm mouth she seems to grieve and might be a type of the more devout of the pilgrims to the shrine of Saint Thomas, seeking intercession for the soul of someone dear to her, a child or a husband, not long dead and still mourned.

From Camilla Lacey we drop down to the A24, to find near the junction a pub called the Stepping-Stones. Southwards the road leads to Dorking.

Dorking is an ancient town with a name of Saxon origin. The termination 'ing' means people and the forepart comes from 'dorce', bright water, so we have 'the people of or by the bright water'. This derivation assumes—and there is no evidence to support the assumption—that the Mole was once called the 'Dorce' or 'Dork'. The town lies so close to the Pilgrims' Way that it would be reasonable to regard it as a convenient place of refreshment and a night halt for pilgrims and other travellers on the Way, as convenient then as it may be today. The town is pleasant in a general view, rather than in the quality of individual buildings. There are several buildings old enough to have seen from their latticed windows the pilgrims trudging in. The short West Street is the most interesting of the town's streets, with a sort of village antiquity in its houses and with a low-slung timbered pub, the King's Arms, that, perhaps optimistically, claims an origin in the fourteenth century. From one of the shops in the town in the seventeenth century a pilgrim of another sort set out for the west, to sail in the *Mayflower* for New England. He was William Mullins. His daughter Priscilla was one of his party. She had a suitor, Miles Standish, who, lacking courage to propose to her on his own account, sent the *Mayflower*'s cooper John Alden to propose on his behalf. 'Speak for yourself, John,' said Priscilla, and so he did and he married her. This is, of course, a cottage version of the old story of Tristram and Iseult, or the Gaelic legend of Diarmuid and Gráinne.

Dorking's church of Saint Martin was built entirely in the five years between 1868 and 1873, the tall stone spire having been completed in the latter year as a memorial to Bishop Samuel Wilberforce of Winchester, who, as I have already recounted, was killed in falling from his horse in Evershed's Rough. The church is regarded as one of the best of the works of Woodyer, the Victorian architect who had been a pupil of the inventive and until recently frequently maligned Butterfield. The Dorking church is in a Decorated style, and like a good deal of Victorian architecture, it seems to attract liking and dislike in about equal amounts.

9 Dorking to Titsey

12 MILES

We stand by the pub called the Stepping-Stones at Burford, in the valley of the river Mole. To the north, just beyond the Burford bridge, sprawls the long white, Georgian, Burford Bridge Hotel, in which Keats once stayed and wrote part of *Endymion*. Ahead of us and round behind the hotel, like a theatrical backcloth, rises the precipitous, tree-clothed breast of Box Hill, its steepness represented on the map by a combed switch of close contours. Unseen along its base runs the river Mole, furrowing its way through the chalk downs in a quite remarkable manner towards the north, making a convenient and easy pass from the Weald towards the Thames valley. The downs gather their skirts away from the river and its valley like old ladies lifting their hems clear of a runnel.

Ancient man on the Old Road, the Romans on Stane Street, and pilgrims on the Pilgrims' Way all had to face the problem of crossing the Mole and of overcoming the precipitous down. The modern motor road follows through the valley, winding with it. Having once crossed over at Burford, it avoids crossing again, but in places runs beside the water. Stane Street also crossed at Burford, coming down the slopes from the south-west; beyond the river it went for a short distance along the line of the Mickleham road, but before the village is reached, Stane Street turns off to the north-east, taking to the hills to climb up over Mickleham Down. For the Romans a straight line was a military command to be followed no matter what lay in the way—or so it seems, though scholars have denied it. In the Lake District the Roman engineers even drove a road up and along the ridge of a rocky mountain, which is called High Street in memory of that unintelligent achievement; one may imagine the uninhibited comments of Roman soldiers as they toiled up to 2,700 feet in the bitter winter winds or in the heat of summer.

Some writers suppose that the Pilgrims' Way went along the

top of Box Hill. A modern surfaced road takes this line, swoop-
ing up the side of the down in spectacular *lacets* that will
astonish any Highlander or Pennine man who regards our
southern downs with derision. The summit is a favourite place
with motorists, who come here in droves in the summer to park
among the roadside trees and to enjoy the panorama over the
Weald. The height is modest, less than 700 feet, but the view is
magnificent. Along the road there are a caravan site, cafés, a
pub, and a tourist shop or two. You may also find a curiosity, a
rectangular block of stone marking the place where one Peter
Labellière, a land-owner about here, was buried head down in
the year 1800. He was placed so at his own wish so that he should
be the right way up at the Last Trump, when he believed that
the world would be turned topsy-turvy. According to local
tradition, his head rests on a fortune, which he took with him
so that he might maintain in the next world the status he enjoyed
in this.

The OS 2½-inch map shows the Pilgrims' Way taking a
straight line between the 200-foot and 300-foot contours of the
south side of Box Hill. To reach this line we would have to go
partly south and then east around the south-west bastion of the
hill. At the south-east corner of Burford bridge we pass over a
stile into a tumbled field and take a path by the Mole. From the
far side of the river rises the steepest slope of Box Hill, called the
Whites. This name suggests the chalk and chalk is confirmed by
the white blazes seen through the covering of trees and bushes,
made either by falls of material down the slope or by the sliding
down of adventurous youngsters (usually on their backsides).
The bank along which we walk is commonly occupied by
anglers, fishing in the little river for fish of small size, but enjoying themselves, as anglers will, in contemplation of the silky
deeps and the rippling shallows.

Along this part of the Mole and from here to the Stepping-
Stones grow colonies of a plant with a pretty pink flower like
those of an antirrhinum, but the plant has dark lanceolate
leaves. The fruit is a long, beak-like container which bursts
with a snap the moment it is touched. I have not seen these
flowers anywhere else on the Way and they are not common
anywhere; called Himalayan balsam, or, popularly, jumping

jack, they are, I suspect, a garden escape. The path curves with the river and comes to a stile (*plate* 6), which we cross into a wood. A few steps bring us to an iron footbridge over the Mole, built as a memorial to members of the Ramblers Association killed in the wars. This bridge is the one with which our alternative route 8a came to an end.

We cross the bridge and turn to the right, upstream, and shortly come to the stepping-stones. In their present form these stones date only from 1946, when they were erected at the cost of Mr Chuter Ede, who held the office of Home Secretary; they take the place of a series of stones that have crossed the river here for many years. No stones, however, are mentioned by either Belloc or Julia Cartwright, who must have seen them if they existed at the time they wrote. Near the stones and the path grows a large and prosperous walnut tree, in September a magnet for small boys.

The path turns away from the river at the stepping-stones and heads for the hillside, which it begins to climb at an angle along a terrace, and soon comes under the shade of a variety of trees, among which yews are numerous, together with over-grown box-bushes—the bushes from which Box Hill takes its name. The slope on our right hand falls away more and more steeply, and there are views occasionally down to the Mole shining along its sinuous course. We avoid a path that leads downhill towards the river and, climbing still, come out on to a bare hillside on the lower slope of which a path runs along the north side of a hedge. On this hillside Mr Dorp took the colour photograph for the wrapper of this book.

The path we are following is not, according to the Ordnance Survey or according to Belloc, who is in many instances followed by the Ordnance Survey, the true line of the Way. The accepted line runs across a field a hundred feet lower down, a line now marked by a row of electricity pylons and their slung wires. These pylons, however, run across ploughed land, land that Belloc also found under the plough, and there is no way and no right of way down there. This lost or inaccessible part of the way diverges from the pylons below Duke's Plantation and soon thereafter falls into a huge chalk-pit, from which it emerges only to fall into another. These two pits show as great gashes in the flanks of the downs, white pyramids of chalk that are visible for many miles over the Weald and seize with astonishment motorists driving along the Dorking to Reigate road. I used to see them frequently for many years, and never ceased to wonder about them. Among the largest along the downs, these pits may also be ancient in their origin, for chalk has been a useful material since men began. Primitive man dug into it to find the best kinds of flint for his tools, flint that was hard and would take a sharp edge. With these flint tools he felled trees and dug out the trunks to make boats, he killed his prey or his domestic animals as needed, and he defended himself with flint knives and axes and with arrows tipped with neatly made barbed flint heads. The Romans used chalk for the foundations of their roads and burnt it for lime to make their hard cement. Medieval and later men dug out the chalk and used it either as blocks or as rubble to build cottages, houses, and churches, and even castles.

You will find that in many places along the downs chalk-pits like these, but mostly smaller (some of them mere small hollows), exist and point to a conclusion underlined by Belloc. When these pits were begun, digging was started where it was because the Old Road was already in existence and gave ready access and a means by which the chalk could be carried out, first on men's backs and then in panniers on the backs of horses or asses and later in carts. Later still, as lower roads were made and lanes or paths came into being leading directly from the pits down to those roads, the value of the Old Road as an access was diminished. Then the floors of the pits, formerly at the level of the road—because no sensible miner would dig up his access—were dug deeper down and an interruption of the Old Road came about. Any subsequent travellers following the Old Road had to circumvent the pits either by going above them or down below them. The Ordnance Survey traces and marks as the Pilgrims' Way paths that run below or through the pits, to emerge in the Pebblehill Road a little above Betchworth station. Alternatively you may go north of and above the pits, but these paths will bring you up to the Box Hill road somewhere near the Hand in Hand. From here you may walk along to Pebble Combe, a road-junction hamlet at the head of a deep indentation into the downs that well deserves the name of 'combe'. Through it and over Pebble Hill goes the modern road from Betchworth to Walton-on-the-Hill and London.

Here we are once more set a problem. If the exit from the quarries above Betchworth station is correct, then the Pilgrims' Way ought to continue on the other side of the main road. A lane is indeed to be found there, leading to Wildcroft. From Wildcroft it is possible to continue alongside the railway and then to ascend by Kemp's Farm and Bridlecombe barn (or Bridlecombe bungalow) and so on to the steeps of the downs. But this cannot be quite right. No ancient path would waste time in this way, that is by describing two sides of a rectangle before it again took an easterly direction. If the exit from the Betchworth quarries is really correct, then we should look for signs of a route taking a north-easterly direction past Bridle-combe barn to the abandoned quarry in the western slopes of Lady Hill. No such path is to be observed.

Let us examine the beautiful range of downs between Pebble Combe and Reigate Hill. They are named in sequence from west to east: Lady Hill, Buckland Hills, Juniper Hill, Colley Hill, and Reigate Hill. This sequence extends for some three miles. The downs in this length are notable for the irregu-larity of their outline, that outline taking the form of a series of scallops with the consequent re-entrant combes. Any path along the slopes would have to move in and out with the contours. That, in fact, is what the thin footpath that exists along these slopes actually does do. It is used fairly frequently in our day by week-enders and walkers, but there is no evidence that it could have been used much in the middle ages or earlier. Here is no obvious shelf or terrace, no development of a hollow way such as is made by the shuffling feet of centuries. Nonethe-less, the Ordnance Survey one-inch map, taking courage after leaving us without guidance for a large part of the route, does mark this path as the Pilgrims' Way, sweeping around the Saddle Knob of Colley Hill and around the combe known as the Horseshoe. We can assume from this that the Ordnance Survey would agree that the whole of the path running in and out along the lower or mid slopes of the hills may be accepted as the Pilgrims' Way. Belloc did not agree. He suggested that the

Way along these hills would, in order to avoid the scallops of the lower route, have climbed to the top of the downs, and would there have taken a line leading more directly towards the summit of Colley Hill. There is indeed a track up there on the hill-top, a broad track made to serve a farm and its fields. This track, however, is older than its present use, for parts of it derive from the ancient trackways that distinguish these hills. Sometimes these trackways are identical with the Pilgrims' Way, sometimes quite different, and their origin is probably medieval rather than neolithic. They were tracks along which farmers herded their cattle and drove their flocks of sheep, from farm to farm, from pasture to pasture, and at times from farm to market. If the pilgrims came along this high route, they would, in bad weather, have had a cold and slushy time, for the ground is partly clay and holds the water.

Walk the upper way if you wish and are convinced that it is the truer one. It is, however, shut in by trees and less interesting than the lower path, and for this reason we chose to go with the Ordnance Survey along the slopes from Pebble Combe to the north-south road, the A217, above Reigate.

The first question to be answered is how to get on to that lower path from Pebblecome or the Pebblehill road, for it is not extended westwards. It cannot be reached directly by any apparent route that might be claimed as certainly part of the Pilgrims' Way. We may do it by taking the lane to Bridle-combe, where we shall have to turn north and breast the hill among trees; this brings us to the upper route, but, having reached this we have at once to turn back almost on our tracks to go down a steep little sunken lane in the sombre duskiness of a tunnel of trees.

Alternatively, this point may be reached from the main road north of Pebble Combe, where, opposite a strange little lodge half-hidden behind a high hedge, we take an easterly lane alongside a wood, in season rich in bluebells. This lane comes to a junction, where we turn right down another broad lane. Where this turns away to the left our direction is continued by the little sunken lane in the wood at which we arrived at the end of the previous paragraph.

Descending this lane we come to a chalk quarry (*plate* 8), a veritable model of a quarry accessible from the lane without having been worked long enough to eat into that lane. It is not seen, however, large though it may be, unless it is looked for. It occurs at a point where a power line of pylons approaches the sunken lane, and at this point too there is another quarry, so that the path runs between upper quarry and lower quarry. A gap in the trees looks over the half-overgrown mounds, past Bridlecombe, to the much larger pits of Betchworth, their white gashes like wounds in the flank of some vast crouching beast with milk for blood.

A little lower down the lane, at a point where the power line changes its direction towards the south-east, climb up the east bank to find the beginning of a path that runs alongside a wire fence. Here, at last, we may believe ourselves once more on the Pilgrims' Way. We are at least on a path interesting for its variety, its changes of direction and of height, and for its frequent views down into the lower land and over the airy distances of the Weald. As if to confirm to us that the path is ancient we came upon a colony of the large white snails that distinguish these downs and which are said to have been introduced by the Romans as food fit for the table. Pale, swollen, and unlovely, these fat fellows have coarse shells bleached and worn as though here on the hillside they had been hauled to and fro over a sandy beach by the waves of the sea. I cannot tell you whether or not these snails are good to eat. Thrushes and blackbirds certainly think so, for this colony was surrounded by broken and splintered shells hammered and smashed by the vigorous beaks of these birds.

The land to the south of the scarps of the downs is intermittently arable and pasture. Down there in the valley the village of Buckland gathers its houses and its church around a green. The church is Victorian, built by Woodyer, with one of his best interiors. Farther south, the larger village of Betchworth has a church at least as old as the Normans, but, on the evidence of a single carved stone, standing on the site of a Saxon church. The present church is largely Early English, drastically restored in 1851, when the central tower was demolished and another was built in a different position. An ancient chest in the church was dug out from the solid tree, a brass shows a cleric, William Wardysworth, who was vicar until his death in 1533, and there is a modern font carved in 1951 by Eric Kennington, a pupil of Eric Gill and rather too much influenced by his master. The village has some restful old houses and a pub called the Dolphin built about 1700. Betchworth castle, well away from the village and nearer to Dorking, is represented only by a number of fifteenth-century fragments, which appear to have belonged to a manor-house rather than a castle. Built about 1440, it is said to have been demolished in 1700 or 1705.

There are views from the path along the slopes of the downs of the expanded town of Reigate, once a country market town and now by grace of the railway a dormitory town for London, that sprawling city whose conurbation begins with Banstead and Sutton to the north of the downs. Reigate joins hands to the east with the modern town of Redhill. From the Pilgrims' Way you may also catch a glimpse, to the west of Reigate, of Reigate Heath, with the sails of its windmill rising above the dark branches of pine trees. The mill, a post-mill, no longer working, was built in 1765, possibly on the site of an older one. Since 1880 the brick-built roundhouse on which the timber structure rests has been fitted out as a chapel of an unusual kind, holding a congregation of about sixty. There are still regular services, though not every Sunday, services in which the prayers and the singing of the choir and congregation rise and seem to circle in the complex timbers like smoke from a fire.

The path on which we walk winds round under Saddle Knob and into the combe of the Horseshoe on Colley Hill, the mouth of which is opened wider by a chalk pit. A little later the path becomes a street passing among modern houses. To avoid these you may climb up the face of the grassy down—and you may have to go on hands and knees!—to come to the level, close-bitten summit of the hill. The land around here belongs to the National Trust and is counted as a beauty spot. So indeed it is, for itself on account of the sloping hillsides with their scattered bushes and little woods, but rather more for the view, which is far and wide and breath-taking. The view, from a height of 700 feet, ranges from Leith Hill in the west round by the Forest Ridges of the gravelly sands, their summits nicked like the edge of a saw with the pointed tops of their many pines. Breath-taking is that great wide expanse of the Weald—the Weald that was once covered by the forest of Andredesweald. You may well suppose that that ancient forest is there still, for trees are the major element of the view, riding up over the hills like marching armies of dour determined soldiers.

Reigate, distinguished now, as Dorking is, by a prominent gasometer, was a town throughout the days of the pilgrimage and like other towns would have received pilgrims of all kinds, coming down from the Way to beg at the monasteries, to eat and to drink, to dance and to sing, or to listen if they had among them a man with a good voice or a lutist who might improvise tune and words on the spot, like a troubadour of France.

The name of Reigate has puzzled semantists. The town appears in Domesday Book as Cherchefell, and later it was Crechesfeld. By 1199 the name had been changed to Reigat or Regat. The first syllable may come from Saxon *raege*, the female of the roe deer, and 'gate' may be a gate as commonly understood, or be from the Icelandic, where it would mean a pass or path. In this latter sense the word remains in many placenames in the north, especially for paths over the moors. The name of Gatton, a place we shall come to very soon, may also be from this secondary meaning of 'gate'. What is an Icelandic word doing so far south in Surrey? What indeed—yet it is not alone. Another old word from the north that is encountered here in the south, and more frequently as we come into Kent, is 'shaw', which means a thicket or copse.

In the middle of the main street of old Reigate the pilgrims found a chapel of Saint Thomas of Canterbury, and here they would enter to worship in anticipation of the miraculous shrine still some sixty miles distant—three days' journey for a good traveller, more for the slow and old and the dawdling. The chapel was desecrated at the Reformation and later demolished and on its site now stands Reigate's picturesque old town hall or market-house, built in 1728. An urbane structure of brick, with its lower storey open on round-headed arches, and topped by a later clock cupola, the building is always in peril because it is an obstruction to traffic in the High Street. I daresay that its demolition has been tentatively broached many times over, though it is one of the few buildings in this town that has any measure of excellence.

Behind the town hall, a large Norman motte rises like a backdrop. It bore a castle, built in the eleventh century by the Norman William de Warenne; a kinsman of the Conqueror, he received from him more than three hundred manors in Yorkshire, Norfolk, Surrey, and Sussex, and in addition was created Earl of Surrey. His castle at Reigate commanded the pass through the downs at Merstham and controlled the long west to east valley called Holmesdale. The castle was one of those taken by Louis, the Dauphin of France, in his bid to win the crown of England, and it was later one of the many strongholds slighted or destroyed by the Cromwellians.

One of the de Warenne family, Earl Hammelin, as natural son of Geoffrey, Count of Anjou, was half-brother to Henry II, and at the council of Northampton he took the king's part in reviling and denouncing Thomas Becket as a traitor. A later de Warenne in 1235 founded at Reigate a priory of Augustinian canons. This was dissolved by Henry VIII and the buildings were granted to Lord Howard of Effingham, father of that Lord Howard who earned enduring glory as commander of the English fleet of small warships and smaller private boats that made mincemeat of the Spanish Armada. The building now called 'the Priory' is apparently a Palladian house, but it incorporates some Tudor and perhaps earlier portions from the monastery, with some later additions. A superb fireplace, for no particular reason attributed to Holbein, was said by John Evelyn to have come from the house of Catherine Parr at Bletchingley. Henry VIII's Nonsuch Palace, demolished before 1688, has also been suggested as the original home of the fireplace. A magnificent painted staircase dates from the first years of the eighteenth century.

Reigate has, as other Surrey towns, a number of old houses disguised by later frontages. Among the oldest is No. 15 in Bell Street, which has a fourteenth-century timber roof that originally sheltered a chapel of Saint Lawrence.

The parish church of Saint Mary, a spacious building, appears on the outside to be of the late Decorated to early

Perpendicular periods, but inside there are Norman arcades of unusual quality, with a series of capitals that may be taken as showing the development in one place of the thirteenth-century ornament known as stiff-leaf. Other periods have left their mark on this church, but none so harshly as the restoration job done by Woodyer in 1845 and a later restoration by Gilbert Scott junior, which attempted to correct some of the more heavy-handed things due to Woodyer. Scott's work included rebuilding the nave arcades. There are Elizabethan, Jacobean, and Caroline monuments that seem to have been shuffled like a pack of cards and not rearranged in their correct suits. In a crypt under the chancel lies the body of Elizabeth's admiral, Lord Howard of Effingham, victor over the Armada; as there was no monument to him—and why not for this man who had deserved so well of his country?—a lettered brass was put up in the nineteenth century with wording following that on the coffin plate.

Each time we have come to a gap in the line of the downs or to a north to south road, we have been presented with problems concerning the true projection of the Pilgrims' Way. The road that runs north from Reigate and across the Way is no exception. This is an exceptionally steep road, climbing up to a junction at the north-west corner of Gatton Park. Belloc and those who follow him considered that the Old Road went through the park, and there does appear to be evidence that this was so. This part of the park, however, is not open to the public—not open, that is, in the sense that the Pilgrims' Way may be pursued through it. Here, for the first time, we come upon an example of the abolition of a right of way by the enclosure of land for the park of a great house. We shall meet other examples as we pass through Kent—at Titsey, Chevening, and Chilham—in which the convenience of a wealthy man or a man of power or importance has been put before the ancient right of the public to pass over land. In those instances it happened long ago, so long ago that memories of such past affronts may have been dissipated by time; but the fences remain.

I am not sure that it is less easy in the present day to close a footpath, but I am certain that it is not as difficult as it should

12. *A rutted section of the Way north of West Yaldham*

13. *Crinkle-crankle wall at Kemsing*

14. *Coldrum Stones: the burial chamber*

15. *Trottiscliffe: chancel, with pulpit from Westminster Abbey*

be. Where the abolition of a right of way causes inconvenience to the public, the provision of a substitute way may be required, but, in the past at least, such substitute ways have not always been as convenient or as comfortable to travel over as was the original path.

At Gatton the substitute lies along the northern side of Gatton Park, a surfaced minor road called at first Tower Lane and then Gatton Bottom. It is a pleasant road, running in a valley between low downs and trees, with Wingate Hill in Gatton Park to the south and the slopes of Upper Gatton Park to the north. A mile along this road we come to the lodge of Gatton Park and enter the grounds to see Gatton church, a church without a village.

For William Cobbett, Gatton was one of the vilest places on earth (Reigate was such another). The political inequality that Gatton represented for him clouded his view and he would have admitted only grudgingly that there might be fine buildings, good country, and competent farming at Gatton. Cobbett would have you believe that Gatton was 'a very rascally spot of earth', that the rottenness of Gatton and other such boroughs made his flesh crawl. The rottenness was the system that allowed the injustice of the election of members of Parliament by only a handful of influential people or, as in the case of Gatton, by only one man, the landowner himself. At Gatton the two members representing the borough were rather appointed than elected.

Gatton was created a borough in 1450 by Henry VI for the benefit of his steward as a reward for his services in the negotiations concerning Henry's marriage to Margaret of Anjou. From that date until the Reform Bill of 1832 Gatton regularly sent its two members to Parliament, though there seems never to have been more than a couple of dozen houses in the parish, most of them and sometimes all of them, other than Gatton House itself, inhabited by persons not qualified to vote. The right to nominate members of Parliament in this manner was valued by landowners, and in 1830, when he bought Gatton, Lord Monson paid a hundred thousand pounds for it, twice the value of the land, on account of its representation in Parliament. Two years later the Reform Bill abolished the

MPW

borough of Gatton, to the disgust and considerable loss of its
noble owner. The estate of Gatton, and also of Upper Gatton,
later came into the possession of Sir Jeremiah Colman, the
gentleman who found the manufacture of mustard so profitable
a business.

The house was rebuilt by Lord Monson in high style, with a
lush marble hall that Julia Cartwright describes as an imitation
of the Orsini chapel in Rome. In 1891 Sir Jeremiah Colman
added a pillared portico of high quality. This survived the
burning of the house in 1934 and the subsequent rebuilding.
Gatton House is now the Royal Alexander and Albert School
for deprived and erring children, and various modern buildings,
not all worth looking at, have sprung up in the grounds around
the original house.

The oldest building of Gatton is the little fifteenth-century
parish church. Lord Monson, with eclectic but undiscerning
taste, lavished money and attention on this church, and transformed the interior with a variety of woodwork from several
sources in England and on the Continent. There are screens
of the fifteenth century from some unknown English church;
altar rails from Tongres in Belgium; stalls of Flemish gothic
from Ghent, set lengthwise as in a college chapel, because they
would not otherwise go in; panelling of 1515 from Aarschot
cathedral; and a great deal more, including a sixteenth-century
pulpit raised prominently in the air, fixed to the gallery of the
south transept (*plate* 7). The windows include ancient glass,
with a good Virgin and Child in the north transept, from
Flanders, and in the sombre west window the arms of Henry
VII. The only things that seem to have survived from the old
church, indeed from an older church on this site, are the
thirteenth-century piscina and font.

The north transept was the private pew for the noble owners
of the manor, who came into the church along a covered passage
connecting with the house. They sat in comfortably padded
seats, and in winter were warmed by a fire in the fireplace in the
transept wall. The parishioners and the staff of the great house
might freeze elsewhere in the church, but the owners of Gatton
would be warm. The upper floor of each of the transepts was
intended for the servants, and each was furnished with a rail

and curtains that could be drawn across so that the sight of these lower beings should not distress their betters below. That indignity must sometimes have been an advantage for servants nodding off to sleep during the long and tedious Victorian sermons or for bright sparks paying more attention to the maids than to the service.

We went round the back of the church to find a way through to the grounds in front of the house and to see the famous Gatton town hall, which—and it will please those who like superlatives—is very likely the smallest town hall in this country. It stands on a mound within a grove of heavy, mature horse-chestnut trees. A little classical folly, a delectable trifle, it was built in 1765 in the form of a rectangular open temple in the Doric manner, sheltering a large urn inscribed in Latin with a pompous and cynical phrase that may be paraphrased as: 'The lots are drawn from the urn. Let the good of the people be the supreme law.'

Beyond the north lodge of Gatton, Gatton Bottom curves round to the right and passes south of Merstham's church of Saint Catherine, raised on a hill. With its shingled spire and flecked flint and stone walls, the church is picturesque, and a view of it must have cheered weary pilgrims passing along the Way through Gatton Park. They might, too, or at least those who came this way during the fourteenth century and after, have taken a rest on the stone benches in the porch. In the church some curious capitals with primitive acanthus patterns point the way to Early English stiff-leaf. There are some late, minor brasses, and a strange effigy of a primitive kind, a bas-relief with flat top and vertical sides, like a ginger-bread man.

In the middle ages Merstham was a quarry village, famous for its fine stone, quantities of which were used in the building of Henry VII's chapel in Westminster Abbey and in some of the extensive alterations carried out at Windsor Castle. Merstham today is largely modern, inhabited by commuters to London, but there remain fragments of old houses concealed under later additions. A vast road junction has been planned for Merstham, with the South Orbital Way meeting the M23 at a multi-storey fly-over.

East of Merstham church a conjunction of factors—the A23, two railway cuttings, and a huge quarry—have obliterated the continuation of the Pilgrims' Way. The Way is found again to the north-east, on Ockley Hill, at a height of 660 feet, and it is likely that the path from Merstham or from Gatton Park climbed in that direction across the site of the quarry. We reach the Way again by taking the minor road leaving the A23 almost opposite the exit of Gatton Bottom. Half a mile along this road, we turn left on to a path that shortly begins to climb the breast of the hill through arable fields and through linear segments of woodland that serve as broad, high hedges between field and field. The fields are arable and are ploughed out each year, but the right of way is reinstated very soon by walkers. When we came here it was to find the path a little canyon between walls of wheat or barley, with a white blaze of chalk in the bottom like a river in a gorge. On the summit of Ockley Hill we joined a broad lane between Tollsworth Manor and Hilltop Farm. This lane goes east and we are on the Pilgrims' Way once more. To the north of us are the encroaching streets of Chaldon, Caterham, and Coulsdon, and to the south is country less affected by the sprawl of London, as though the ancient Way were a boundary with some magic that keeps the developers at bay.

Nutfield has an ancient industry of digging and preparing fuller's earth, an industry that continues to this day. The earth, found here in the Cretaceous strata, has its name from its having been used to absorb grease and oil in the preparation of woollen materials; it is not now so much employed in the woollen industry, but it finds uses in various industrial processes as a filter medium and in making soaps, pigments, and toilet preparations.

Nutfield and the next village, Bletchingley, are main-road villages on the A25, bedevilled by traffic. Bletchingley, once one of the widespread properties of Christ Church at Canterbury, is worth a visit for its fine Norman and thirteenth-century church, in which you will see the magniloquent marble monument erected by Sir Robert Clayton for himself and his wife. As he did not die until several years later, he had time to admire the skill of the carver, Richard Crutcher, who displayed the noble knight in his robes as Lord Mayor of London. He might also have admired the little figure of a child, eyes closed in death, lying there in a lace bonnet and gown. This piece does not seem to have been made by the same sculptor as the rest of the monument. Sir Thomas Cawarden, who died in 1559, has a lettered brass beautifully inscribed in chancery italics. This brass plate was for some reason removed once to Loseley House (which we passed near Compton), and was brought back to the church in 1836. Sir Thomas was steward to Anne of Cleves, who held the manor of Bletchingley. In the south wall of the chancel is a small quatrefoil opening of no obvious purpose if it was not for the cell of an anchorite called Roger, who in 1233 was granted a bushel of wheat by Henry III. We saw a similar foiled opening earlier, at Shere, for Christine Carpenter's cell. Note as you come from the church the wooden door in the south doorway, with its iron handle; door and handle are believed to date from 1460; your hand turns the very handle turned by pilgrims who came down from the Way to enter the church. Some of them may have put up in the Whyte Hart inn, which was in existence in 1388. There are other attractive buildings in Bletchingley and Middle Row; by the churchyard gate is a pretty row of old houses, tile-hung and timber-framed. The broad main street of this village suggests the site of a market or fair.

Bletchingley Castle remains only in fragments; it was wrecked in 1264 during the baronial wars. It is most remarkable now for the view from its elevated site.

The manor was held by the enormously wealthy family of Clare, whose forebears came with William the Conqueror and were well rewarded for that. By the twelfth century it could be said that nearly all the nobles of England were related to the Clares. One of this family was a girl so lovely that she was reputed the most beautiful in England, and FitzAlan commented that 'she had long been desired by King Henry II'. The manor of Bletchingley passed from the Clares to the Staffords, their relatives, who held it until Edmond, third Duke of Buckingham, was attainted for treason to Henry VIII and was beheaded in 1521. The next owner of Bletchingley, Sir Nicholas Carew, also fell foul of Henry and had his head struck off. Henry then gave the manor to his wife of a few months, Anne of Cleves, whom he had married reluctantly and with limitless imprecations against his minister Thomas Cromwell, who had recommended the match, persuading Henry by means of a too-complimentary portrait of Anne by Holbein, a portrait you may see in the Louvre. Cromwell must have shuddered with fear on that first day of January 1540 when Henry travelled down from London and met his future wife at Rochester. The king, dismayed and furious, wriggled to get out of the agreement to marry Anne, but feared that he might offend rulers on the Continent if the marriage did not take place. Marry her he did, leading his 'Flanders mare' to the altar with gritted teeth. Determined from that moment to have his freedom again, he succeeded on the 9th of June in having the marriage declared void and unconsummated. Yet Anne, plain, simple, unintellectual, pleasant Anne, who when she arrived spoke no language but her own and had no accomplishment but needlework, might well have made him the best of wives and might have given him the strong sons for whom he craved. She was apt enough to drive a good bargain in manors and income for her support in exchange for her agreement to the divorce.

After the divorce Anne came to live a quiet, independent life in her manor of Bletchingley, and if she had lovers, as she may have had, it was only necessary to be discreet so that they might preserve their heads upon their shoulders. When she visited the Court, as sometimes she did, it was remarked how cheerful, how happy she was, and that she wore a new gown every day. Even Henry, made miserable by his own lusts, by disease and premature old age, and by another unsatisfactory wife, Catherine Howard, might have come to think he had made a mistake.

After Anne the manor belonged to her steward, Sir Thomas Cawarden, who served as master of the King's Revels, and who has his beautifully lettered brass in the church. At the outbreak of the Civil War, the manor was in the hands of the Howards of Effingham, who were fined £10,000 by Parliament for supporting the royal cause. In order to raise the money Bletchingley was sold to Sir Robert Clayton, a successful City merchant, the man responsible for the overblown monument in the church.

We can recover the Pilgrims' Way once more by turning north up Workhouse Lane to take a footpath on the left beyond the mental hospital. This path leads over to the hamlet of Brewer Street, to the north of which is a beautiful timber-studded, stone-roofed farmhouse of the fifteenth century; it was being restored when I last saw it in 1970. A few yards down a side road is Place Farm, which retains elements of the manor-house of Anne of Cleves. The manor house, originally built in 1296, was 'newly builded' in 1521; Anne came in 1540.

We left the Pilgrims' Way at Hilltop Farm on the Bletchingley–Chaldon road. The nearest point of the Way to Brewer Street would be on White Hill, but this would mean that we had skipped a mile of the Pilgrims' Way. With little more trouble we can return to Hilltop Farm by means of footpaths across the fields from Brewer Street towards a house called Rockshaw, and then up the rising Chaldon road to the farm. The double-headed lane that begins here and runs east represents the Pilgrims' Way and is suitably called Pilgrim Lane. A grassy lane between hedges and trees, it maintains a good width until for no obvious reason, it suddenly widens still further and runs so for many yards before narrowing once more to its former width (*plate* 9). I thought that this wider part of the Way should have some special meaning, but I have found no useful explanation other than that there is a junction here with an overgrown bridle-way that leaves in a northerly direction. As the Pilgrims' Way here is also the line of a track-way, it is possible that this wider portion was used as a resting-place by drovers and their cattle, but I admit that the idea is thin.

The lane leads to Willey Farm, whose seventeenth-century or eighteenth-century farmhouse is half-hidden, or half-obliterated, by an enormous chestnut tree. Just beyond the farm behind the hedge and beside a tiny, reedy pool, rises a small flint-built tower of a form apparently inspired by the much larger round towers of Ireland; it seems to be a folly.

At this point the Pilgrims' Way turns south-east on a roughly surfaced track between hedges. A little farther on, the track comes to a crossing and continues on the far side as a narrow surfaced lane. It passes White Hill Tower, which has a function in connection with a water-works. Opposite this, Arthur's Seat, a not easily perceived or universally admitted earthwork, takes its name from some tenuous legendary connection with King Arthur. A more distinct earthwork, Cardinal's Cap, is found farther on, enclosing the garden of a house. Here, too, is War Coppice Garden Village, an upper-middle-class estate of expensive houses built along a few steeply falling streets. The name 'War Copse' is mentioned by Aubrey; 'war' may come from an old Norse word meaning 'beacon'.

The Pilgrims' Way now goes along the south flank of Gravelly Hill about 700 feet above sea-level, to a sharp bend in the lane, where once more the route becomes uncertain. You may follow the surfaced road round three sides of a rectangle to come to the A22, the Godstone–Caterham road, or take a path to the right around Fosterdown Fort, to come to the same place. The path through the woods is confusing. The wood has fine beech trees and a number of yews and under them tracks go in various directions. If you descend too much along the slope of the hill, you may arrive at a wire-fenced dogs' cemetery, which contains a number of small and dull memorials to various dogs that were once much-loved pets. If you find yourself at this cemetery you have come too low on the hill in the wood, and you must retrace your steps to go round and above the cemetery and come out into the surfaced lane or directly on to the A22, which comes up from Godstone.

Godstone has been more sadly divided by motor traffic than has most villages. It is at a junction of main roads all of which funnel their traffic through the few streets of Godstone, winding in a one-way system. The traffic comes from London in the north, from Redhill and Reigate in the west, from the south coast by way of East Grinstead, and from Kent by way of Maidstone and Westerham. With all this it is surprising how well Godstone has maintained its village character, how it has kept as alien and apart all that pours through. The village has an unusual history, with the church half a mile away from the main street, in a hamlet of its own. This hamlet at Church Town was known in the tenth century as Wolcnesstede, or

Walkingstead. At that time the church and its accompanying houses were the village and the lower settlement was Goda's tun, from Godgifu, daughter of the Saxon King Edward the Confessor. The Romans, however, had chosen to build a road through here, going north towards London, and when, after centuries of disturbance and neglect, this road began to be used again, it was Godgifu's hamlet that grew, while Church Town, away from the road, remained small.

At Church Town the Normans built a church, as a few stones testify, and probably this church took the place of a Saxon predecessor. The present church is nearly all the work of Sir George Gilbert Scott, who built it between 1872 and 1873 in a late Decorated style. In it there are monuments of a branch of the Evelyn family, including one for Sir John Evelyn and Dame Thomasin his wife, who were married in 1618 and appear as recumbent figures on a tomb-chest. A sarsen stone in the churchyard was raised in memory of Walker Miles, otherwise S. F. Taylor, who died in 1908. He is considered the father of rambling societies and clubs and must surely have known every inch of the Pilgrims' Way.

Next to the churchyard, a charming set of old folks' almshouses called Saint Mary's Homes, with a well and a chapel, is also by Scott; these almshouses show that determined medievalist in a lighter and happier mood in which he created a design gothic in general feeling but in detail not an imitation of the middle ages.

The main part of the village is reached from the church by a path past the extensive town pond, a reedy stretch of water now preserved as a nature reserve by the Surrey Naturalists' Trust. There is another pond in the village, on a corner of the wide village green, a green on which cricket is played in peaceful disdain of the surrounding traffic. That pond, with a border of good trees, has been photographed, drawn, and painted innumerable times, the reflections in it of the old White Hart Hotel being one of its attractions. The White Hart Hotel was once the White Hart Inn, and for a time it was known as the Clayton Arms. Its present building appears to belong to the sixteenth century, but the inn claims to have been established in the reign of Richard II, that is before 1399. It could therefore have served pilgrims for more than a hundred years before the dissolution of the monasteries and the end of the pilgrimage.

The continuation of the Pilgrims' Way after it comes on to the A22 north of Godstone is altogether lost. First the Romans, making their road through here, then a quarry, and lastly the modern main road have between them so churned up the ground and eroded it and cast it aside that any definite clue of the direction of the Old Road, of the Pilgrims' Way, is difficult to find. The Way can be recovered by descending the hill a short distance and turning into the quarry drive; this runs a little above a leafy valley in which Quarry Farm appears as a modest brick-built seventeenth- or eighteenth-century house. The drive we are pursuing passes the opening of the quarry, and turns as a lane along the flank of Winders Hill. In a few steps we come to a division of roads, where, opposite an air-shaft, a footpath leads off and connects with the higher part of Flower Lane on the north side of Hanging Wood. Alternatively we may follow the track from the air-shaft towards Flint Hall Farm to the apex of the hairpin in Flower Lane; and then along that lane uphill to seek a footpath at a bend in the lane, leading east towards Laundry Cottage. This short path is in all probability part of the Pilgrims' Way, but as for the rest, there can be no assurance. The name of the wood to the south, Palmers' Wood, has been at times quoted as evidence for the Pilgrims' Way having passed by here, but it is poor and unsatisfactory evidence, a straw clutched at where nothing of the Way is known for a mile at least. It was perhaps this evidence that led the cartographers of the Ordnance Survey to mark on the $2\frac{1}{2}$-inch map two disjointed half-mile sections of the Pilgrims' Way. The first of these sections is shown as passing above the mouth of the Oxted railway tunnel, which runs more than a mile from here under the chalk of the down. The second section is a continuation, after a gap, of the first, ending at Limpsfield Lodge on the border of Titsey Park, just above the junction of Water Lane and Pitchfont Lane. On the map each of these two sections is drawn ruler straight, and each has the same obtuse angle, as though the line were theoretical or conventional rather than an actual course on the ground. In fact the two sections are isolated, inaccessible, and invisible, on ploughed land. However, I have been told by a local resident that the eastern section at least may be seen as a cropmark in the summer, and that a spring on the western section is known as Saint Thomas's Well. Julia Cartwright, writing in 1895, says that the eastern part, to Limpsfield Lodge, was a farm track between hedges until 1875.

The continuation of the line indicated by these two lost sections would be straight across Titsey Park, passing by a Roman villa and south of Titsey House and south of the site of Saint James's old church.

Some of the evidence that might have remained under the ground to prove that there was indeed an old road here must have been destroyed when a pipe line was laid in 1890, and much more bedevilled in 1970, when a broad swathe was cut over the landscape, over hill and dale, for the laying of pipes for North Sea gas. The next item of destruction on the agenda is the M20, which is planned to run between the scarp of the North Downs and the Godstone–Westerham road. Old John Aubrey, who praised the peace and pure air of Titsey, must now be stirring; may he gibber in the ears of the planners!

For the moment Titsey is a pleasant estate. It was once famous for its gardens around the house against the dark, wooded background of the downs. The name is derived from a Saxon called Tydic, who is said to have had an island (*ey*) here; the derivation sounds improbable in relation to this dry ground, but in fact there is an ornamental lake with an island in it, a lake made long after the time of Tydic but perhaps on the site of a marsh in which there rose sufficient firm ground for a house to be built. The Conqueror gave Tydic's land to the Earl of Clare, whose family we have already met at Bletchingley, from whom it passed in the fourteenth century to the Uvedales, and in the sixteenth century to the Greshams. One of this latter family, Sir John Gresham, rebuilt the house, or most of it, in 1775. He pulled down the old church of Saint James because it was too near his house, bringing the parishioners into his grounds. Not much of the house may be seen from the public road, but there is a view of it from a footpath (not the Pilgrims' Way) through the park. It appears as a dull building, altered for the worse in 1832. In the centre of the park there is the site of a Roman villa, which in the fourth century was used as a fulling-mill and dyeworks—or so the remains, excavated in 1864, suggest. Farther south, and again to the south-west, neolithic implements have been discovered.

Opposite the house and the site of the old church rises Titsey's new church, with a few old cottages for neighbours. The surfaced lane between the church and the cottages is the Pilgrims' Way.

But I have left you in Flower Lane or near it, on a path you cannot follow. We have need of a practical diversion.

Alternative 9a. The north way round Titsey Park

This alternative way is a surfaced lane throughout. I think it probable that a primitive road might seek this route along the upper slopes of the downs and near the summit, rather than, or instead of, the line indicated by the two lost sections in the field below on the 450-foot contour. The ground down there is soft and heavy and good for ploughing and for the growing of grain, but it could not have been good for walking, nor for riding. Some generations of travellers have thought so too, for they have used and preserved the higher route and kept it in being, so that the whole is now well established between Flinthall Farm on the hairpin bend of Flower Lane to Botley Hill and beyond. The lane rises through woodland, with occasional spectacular views over the valley to the south. It is a breathless climb for pedestrians and, in summer week-ends, when many cars use this road, not a pleasant one, and even an alarming one, with no sidewalks or refuges in the narrow sunk lane. To the north is the mostly modern town of Woldingham, with its many new houses hidden away in leafy valleys so that you do not see by how much the old village has been extended.

Our road comes over a summit to a viewpoint and a small car park 870 feet up on the lip of a vast quarry. The view is splendid. On a road with so many viewpoints as has the Pilgrims' Way, this is well called superlative, despite the presence of a prominent pale blue gasometer in the valley below. A great part of the Weald is spread out before the viewer, and graphic-

ally exhibits the formation of that country. It is not rolling
country, as some people suppose, but country of emphatic
contrasts of heights and valleys, of ridges of ragstone and of
gravel and gault disposed parallel with the North Downs—
the Ragstone Ridge and farther south the Forest Ridges—and
beyond them the distant line of the South Downs, whose summit
seems from our viewpoint to form an horizon as straight as that
of an ocean. From this high viewpoint you might suppose, as
we have previously seen, that the medieval description of the
Weald as forest still applies, and you may easily suppose that
the ancient forest of Andredesweald still covers much of the
land. But among those trees and among those upland ridges
and in the valleys between lie dozens of villages and towns with
a total population as large as that of the whole of England in
the time of Becket. Nearest to hand, below the downs, lie the
villages of Oxted and Limpsfield.

We continue on the surfaced road towards Botley Hill.
You may, if you wish, walk for a time along parallel footpaths
through the woodlands of Titsey Plantation, but they will not
save you either time or distance. The road comes to a junction
of four roads at Botley Hill, at a spot that was formerly called
Coldharbour Green. That lost name is one we should pause to
examine, for it is relevant to our travellers and to our pilgrims.
A 'cold harbour' was just what the words say, a shelter or
refuge for travellers, but a cold one and probably wretched.
Not an inn, with its cheerful and warming fire and welcoming
host, but a mere enclosure that may not have had a roof, and
may or may not have had an attendant keeper—any keeper
would, anyway, have been a miserable fellow who could ask
for and could expect little for such cheerless service up here on
the hill. It is said that some of these 'cold harbours'—for there
are many places of this name throughout the country—were
ruined Roman villas, roughly fettled for their new service,
with their broken or collapsing tiled roofs stopped with sod
or thatch, and their hypocausts dead and cold for centuries.

The road bearing off to the right at Botley Hill loops down
and around Titsey Park to Titsey new church and the continuation of the Pilgrims' Way. Instead of taking this, and losing
ground, you may continue ahead on the B2024 along the line

of a trackway, now a surfaced lane, and join the Pilgrims' Way two miles farther on.

This upper road passes by a neolithic site and within a few yards of the isolated Norman church of Tatsfield, which has kept well clear of the bungalow town that Tatsfield has become between the wars and since. Tatsfield church is distinguished by two unusually richly ornamented lancet windows in the chancel, one of which remains intact. These windows have been a puzzle to ecclesiologists and students of architecture: why should a small country church have been so favoured? It appears that these windows were intended to do honour to something unusual; this chancel contained something especially holy. So one may suppose, believing that here again rested one of those relics, displayed to attract pilgrims into the church.

The surfaced lane we have followed from Botley Hill continues east past Tatsfield Court Farm to a cross-roads where the road from Titsey new church, the Pilgrims' Way, comes in and continues towards the east.

Alternative 9b. The route by Oxted and Limpsfield

Oxted may be reached by road from Tandridge Hill or by footpaths descending through Rye Wood and Robin Grove and coming into Barrow Green Road by Castle Mound. The latter is a hillock variously said to be prehistoric, to have been built by the Danes, or to be a natural feature: for either of the first two of these attributions it would be bigger than usual, while for the last it would be, at least, odd. The old village of Oxted, at a cross-roads, with some sixteenth-century buildings, notably the Crown and the Old Bell inns, is a bottleneck on the A25. A newer Oxted, inhabited by London commuters, has grown up to the east, astride the railway, and the church clings to this as though it had abandoned the old village, as the village, at the time of the Black Death perhaps, abandoned the neighbourhood of the church. The church has a broad and low Norman tower and a thirteenth-century chancel. The rest is of various periods, after the general fashion of English churches that have grown organically, the sum of additions and changes through centuries rather than the taut result of the plans of

masons or architects and of a single build. There is sinuous
fourteenth-century tracery in the east window, with Evangelists
of the same period in the glass. There are also, for contrast,
windows by Kemp, five hundred years younger, with character-
istic silvery tabernacle work. There is, too, a ponderous iron
chest with twelve bolts shot by a single large key, a chest of
which it may be said that it is at least as old as the middle
ages. The church stands in a circular churchyard, which may
mean that it is built on and has hallowed a pagan site, perhaps
a stone circle. This is not uncommon. I remember seeing at
Ysbyty Cynfyn in Carmarthenshire in Wales just such a churchyard in which the menhirs of a stone circle still stand, rising
from the churchyard wall.

Limpsfield, a close neighbour to new Oxted, on the edge of
that commuter country, is the last village in Surrey—the
Kentish boundary runs between here and Westerham. So
near to Kent, Limpsfield has something of the flavour of that
county, sharing the careful husbandry and the prosperity of the
Men of Kent and the Kentish Men. You may see this in manors
and farmhouses each like a little manor-house such as you may
find in Kent. Those yeomen dated their prosperity and their
independence from a time when, led by Stigand, Archbishop
of Canterbury, and Egelsine, Abbot of Saint Augustine's,
the Men of Kent met William the Conqueror at Swanscombe
and defied him to his face, though circumspectly. In order to
impress they had cut leafy branches and had borne these before
them so that to William it seemed that the woods were moving
against him, as the Wood of Birnam moved towards Dunsin-
ane. 'But', writes Lambarde in 1576, 'they as soone as he came
within hearing caste away their boughes from them, and at the
sound of a trumpet bewraied their weapons.' They offered the
king peace and loyalty if they might preserve their ancient
customs and inheritance, but threatened the worst they
could do 'and that most deadly', if he did not accept. The story
is legend. I do not think that triumphant William was a man
who could be threatened in such a manner. On the other hand,
customs certainly survived in Kent that were abolished elsewhere. Among the more important of these was gavelkind, a
system of inheritance in which all the sons of the house shared

alike. In other countries such a system has proved a weakness, fragmenting estates and farms and provoking dissension. The Norman system of primogeniture, though patently unfair, tended to preserve the strength of the family and to transmit its property safely and intact from generation to generation. Sometimes William and his successors on the throne must have wished that gavelkind had continued in force throughout the country; the great Norman barons might not so easily have preserved their power without their economic background of many manors and broad lands.

Limpsfield village, off the A25, compensates for a formless plan with delightful houses of timber and brick dating from the sixteenth century and in some instances from an earlier period. The Court House, the Old Court House, and Detillens are fifteenth-century hall houses, in which the family of those days dwelt during the day in the great hall, which, open to the roof, may even so late have been warmed only by a central fire, the smoke from which rose into the timbers of the roof and escaped through louvred turrets. Pilgrims, coming down from the Pilgrims' Way, would have known such houses. Now these houses hide their antiquity behind later façades. Limpsfield's church of Saint Peter, standing above the road, in a churchyard entered through a fourteenth-century lych-gate, has an unusual plan. What is unusual is that the tower rises from the south side, up against the chancel, and to English eyes accustomed to towers on the crossing of a cruciform church or more commonly at the west end, the effect is strange. It would not so surprise a native of Gower, in south Wales, where towers placed at one side are not uncommon. Limpsfield's tower is Norman, built about 1180, with a tall pyramid roof that is itself untypical of English church towers. The church is sturdy and blunt, with a roof of Horsham stone slabs, which, as the fashion was with such roofs, grow progressively smaller as they approach the ridge: the effect is subtle and studied, and was so adopted despite the fact that the smaller the slabs the greater must be the load on the beams below. The nave is also of the twelfth century. It was given a south aisle in the thirteenth century by the perilous process of hacking through the thick Norman walls and inserting pillars and arches; the same thing was done on the north side in the nineteenth century, when the church was restored.

Among the interesting things in this church is a wafer oven, a small rectangular recess on the east wall of the chancel, by the altar, with a chimney to take the fumes away. It is by no means unique, and I wonder why some churches apparently baked their communion wafers on the spot (during a service?) while others had them made elsewhere.

The manor of Limpsfield and its Saxon church were estates of the Saxon King Harold. As such they became by conquest the property of Norman William, who gave the manor to Battle Abbey as part of the endowment of that monastery founded where the battle of Hastings was fought.

In the churchyard, in a simple grave, are buried that touchy genius Delius, the composer, and his patient and much-wronged wife Jelka, who died only a year after her husband, in 1935. I believe they had no particular connection with this parish, but Delius had desired to be buried in England and he was allowed to rest here.

The road north out of Limpsfield passes a neolithic site and comes to the new church of Titsey, outside Titsey Park. The church is new in the sense that it succeeded the old church, which stood within the park opposite, across the road. The new church was built in 1861 to a design by J. L. Pearson, competently gothic, but sharp and unsympathetic, its hardness contrasting with the homeliness of the old cottages just below. You are likely to find this church locked because it stands beside a busy road and so is easily accessible to the kind of idiots who are too much dignified by the name of vandals.

The little lane running east, south of the church, is the Pilgrims' Way, and we follow this now, past Pilgrims' Farm, to the cross-roads east of Tatsfield Court Farm.

East from Titsey, all the way through Kent to Canterbury, the Pilgrims' Way is for the most part clearly marked and only occasionally lost. I do not mean by this the signposting that has been done by the Kent County Council, more thorough than anything that Hampshire and Surrey have provided (the signs are distinguished by a scallop shell, but some symbol more directly related to Canterbury and Saint Thomas would have been appropriate). I do not mean this sign-posting and lane-naming, useful though it is: I mean that usage from ancient times to our own day has preserved the Way and kept it in being so that much of it is now surfaced road (but country lane rather than main road), and the rest is distinct lane or path or track. For here in Kent we come to that part of the Old Road more frequented than the rest because it is joined by important tributary ways coming in from London and the Thames valley and bringing not only travellers originating from that valley but also many who came from farther north and had of necessity to seek a crossing of the Thames to continue their journey. And this was so from very ancient times. On either side of the road numerous stone-age tools and implements and other remains have been found, and on the downs facing across the Medway neolithic megaliths remain to show that the Old Road was a route along which the dead were carried to be laid to rest. The Romans or Romano-Britains had villas connecting with the road by short lanes, villas that flourished in the long Roman peace and were well built and handsome and well warmed—yet these houses, and it has always puzzled me that it should be so, seem to have been of little interest as dwellings to the Saxons or Jutes who came raiding and invading through Kent.

Kent, as history and archaeology show, was the common entry for nearly all the invaders of this island. Neolithic men and their bronze-age successors came this way, to be followed and overcome by Celts bearing weapons of iron. The Romans under Julius Caesar landed on two occasions in Kent, and a century later the Romans came again, to conquer and settle the country. Then, as the Romans left, by way of Kent, the Saxons poured in, coming ashore at Ebbsfleet. They in turn had to defend their lands against further invaders, this time the wild men of the long ships, the Danes. At Otford, Edmund Ironside, victor over Canute in several battles, defeated him again in 1016 and drove the Danish army like sheep to Aylesford, to the ford across the Medway.

All these people, moving and fighting, could not but have used the Old Road. In later times the Old Road, the Pilgrims' Way, was joined by bands of pilgrims, some from London, others from farther north who used ferries across the Thames estuary. Kings and nobles also passed this way, coming from and going to the Continent. Henry VIII, for example, on his way to the Field of the Cloth of Gold, in 1520, travelled by boat from London to Greenwich, then on horseback up the valley of the Darent to Otford, and so by the Pilgrims' Way to Canterbury and a port for France. The ancient Way can never before or since have seen so splendid, so extravagant, and so large a cavalcade, so numerous that in France Henry's followers managed to consume in a month the mutton of 2,200 sheep, with other goods in proportion.

Henry's company comprised 3,400 of England's nobility and their servants, and his queen Catherine of Aragon with 1,200 ladies. Then came the train of Cardinal Wolsey, preceded by a man in scarlet bearing a large jewelled cross, after whom stepped fifty mace-bearers, two hundred gentlemen, and two hundred archers, with the cardinal himself bringing up the rear dressed in scarlet from head to foot. The Archbishops of Canterbury certainly used the Way, with their retinues— retinues large enough in all conscience but nothing like Henry's —streaming in serpentine line along the slopes of the downs. The archbishops, it seems, had palaces everywhere, with fifteen at least in Kent, of which four lay along the line of the Way—at Otford, where Henry VIII often came in the days before the Reformation, and afterwards, at Wrotham, at Maidstone, and at Charing, while the Bishop of Rochester had a palace, or at least a manor-house, at Trottiscliffe. Along the Way there were many properties of the archbishops and of the monasteries of Christ Church and Saint Augustine of Canterbury, some of which had been presented to them by Saxon kings long before the Conquest, as Offa, King of Mercia, in 791 gave Otford (where, twenty years earlier he had defeated Aldric, King of Kent), and as Athelstan gave Wrotham in 964. There were also monasteries ready to welcome both bishops and pilgrims—Boxley, Malling, Charing, etc.

All these palaces, all these ancient monasteries, fell to the grasping hands of Henry VIII, gross, diseased, wenching, subtle, totalitarian Henry, the very embodiment of Machiavelli's Prince, for whom the State was transcendent. In England Henry, in his own opinion, *was* the State. His achievement was to impose the authority of the Crown not only on the Church and its princes, but also on certain barons or nobles, especially in the north, who enjoyed powers, inherited from the middle ages, that Henry considered to be excessive. With his drastic action against the organization and the property of the Church he overcame in a short time those ecclesiastical limitations and hindrances to the secular law that Henry II had attempted to destroy and which the murder of Becket seemed to have confirmed for ever. Henceforth the Church was to be subject to the Crown and the king was head of the English Church on earth.

All these many movements throughout generations, these marching feet and shuffling hooves, so marked the Pilgrims' Way that henceforward we shall not lose it again except where by deliberate intent and form of law right of passage has been abolished, as happened at Chevening and at Chilham.

The lane beginning at the church at Titsey is marked by the Ordnance Survey as both trackway and Pilgrims' Way. In parts very narrow and sunk between hedges, it leads uneventfully to the junction with the B2024 on the boundary between Surrey and Kent. This road leads down to Westerham on the A25.

Westerham, once called 'Oisterham', was a Saxon place, and had a Saxon church, which seems to have given way to a thirteenth-century rebuilding without the usual intercalation of a Norman church. The church of the thirteenth century remains, with some Decorated details, but it has been so altered to follow the gothic evolution that now it seems at first glance to be mainly of the Perpendicular style that came into fashion after the Black Death. It has a broad, low tower with a short and sturdy broached spire over a belfry, to which, inside, a distinctive spiral staircase of *c.* 1400 climbs in a cage of wooden uprights. There are several minor brasses, one of them showing a post-Reformation priest, William Dye, who died in 1567; he wears canonicals, rarely seen on brasses of this time. The fourteenth-century octagonal font is one in which James Wolfe was baptized, the James Wolfe who became General Wolfe and died in the capture of Quebec for the English, by which it turns out he founded a sequence of troubles. A statue of Wolfe brandishes a sword at the head of the sloping, triangular green on which a bronze figure of Winston Churchill, by Oscar Nemon, crouches in a chair and glowers at the grass. Wolfe, born at the rectory, lived for the first eleven years of his life at Quebec House, which he knew as Spiers, whose gables rise beside the A25 just below the green. Chartwell, Churchill's home from 1922 until his death, is about two miles to the south. Both houses are open to the public.

The Darent, a river whose name is older than the Romans and means the river of oaks (it is the same as 'Derwent'), is a stream that runs peacefully and as it should in its obvious valley, and then at Otford turns and charges northwards as if it meant to overwhelm the downs on its little flood; but it goes through that range just as surprisingly as we have seen the Mole do so. Just as they do for the Mole, the chalk downs draw aside to let the river pass. The upper reaches of the stream, from ancient times, and the A25 today, no doubt on the line of an old valley track, link the villages of Brasted, Sundridge, and Chevening, all of which have churches whose livings are in the gift of the Archbishop of Canterbury, though not in his diocese—they belong to Rochester—and on account of that fact this part of the valley of the Darent came to be known as the Archbishop's Garden.

Brasted is a large village with a church rebuilt in 1880 to the design of Alfred Waterhouse, all except the tower, which is

Norman of the twelfth century in its lower part, and fourteenth century above. Clearly there was a time when the tower was about to fall over, for no less than seven huge buttresses lean up against it, with the central one on the west side arching to give admission through its bulk to the west door, an unusual ploy.

The church has a south chapel that, as we saw was the case with the north chapel at Tichborne, belonged to the lords of the manor, who owned it from the thirteenth century to 1919, when there was a proposal to sell it. A situation arose in which this chapel could have been bought by anybody, since it was in no wise the property of the church; it could have been bought by a Catholic and used for the service of the mass; it might, indeed, have been bought by a Muslim and used as a mosque. In the end, after some alarms, a local resident purchased it and presented it to the church. Brasted was formerly known for its old armorial glass, but all of this was broken by a bomb during the war and the windows now contain conventional modern glass. In one of them appears Saint Martin, patron saint of the church, slicing his cloak to share it with a beggar, and in the clear quarrels around him are several little drawn figures of the characters of Chaucer's *Canterbury Tales*.

Sundridge, spread along the main road, has a thirteenth-century church nicely placed on a rise.

The Pilgrims' Way runs approximately parallel with the A25 about a mile to a mile and a half to the north. Its character as a country lane has been preserved by reason of the easier gradients and greater convenience of that main road to the south. As Belloc remarks, we have here and to the east, as we shall presently see, a demonstration of the history of the Old Road in its later days. At first the only through route, keeping above the valley on the drier land and avoiding the tangle and the shadows of the great forest, it gave place as the forest was cleared to a lower and easier road, and itself continued in use only for lighter traffic.

The Pilgrims' Way, keeping on as a surfaced lane between hedges, passes a quarry at a cross-roads, crosses over north-south roads coming up from the Darent valley, and at the junction with Sundridge Hill road comes to the fence enclosing

Chevening Park. The Way should go straight on, pursuing the line north of east that it has maintained for the last few miles, but here we find only a gate into a field and a notice declaring that the land is private. It may be seen through the gate, however, that in the field there is a slight terrace bearing a faint track, a terrace marked by the OS $2\frac{1}{2}$-inch map as continuing directly across the park and passing north of Chevening House. A few yards up the hill a parallel lane to the Home Farm could also represent a continuation or convenient alternative to the Way, but this too is marked 'private'. We know, we can *see*, how the Way continues, but we are forbidden to follow it. The right of way across Chevening Park was extinguished in 1792, when the landowner and lord of the manor, the third Lord Stanhope, built a new road from Sundridge to Chevening cross-roads and beyond to take the place of the path through his park. It was an expensive exchange for Stanhope in terms of money and for walkers in terms of distance, for the new road, equivalent to three sides of a square, trebles the mileage of the fourth side, which is the Way.

Chevening House, the few houses of Chevening village (interesting as an example of an estate village), and Chevening's church of Saint Botolph are all on the east side of the park. The word 'Chevening' comes from a Celtic word, *cefn*, a ridge, with the addition of *ing*, people; so we have 'the people by the ridge', which is apt enough, for the downs rise to the north. It is interesting that this name is evidence that there was a village here before the time of the Saxons, and one may speculate that it may have existed in the iron age, when the Celtic tongue was brought into this country. The manor was bought in 1551 by John Lennard, whose grandson became the twelfth Baron Dacre. His son built a new house at Chevening, and this still exists in the fabric of the present house, which is said to have been designed by Inigo Jones—but then, anything that reasonably might be his and a great deal that could not possibly be his, are attributed to Jones. The Dacres remained until 1717, when General Stanhope, of a family originating in the north of England, bought the estate.

It was the general's grandson, Charles, third Earl Stanhope, who closed the Pilgrims' Way through the park. A strange, eccentric, inventive, and often absurd man, he sadly altered the house by covering the exterior with his own design of white 'mathematical' wall tiles (which have now been removed). He conceived ideas for progress in various industries and among other things designed and built the first iron printing-press, a practical machine and an undoubted improvement on the wooden hand-presses of the day. It was placed on the market and a number were sold. Balzac mentions one in use in the printing-house of David Séchard in *Illusions Perdues*. The Stanhope press, however, did not survive competition with the later and handier Albion and Columbian presses, and not many Stanhope presses remain today, even as museum exhibits.

The last Earl Stanhope died in 1967, bequeathing the house, with 3,500 acres of land and the sum of £250,000, to the nation. The house was to be used for (a) the Prime Minister, (b) the royal family, (c) certain politicians, (d) the High Commissioner of Canada, or (e) the Ambassador of the United States. Two small boys sitting on new bicycles by the churchyard gate told me that the house, then under repair, was to become the country home of Prince Charles. I inquired of Buckingham Palace, and was informed that this was a possibility but that nothing was certainly decided for the present. Nor was there any information about what might happen concerning the Pilgrims' Way and some other public paths through the park.

From one of these paths there is an excellent view of the north front of the house, and in the opposite direction of a strange artificial feature, a gap known as the Keyhole cut in the trees on the distant skyline of the down.

Chevening's church of Saint Botolph, built in the thirteenth century, was subsequently altered, so that the principal impression now is Perpendicular, of the time when the fine west tower was added. As with so many churches close to a great house, Saint Botolph's serves as a memorial chapel for the lords of the manor, with their hatchments and monuments. The south chancel chapel is the Stanhope chapel, shut off by glazed screens. It contains interesting monuments of the Lennards and Stanhopes, including an affecting white marble figure— a notable work of Sir Francis Chantrey—of Lady Frederica

Stanhope, who died in childbirth in 1823; she appears reclining with her child in her arms.

The Pilgrims' Way runs a short distance north of the church. We wandered in the deserted estate more freely than perhaps we should have done, looking for the Way, only to come up against locked gates and forbidding signs.

The accessible Way may conveniently be regained by taking a footpath through Chevening churchyard south of the church and out through a gate at the east end. This path leads to Turvin's Farm at a corner of the B2211. The Way may now be recovered by footpaths going up the hill to the north, or by road at the next junction.

The Way, a surfaced lane, winds eastwards to pass a still active quarry. Here motor access along the Way is cancelled to allow the A21 to pass. We pick up the surfaced Way again on the other side of this main road. In about a mile it descends to cross two arms of the Darent and enter Otford. Otford village is nowadays bedevilled by the traffic of the A225, but the centre, with old cottages, a pub and the church is still picturesque, with a well-kept green and a pond into which a graceful willow weeps. Just off the green is the former palace of the Archbishops of Canterbury. In the previous building on this site Thomas Becket used to stay and enjoy the scenery and the quiet air of this fertile valley. Here he performed what Lambarde calls one of his 'spitefull miracles', commanding to silence—and that henceforth no bird should sing at Otford—a nightingale that interrupted his evening prayers. The greater part of the present building dates from the year 1501. Built by Archbishop Dene in his short reign of two years, it was subsequently altered on a more ambitious scale by Archbishop William Warham at a cost of over £30,000. Here on several occasions Warham was host to Henry VIII. There remains a broken but impressive tower of brick coigned with stone, attached to a lower range that is now a terrace of cottages, and another ancient portion, also in brick. A covered spring east of the palace and of the church is known as Becket's Well, and is said to have been brought into being by the archbishop himself, in the usual manner in which saints create springs, by striking his staff on the ground.

Henry VIII appropriated the palace from Archbishop Cranmer and used it, but soon found that the low-lying ground was too damp and aggravated his rheumatism. Seeking relief, his gaze turned southwards to another house of the archbishop, Knole, on higher ground beyond Sevenoaks. This house too he compelled the unwilling Cranmer to concede to the Crown. The exchange appears in Henry's own words: 'The house [Otford] standeth low, and is rheumatik like unto Croydon, where I wuld never be without sicknes, and I will live at Knole, and most of my house shall live at Otford.'

The lead roof of Otford's palace was stripped off in the time of Henry's son Edward VI, and since that time the palace has been in ruins. According to Hasted, the ruins covered an acre of ground. The Romans, who had two villas near Otford, in the Darent valley, perhaps escaped rheumatism by reason of their hypocausts.

There was a church at Otford in Saxon times, part of which may remain in the present building. The fat west tower was added about 1175. Thereafter there was the usual progression of additions and changes until a fire in 1630 caused considerable destruction. An unusual and charming feature of this church is that it is still lighted by candles, which are set in no less than thirteen brass chandeliers, all of which, except for the eighteenth-century example in the chancel, were introduced into the church in 1912. Their soft, shadowy light gleams on hatchments of the Pilhill family, on their monuments, and on a Tudor tomb doubling as an Easter sepulchre, on which, with Henry's Tudor rose, appears the pomegranate badge of Catherine of Aragon, first and and most enduring of the six wives of Henry VIII. She married Henry in 1509, as the widow of Henry's brother, and was rejected (rather than divorced) by him in 1531 when, tardily, it occurred to him that he and Catherine had been living in incest; so this tomb must have been made between those dates, late in the history of the Canterbury pilgrimage, but early enough to have been used as an Easter sepulchre at services that pilgrims attended.

Otford is one of those few settlements through which the Pilgrims' Way passes directly, forming, as we saw at Bentley and at Farnham, the main street. Travellers of all kinds on the

Way therefore had to pass through Otford, whether coming from the east or the west, or from the north through the Shoreham gap, for Otford stands only a little above the turn where the Darent swings around to flow through that gap, where road and railway now go together, burrowing one under the other. River, road, and railway pass by Shoreham's Perpendicular church, whose fine south porch of timber has an arch formed by only two slabs of oak cut directly from the tree. To the north beside the river there stood a Roman villa, and farther north again, at Lullingstone, yet another. This latter example has been excavated and covered over by a large shed by the Department of the Environment and it is open to the public regularly. It has good mosaics and a fresco of a water-nymph in a room that seems to have been used for worship. Lullingstone Castle, largely rebuilt in the time of Queen Anne, has descended directly, though twice by the female side, since 1361, and fine tombs of the family, under the names of Peche, Hart, and Dyke, are to be seen in Lullingstone's fourteenth-century and sixteenth-century church of Saint Botolph, close to the house. A beautiful altar frontal was made from silk spun on a silk farm at the castle. A seventh-century bronze bowl, very handsome in the Celtic style that derives from the La Tène manner, was found at Lullingstone in 1860, when the railway was building; it may be seen in the British Museum.

The Pilgrims' Way winds through the village of Otford and beyond the station turns off to sidle along the steep North Downs, which have, on the map, in this area a curved and re-entrant outline as though instancing the scallop that is the symbol of pilgrimage. Kemsing is two miles away, its church only a few yards below the lane that is the Pilgrims' Way. It is a pleasant village, whose church originally stood alone a little distance off, but now has the company of a group of modern bungalows and houses. All around, except on the slopes to the north, is good farm country, with patches of orchards—apples and cherries—and spinneys of woodland. I was delighted to find here, along one side of the churchyard, a crinkle-crankle wall with the warm colour of eighteenth-century brick (*plate* 13). Its looping outline presents to the churchyard a series of convex surfaces contrasting with the rigidity of the tombstones.

These curving walls have been said to be stronger than simple straight ones, the curves conferring a stiffness derived from compression, as in ordinary arcades. I think this is nonsense. It is much more likely that crinkle-crankle walls were built to form on the concave side a series of arbours in which fruit and flowers would take the best advantage of the sun's heat gathered in and reflected from the curves.

Saint Mary's church has stood here for at least eight hundred years, for some of the masonry is Norman and some perhaps Saxon. It contains a brass demi-figure of Thomas de Hop, who was rector of Kemsing from 1341 to 1347; he appears in eucharistic vestments, with an amice about his neck. Visitors may be surprised to see that the amice is decorated with a line of swastikas. Recent history has endowed the swastika with a malign aura, but Hitler, for all his crimes and the magnitude of the conflict he engendered, was no more than a moment in time, a mere page, if as much as that, in the long history of the swastika, which is called also the gammadion and the fylfot. More than five thousand years earlier than Hitler's day, the swastika was known to and used by men of the bronze age who tramped the Old Road along the hills, and by their successors who built the great iron-age hill-fort of Oldbury (which Benjamin Harrison called 'the Gibraltar of Kent') two miles south of the Way; and, who knows, it may have come about by an idle scratching in the sand by those primitive hunters of the distant palaeolithic age who are known to have crouched in the rock shelters on the east side of Oldbury Hill. The swastika was also a symbol used in oriental religions and was without doubt borrowed from them for Christian use. Its Christian significance is the reason for its appearance on the amice of Thomas de Hop.

Montagu Norman, or Baron Norman of Saint Clere, governor of the Bank of England between the wars and a tantalizing mystery man to the economists and politicians of his time, is commemorated by a plaque which is here because Norman lived, as his family still live, at the house of Saint Clere, which lies to the east beyond Heaverham, and which we shall come to presently.

The church of Kemsing has two interesting representations

of the Virgin. An incomplete one dates from the fourteenth century, while the other, more charming, with Mary in a green skirt and an underskirt of yellow, was made about the year 1220; generations of pilgrims would have halted to admire that figure in coloured glass, put there in the year in which the body of Thomas Becket was translated from the crypt of Canterbury cathedral into the new shrine behind the main altar. A modern window (1911) shows Saint Thomas Becket in company with Saint Richard of Chichester.

The churchyard has rows of those curious tombs in which a headstone and a footstone are connected by a rounded coffin-shaped 'sleeper' stone. Common in Kent, this arrangement is also seen farther afield, in Surrey and in Sussex, and occasionally even in Hampshire, but examples are so much more numerous in Kent that this county must be their origin. Dickens made use of some of these stones at Cooling, north-east of Rochester, as a hiding-place from which the convict sprang out to terrify Pip.

Kemsing was once an object of pilgrimage on its own account, for Saint Edith, daughter of King Edgar the Peaceful and Wulfrith his wife, was born here in 961. Until her early death (at the age of twenty-four) she impressed everyone by her notable piety, and, as was the common thing with medieval saints, her sanctity was made apparent after her death by the miracles that were wrought for those who prayed to her. A shrine was made in the churchyard with a statue of Edith, and this could not have failed to attract devout pilgrims coming along the Pilgrims' Way; but Edith's bounty was really for the local people, who brought grain to be blessed at the shrine, which was then mixed with other grain to ensure a fortunate harvest. Lambarde writes of it, with becoming scepticism for his time, fifty years after the Reformation: 'the Image of Edith (the daughter of King Edgar, and sometime Prioress of Wylton in the West Countrie) was religiously frequented in the Church-yarde at Kemsing, for the preservation of Corne and Graine, from Blasting, Myldew, Brandeare, and such other harmes as commonly do annoy it. The manner of the whiche sacrifice was this: Some seelie bodie brought a pecke, or two, or a Bushell of Corne, to the Church: and (after praiers made) offered it to the Image of the Saint: Of this offering, the Priest used to toll the greatest portion, and then to take one handful, or a little more of the residue (for which you must consider he woulde be sure to gaine by the bargaine) the which after aspersion of holy water, and mumbling of a few woordes of conjuration, he first dedicated to the Image of Saint Edith, and then delivered it back, to the partie that brought it: who then departed with full persuasion, that if he mingled that hallowed handfull with his seede Corne, it woulde preserve from harme, and prosper in growthe, the whole heape that he should sowe, were it never so great a Stacke, or mowgh.'

Saint Edith's Well and Saint Edith's Farm preserve her name.

At the hamlet of Heaverham the lower road is represented by a drive across the Saint Clere grounds, accessible as a footpath, but a surfaced road goes north to the Way and people wishing to drive from Heaverham to Yaldham have to go by three sides of a rectangle. This is a convenient demonstration of the ancient necessity of the Way as a means of communication between village and village. If you will look at the map you will see that from Otford to the first side-road on the south the Pilgrims' Way is the sole way and nothing has come about to compete with it; but from that side-road on to Heaverham there are two parallel roads connected by short north and south roads: the Pilgrims' Way on the slopes, and, some fifty feet lower, the later road, which came into use as a matter of convenience to avoid having to describe three sides of a rectangle in going from one village to the next. But at Heaverham the ancient upper way prevails for a mile as the good way between village and village. But now something very odd and very illuminating happens: there is a counter-change, the lower road regaining its surface and continuing as a surfaced road into Wrotham, while the upper road, the Pilgrims' Way, becomes a mere path or track (*plate* 12) once more and does not become surfaced again until it is almost at Wrotham. It could be said that this arrangement has come about partly by the shopping and market needs of the villages and hamlets concerned, with Heaverham acting as it were as a divide. From Heaverham and points west people have gone to market in Otford, while those from West Yaldham and Yaldham have gone east into Wrotham. Nowhere else is the evolution of the Pilgrims' Way and its relation to the communities along it so graphically displayed.

From the length of the Way between Heaverham and West Yaldham you will have a good view of the house of Saint Clere, which is set down on a pleasant site in a well timbered park. Built in the seventeenth century on the site of an earlier house, Saint Clere is of the type known as a double pile, the type of Chevening on the Pilgrims' Way and of Coleshill in Berkshire, which was designed by Roger Pratt and Inigo Jones about 1652 (now demolished after a fire). An oddity about Saint Clere is that, although a classical house, it has polygonal corner towers of Tudor fashion, which, in that fashion, were formerly topped by cupolas.

Among neighbours of Saint Clere as the homes of affluent country gentlemen are Ightham Court and Ightham Mote. Ightham Court is a Tudor house exhibiting rather more markedly than usual the naïveté of the period concerning classical architecture; its classical details, such as pediments and pillars of the various orders, are applied as though simply by adhesive. Ightham Mote is indeed a moated house, with its fourteenth-century walls rising directly from their reflections in the moat as though for ever narcissistic; but the name comes rather from 'mote' or 'moot', a meeting-place. The house may date back as far as the twelfth century. From 1370 it was in the possession of the family of de Haut, one of whom, taking the side of the unfortunate Edward V against the Duke of Gloucester, was executed when that duke took the throne as Richard III. Richard turned the de Hauts out of their house and gave it to a supporter of his, Sir Robert Brakenbury, the man who, according to Shakespeare, surrendered the Duke of Clarence to the two murderers and also, probably, the two young princes; but not many months afterwards Richard and Brakenbury fell in the bloody fray of Bosworth Field and the de Haut family got their house back.

Ightham village is spectacularly attractive, with timber-framed cottages of the fifteenth and sixteenth centuries grouped around the church. Among them is the George and Dragon inn, built in 1515. Just as Kemsing church, and indeed many other churches, stands apart from its village, so too does Saint Peter's at Ightham. It was originally built about the year 1100, but was altered subsequently, a large part being rebuilt or rewindowed in the fifteenth century. Above the recess in which Sir Thomas Cawne lies in effigy with his emblem, a forked-tailed lion, on his breast, is a window with unusual tracery, the cost of which was defrayed by a bequest from Sir Thomas *c*. 1374. There are some other interesting monuments, and in particular one to Dame Dorothy Selby, who died in 1641 and was in life an assiduous needlewoman. A relief of Adam and Eve, of the Armada, and of the Gunpowder Plot, on her monument is based on an elaborate piece of her embroidery that is still in existence.

The Pilgrims' Way from above West Yaldham to Wrotham is an unmetalled lane or footpath, hedged at first, but later becoming open on the south side, with good views of the country-side and of the Wealden hills. A large variety of plants and trees grow along this section, including ash, oak, sycamore, and field maple, hawthorn and wild roses, mallow, campions, thistles with impressive fruit, meadowsweet and other umbels, and of course, quantities of nettles, which do not, however, block the path. On the north side the downs lie in folds blunt and rounded as the soft drapes of velvet.

For some distance the path is bordered on the north by a wire link fence, and in this you may see a small, top-swung door or hatch, of the kind some people have in their house doors for the admission of cats or small dogs. This particular door must have been made and placed here by an enlightened farmer, for it is meant for the passage of badgers in their foraging expeditions. Some farmers trap or shoot badgers, though it has been shown more than once that the slight amount of damage badgers do is more than compensated by the valuable services they unconsciously render to the farmer in killing various pests.

The Way crosses the Ightham road, which north of the track describes a dog-leg bend to overcome the severe gradient of the down. The Way then becomes a street, which continues to the complex of modern roads north-west of Wrotham towards Rochester. As it does with so many villages, the Way leaves Wrotham aside, though very near, but Wrotham was of some importance to the pilgrims because here there was another palace, or at least a manor-house, of the Archbishops of Canterbury. The greater part of the building was demolished by Archbishop Simon Islip in the mid-fourteenth century to provide material for the building of the palace at Maidstone, and today only the merest vestiges may be seen, south of the church and behind the Black Bull hotel; a roofless wing attached to a house appears to be part of it. In the palace at Wrotham, Lambarde recounts, Becket's successor in the archbishopric, Richard, had a terrible vision of a vengeful spectre which haunted him from here towards Rochester and brought about his death at Halling.

Wrotham, facing on to constricted streets with too much traffic, despite the by-pass of the A20 north of the village, has old pubs, including the Rose and Crown and the George and Dragon, and many old houses. The church, dedicated to Saint George, stands above on a slight hill, with its fifteenth-century tower butting on to the roadway. The tower was built over an open passage so that the processions the middle ages loved to mount, to take part in, and to watch, might move round the church without leaving consecrated ground. A stone in the wall of the tunnel has a number of the little crosses such as we saw at the church of Saint Martha above Albury, crosses said to have been scratched by crusaders going to the Holy Land, or by pilgrims marking their presence on the pilgrimage; but this stone at Wrotham is supposed to have come from Canterbury cathedral, where pilgrims might have cut the crosses to show that they had achieved their goal, the successful arrival at the shrine of Saint Thomas. The rest of the church derives from the thirteenth century, when it was built in place of a Saxon church of the year 964. There is a series of good brasses ranging in date from 1498 to 1611, and some good monuments, but the most interesting feature of this church is the passage known as the Nun's Gallery, which runs across the width of the church above the chancel arch, and is reached by a continuation of the rood stair above the fourteenth-century screen. It is unlikely that nuns customarily came up here either to worship or to contemplate. There are openings looking into the church to east and west, and it seems more

OPW

reasonable to think that this was a watching-chamber, from which a sacristan could keep guard over the church's treasures, or possibly over some holy relic kept in the chancel for pilgrims and other travellers to revere and to which they would duly contribute sums of money, to the enrichment of the church. There is a similar arrangement at Hythe, and in other churches may be found the more frequent type of watching-chamber set above the sacristy, with a window into the chancel.

At Wrotham, the Pilgrims' Way is rejoined at the road junction north of the village. It leaves as a slender, surfaced lane between hedges, passing a house called Chaucers, inappropriately, since this is not on the route taken by Chaucer's Canterbury pilgrims. The lane winds along the slopes of the downs, marking, as it has so often done, the dividing line between the uncultivated hill and the arable fields. Along this length miles of the downs are covered with trees—Hognore Wood, Downs Wood, Great Wood, and the extensive White Horse Wood. The tendency of the Way is now towards the north-east following the great curving cape of the downs. Already, in anticipation, the hills seem to be gathering their skirts to hold them clear of the Medway, where it flows freely northwards, a smooth, brimming river drained twice in the day by the ebb of the tides. We have seen this same recoil of the chalk hills twice before, for the benefit of the Mole and of the Darent, but those instances were not on the scale that now faces us, and nothing quite so formidable has previously been placed in the way of the pilgrims as the marshes and the water of the tidal river.

The surfaced lane that is the Pilgrims' Way loses its surface below Hognore Wood, or rather, it would be more accurate to say, the surface turns away abruptly down to the south, dropping down the hill as Wrotham Water Lane, a name it has from an old pond or reservoir. Wrotham Water Lane passes a delightful Jacobean house called Ford Place, built of low-toned red brick, with shaped gables in the roof. Above Trottiscliffe the Way comes to Pilgrim House, which was once the Kentish Drovers' Inn. Opposite this house a lane descends to Trottiscliffe, which, if you wish to be understood in these parts, that is to speak the local language, you must pronounce as 'Trosley'. The village itself is of no great importance, but its church has interest. The church lies half a mile off to the east, in company with Court Lodge; the rest of the village, once mothered by the church as a hen its chickens, migrated to the present site in the hope of escaping the Black Death, a flea-borne disease that in 1348 killed thirty-two of the Bishop of Rochester's staff. Court Lodge seems to be a house of Georgian flavour, but it stands on the site and fractionally incorporates a palace or manor-house of the Bishops of Rochester. The bishops had a manor-house here probably from the year 774, when the property was granted to them by King Offa, after the victory by which that able Mercian won the Kingdom of Kent. The bishops held the manor through nine hundred years, coming here to find peace and refreshment in their country house on the sunny side of the downs. It was here that one of them, Hamo de Hethe, while staying in his palace of Trosley, lost those thirty-two of his staff to the Black Death. In 1648 the manor, which had escaped confiscation at the Reformation because it was the personal property of the bishops and did not belong to the cathedral or to the Church, was sold to one Nicholas Bond for the precise sum of £1,632 12s. 7¼d., and thenceforwards possession passed through a series of secular owners. Scarcely anything of the medieval house is now to be seen, though there is an old gateway and in front of it a marshy piece of ground that is the reputed site of the bishops' fishponds.

The Saxon church at Trosley was demolished by the Normans, who built a new church on the Saxon founda-tions—the big sarsen stones in the footings probably remain from the Saxon building. The Norman fabric of an unaisled church survives largely intact in the present church, with subsequent alterations to the windows. The west wall, rebuilt in 1885 at a cost of £800, is an interesting example of flintwork in red and black. The flints are squared and closely spaced, and so arranged that the courses become progressively narrower as they approach the gable.

Into this simple little country church some highly sophisticated woodwork was introduced about the beginning of the nineteenth century. The very grand pulpit (*plate* 15), with its canopy resting on a kind of artificial palm tree, was designed for Westminster Abbey in 1781 by Henry Keene, the abbey surveyor. It was in use there until the abbey was cleared and decorated for the coronation of George IV. For some reason not at all plain and decidedly unofficial, the pulpit was given to William Seager, a distiller (Seager's gin), who in 1824 gave it to the church at Trosley. The chancel rails date from the year 1700 and there are other examples of old woodwork in the church, including two Charles II chairs in dark wood given by the Rev. E. J. Shepherd, who held the living for more than forty years, as did his father before him. The two incumbents achieved between them a total of only seven years short of a century—the air of Trosley in the nineteenth century and the peace of the countryside and of the downs clearly made for longevity and content.

In a glass case lie a human skull and small pieces of calcined bones. These belonged to a group of neolithic people who were buried, twenty-two of them, at Coldrum, where in 1910 their bones were found, together with those of ox, cat, deer, rabbit, and fox—the meat diet of a family who lived four thousand years ago. The Old Road was for them already familiar. They were farmers and here in the lower land on the slopes of the hills they would have found good sweet soil to till and to plant, supplies of the flints that were the basis of their lives, for they made of them both tools and weapons, and wild animals to be hunted or snared in the deep woods of the clay and the greensand to supplement their diet.

It was farmers such as these who built the great megalithic tombs that are to be seen close to the Old Road between Trottis-cliffe and Boxley, on the two shores of the Medway. They hauled the huge sarsen stones across the countryside and erected them as they found them, without shaping or tailoring their durable form. They took four or more of the largest and stood them upright and capped the chamber so made with a yet larger stone, and then they covered the whole structure with a huge mound of earth, which they surrounded with spaced-out standing stones in what archaeologists call a peristalith. This huge monument, this veritable house or palace of the dead, they then used for the burial of bodies or of cremated bones and ashes through several generations, providing each corpse with goods and articles of daily use so that in the next world the dead might be as comfortable as in this. The entrance was commonly at the broad end of the mound, which was made to face the east, as though their divinity and their salvation came from the rising sun; but in later days, because the tombs were interfered with and robbed, barrows were built with a sham entrance at the east end, the true entrance being hidden in the side of the mound.

Coldrum could have been so called from a time twelve hundred years later, but there is no evidence that the name is earlier than the building of a nearby farmhouse of that title in 1796. There has been a great deal of speculation concerning the derivation of the names of the Kent megaliths and of Coldrum and Kit's Coty in particular. It is generally agreed that both of these names are probably Celtic, and if that is so they may derive from any time between the arrival of the iron-age invaders in the sixth century BC and the ascendancy of the Saxons after the departure of the Romans in the fifth century AD. But what 'Coldrum' means is not at all clear. It looks like Gaelic rather than Welsh—'drom' in Irish means a ridge, and that would be appropriate enough, since Coldrum is set on the emphatic edge of a steep mound or spur that may be a natural formation partly shaped by man.

The OS one-inch and 2½-inch maps scorn the name of 'Coldrum' and prefer to mark the site simply as 'Burial Chamber', a detail that may give you trouble in finding the monument of which I write. The burial chamber lies south of the Pilgrims' Way half a mile to the east of Trottiscliffe church, in the Ordnance Survey kilometre square 65:60; it may be reached by a track descending from the Way, or by road and track from Trottiscliffe church. The central chamber or box, formed of massive slabs of stone (*plate* 14) stands on the very brink of a terrace that slopes steeply down to the east, under the shade of a fine ash tree. Some observers, as Mr Ronald Jessup points out, have supposed that the monument was built on two levels, and this is what the present form suggests. Of the twenty-four stones of the peristalith, seventeen lie awry at the foot of the slope, as though they had fallen there from the top when the earth was suddenly whipped away from beneath them. The slope and the disarrangement of the stones are difficult to understand. The slope may be partly, but only partly, due to the digging and ferreting of local people, who supposed that there was under the mound a secret passage to Trottiscliffe church, a passage that might contain treasure. However, the slope is not the kind of thing that would be made by people looking for a tunnel. Nor is it easy to assume that the whole of the peristalith was originally all at one level, for that brings other questions that are equally difficult to answer. There is at present a difference of about eighteen feet between the two levels on which the remains of the monument lie. The earthen mound that once covered the chamber has long since disappeared, as it has in so many other examples; it is not easy to imagine that the mound was built on anything but level ground, as with other megaliths, and equally it is not easy to imagine anyone cutting away the ground from beneath it, with the peril of the stones falling upon them. Coldrum, it seems to me, deserves much more attention than it has had, both by archaeologists and by semantists.

Coldrum stands alone, but not very far from other megaliths to the south in what used to be Addington Park. Here are the remains of two other chambers, one known as Addington Long Barrow and the other as the Chestnuts. The latter lies near a country road and a modern farmhouse, and we approached it down the farm drive and across a recently set rose plantation. The Chestnuts, or Stony Warren (or, according to Josiah Colebrook, a temple of the ancient Britons), has suffered far more than Coldrum. Until recently its stones lay in a confused heap such as we shall see later at the Countless Stones. A few years ago a number of the stones were pulled back to vertical without shifting the positions of their bases. So the Chestnuts remains today, still confused and neither as atmospheric nor as moving as the stones of Coldrum. But the site is older, for among things found here were a number of mesolithic flints, and it is younger because long after the neolithic builders abandoned their work the Romans were here, with labourers living in a hut to one side of the megalithic site. All this can be known because, though the tomb was pillaged in the thirteenth century, the collapse of the stones thereafter prevented any further, more casual, interference. Not less than nine persons, including children, were buried in the stone chamber under this barrow, which was used well into the bronze age.

Addington Long Barrow, a little to the north-west of the Chestnuts, is in worse condition. A modern farm-road has been driven through the site and much alteration and damage have been perpetrated during the past half-century. As yet, little has been done to elucidate this monument or to discover what relation it may have had to the Chestnuts and to Coldrum, as well as to the plan of the Medway megaliths as a whole.

In this district people have seen barrows where none existed or which have been confused with irregularities in the earth's surface. Addington's church of Saint Margaret, for example, stands on a large mound that is said to be a barrow. Only excavation can show what is genuine and what is accidentally or naturally similar to ancient work. Excavation, however, is not needed to show that the great stones of Coldrum and of the Chestnuts were set up by no mean people. Whoever they may have been, the dead who lay here must have been notable men or the ruling families of their day to be held deserving of memorials so massive and so enduring. Any who sleep here still may be disturbed by the M20, which is designed to cross this land.

Saint Margaret's church was built in the thirteenth century and considerably altered in the fifteenth century. It contains a number of good brasses, dating from 1378 for one Richard Charlis, who appears as a knight in camail armour, to about 1446 for Thomas Chalkorth, a priest. In the village, by a sloping green, the Angel Inn claims an origin in the fourteenth century.

What could our pilgrims have conceived of those great stone tombs set in mounds some of which must have been complete in their day? For men of the middle ages 'old' and 'ancient' were adjectives of hazy value, referring to a past in which Alexander and Hercules and Julius Caesar and the forebears of the English lived in a jostling world immeasurably smaller than ours, moving about in a murk of time and legends and tradition. A century or a thousand years gone by were much the same for them. They would not have imagined, and might have supposed it a sin to imagine, that the stones of Coldrum and of Addington antedated by millennia the birth of Christ, that here in the familiar Weald of England men worshipped strange gods and believed in an hereafter in which worldly goods were useful and necessary. Even the sophisticated eighteenth century, when archaeology may be said to have begun to find its feet, could not venture to believe that monuments such as Coldrum, the Chestnuts, and Stonehenge could be older than the time of the druids, those mysterious Celtic priests to whom were attributed all kinds of strange crimes and strange structures.

I have already spoken of the mirror image of the landscape either side of the Medway. The reflection extends to the stones of Coldrum and Addington: for to the east of the river, where the downs curve round and away from the water, there are those other antiquities, one of them resembling the tumbled chamber of Addington and called locally the Countless Stones, another the standing dolmen of Kit's Coty, and yet another the White Horse Stone, the name of which links with the White Horse Wood above Coldrum and recalls the legendary symbolic horse of the British, the horse that, after the Greeks, they put upon their first coins or cut so grandly on the summit of the downs above the Vale of the White Horse in Berkshire. The Berkshire horse, however, is on the line of another ancient track, the Ridgeway.

As the Pilgrims' Way continues north of Trottiscliffe and Addington a splendid landscape opens before it, a landscape in which the vast watershed of the Medway is scattered with woods, fields, and villages, with orchards and arable farms, all melting into the haze of the distance, where low hills form the horizon. Among them are the villages of Ryarsh, whose harsh name means a field of rye, and Birling, with a church that has a noble tower of the Kentish kind—one of its lords of the manor in the twelfth century, Ralph de Curva Spina, has left his name and the memory of his deformity in Crookhorn or Crookthorn Wood just north of the Pilgrims' Way. Also in the Weald and in the valley of the Medway are fine houses such as Mereworth, Bradbourne (now a research station), and Clare. Offham still maintains on its village green the quintain set up for horsemen to practise with the lance; if they were imperfect or not spry enough they got for their trouble a clout in the back from the revolving wooden arm. At West Malling, in orchard and hop country, are the remains of Saint Mary's

Abbey, which was founded about the year 1100 by Bishop Gundulph of Rochester. The abbey, on the site of a Saxon manor, was for Benedictine nuns; Anglican Benedictine sisters occupy it today, for about the year 1900 this sisterhood came to take the place of the one driven out by Henry VIII nearly four hundred years earlier. Lambarde darkly suggests that the medieval nunnery was in verity a bawdy house for monks: 'that the monkes . . . might have a convenient place to resort unto, and where they might (*Caute*, at least) quench the heats, kindled of their good cheere and idlenes, God knoweth, and I will not judge. But well I wote, that this was a very common practice in Papistry.' Lambarde was a keen Protestant! A strong tower, in ruins, and some other remnants are to be seen joined to the new buildings of the revived nunnery, which are designed to go with the tower without themselves pretending to be medieval. A little to the south is another tower, Saint Leonard's, a grand keep, which is believed to have been part of a fortified manor-house built by Gundulph. Gundulph's hand may be seen in several places in the diocese of Rochester.

The nuns' abbey of Saint Mary, as was the case with other religious houses, would have been a resort of the pilgrims, and especially of the women among them, a place where they might find comfort, food, and rest before they set out to continue their journey on the far shore of the Medway. Those who came here would not be likely to return to the Pilgrims' Way to cross the river at Snodland, unless they had some special reason to do so. But if they did decide to return northwards, they would pass by the walls of the castle of Leybourne, built in the thirteenth century by the powerful family of Leybourne close to the Norman church of Leybourne village. The family had connections with the wine trade of France, and one of them, Sir Roger, founded there the village of Libourne near Bordeaux. This same Sir Roger went off on pilgrimage to the Holy Land, where he died in 1271; but his heart was cut out and brought back so that this part of his body at least, this chalice of sympathy, might rest in his own church in his own village; there you may still see the heart shrine in which it was placed. The family died out in the fourteenth century with Juliana de Leybourne, who, childless despite three marriages, was so

wealthy and owned so much land in the county that people
called her the Infanta of Kent. What remains of the castle is
incorporated in a modern house.

Those guests of Saint Mary's who had no reason to retrace
their steps to the north would sensibly have made their way
towards Aylesford, where there was a good ford and from an
early date a bridge. From Aylesford they would recover the
Pilgrims' Way near Cossington.

But we are still upon the Pilgrims' Way above Birling (*plate* 16),
looking over the broad panorama of the valley of the Medway,
and seeking for the crossing of the river and the continuation
on the far shore of the ancient track it is our business to follow.
Above us the downs rise to 550 feet in Crookhorn Wood, and
here the uplands curve round to the north in that great cape
or headland following the whim of the river towards Rochester.
From where we stand we may look across the valley and see
on the distant and farther shore a similar formation of downs
and slopes turning a similar cape or headland round Burham
Down and Bluebell Hill. Our pilgrim, and ancient man long
before him, would know that he would have somehow to reach
that farther shore, those distant hills, in order to continue his
journey on a dry and passable track just such as those we have
followed all the way from Winchester, from which he, and we,
have now come more than eighty miles; we still have thirty
miles to travel.

First we have to cross the river and the lowland on either
side, stretches of which were, in the days of the pilgrims, likely
to be marshy or sticky on the gault. Snodland, Halling, and
Cuxton have all been suggested as traditional crossing-places
for the Pilgrims' Way. Of these three, the lowest, Cuxton, was
the most difficult and, at least in the middle ages, a ferry must
be supposed. Even with a ferry Cuxton would not be altogether
satisfactory, for it would involve not only a long detour from
the Way, but, once you had got across the river, the passage of
a broad strip of marshland still marked on the maps as
Wouldham Marshes. Halling had a ferry until recently, and
the supposition that pilgrims crossed here is strengthened by
the presence of a chapel on the west side (now converted into

cottages), while on the east side it was only a short distance to firmer, rising ground and Wouldham church. But even so, Halling still involved a detour, a waste of mileage, and if the pilgrims could cross without danger and with no more trouble on a shorter line, that, human nature being what it is, we must suppose is what they did do. So we will descend down through the hamlet of Paddlesworth towards Snodland. For the moment we leave aside the longer detour to the north, by way of Rochester, for that we shall discuss in the next chapter.

Snodland, with Holborough, is today an industrial town, with tall mill chimneys and large, dull buildings, which appear unwelcome and unwelcoming in this broad, sun-filled, rural landscape of the downs and the Weald and the Medway valley. The Holborough factory of the Blue Circle Group makes cement down there, digging their materials from vast quarries, and by the river Townsend Hook make fine-quality papers in a mill opposite the church. Columns of marching pylons cross in various directions, linked by sagging wires. Snodland church stands by the river, and that fact alone would identify the preferable crossing of the Medway, which you may put together with the view of another church, the old church of Burham, on the far shore.

We saunter along the Way above Birling Place with all this in view, and come to a junction with a surfaced road. Northwards this road gives access by way of Wrangling Lane (lovely name!) to Dode, or Dowde, where there is a little lost Norman church hidden away among trees; its congregation disappeared at the time of the Black Death, either into the grave or in flight, and through the following centuries the little building became more and more a ruin. In 1905–6 it was repaired and re-roofed, and it now belongs to the Roman Catholic faith. The lonely position and the fact that the church is Catholic mean that you are likely to find the door locked, and if you really want to get in you will have to go all the way to Rochester for the key.

At the junction a branch of the Pilgrims' Way continues as a lane, the beginning of the detour to Rochester. We turn off it by a footpath or a little farther on by a lane descending beside two rows of pylons to Paddlesworth, whose tiled and hipped roofs have an air of peace. This hamlet of Paddlesworth once had some importance on the Pilgrims' Way, for here there was another small Norman church, whose position should be as significant for the line of the Way as we found were the positions of Saint Catherine's and Saint Martha's of Guildford. The chapel at Paddlesworth has long since been desecrated and is now a barn attached to a linhay, but the evidence of Norman building is still apparent.

Snodland takes its unattractive name from a Saxon called Snodd, who owned land here where the Romans once had a house (on the site of the gasworks). The small, busy little town has the workaday air more common to the midlands and the north, but it has several interesting houses, including in the High Street an admirable example of Wealden timber-framing and studding (*plate* 17) in a house deriving from the fifteenth century. We follow the High Street along to the church of All Saints, which was built by the Normans and later acquired examples of all the medieval pointed styles down to Perpendicular, this last period being that of the tower. Roman bricks in the fabric announce the proximity of the Roman villa. Inside there are some brasses of interest.

The High Street seems to come to an end at the point where the church tower looks glumly across to the paper mill, but there is a path down by the west wall of the churchyard to a black-painted house, which we skirt to the left to find ourselves on the bank of the Medway. Here we look over to a flat and marshy strip beyond which are seen the two churches of Burham, the old church nearer the river and the newer one beyond on the hillside. The river is sad and miserable, flowing smoothly between sullen banks of mud and bordered by dumped rubbish, among which, when we were there last, was somebody's superannuated settee.

Belloc claimed that he saw at Snodland, in the river, the remains of a hard-bottomed ford, but he did not claim that the hard bottom was necessarily ancient. Eighty years later we could see no sign of any such ford, even with the tide near low ebb. Further, if there was one, it would have led only to marshy ground on the far side. That there was a ferry in historic times is certain, but not, in all probability, a ferry directly across to the other shore. In these reaches between Snodland and Burham the Medway meanders in great loops, as it flows smoothly and lazily between soft banks. The ferry from Snodland probably moved upstream along the northern arm of a horseshoe loop and decanted its passengers at the foot of a level lane that passes for a short distance over soft ground directly to Burham old church.

There is no ferry today. Ferries throughout England have died away and have disappeared since men ceased to be interested in earning mere pennies, with the risk, on bad days, of nothing at all. Years ago a bridge was proposed, but it has not come about. So, unless you choose to swim or to test for yourselves the existence of the ford, with its reputed hard bottom, there is nothing for it but to return through the village to the cross-roads and there to take the road to the north to cross the river by the new motorway bridge on the M2, or still farther north to cross at Rochester, where there has been a bridge since the Romans came.

12 *The Rochester Diversion*

12 MILES

We stand again at the point north of Birling where the Pilgrims'
Way meets and crosses the Paddlesworth road near a small
chalk quarry in the face of the down, in a landscape pieced and
parcelled by pylons and cables, and on a length of the Way dis-
figured by more rubbish and bits of old cars than any other
stretch; a deep hollow beside the Paddlesworth junction is
filled with rejected hardware. To the north of us is the tumbled
country of Meopham and Luddesdown, which, except for the
afforestation of the hills (with hardwoods) and the occasional
cultivation of orchards, cannot have altered much for centuries
—Luddesdown, indeed, has a house claimed to have been
occupied continuously since 1066. This is the hinterland behind
the great cape or headland of the downs that we are about to
turn to enter into the Medway valley. We follow the feet of the
pilgrims who chose, not to go directly by way of Snodland, but to
make the long detour through Rochester. There are good reasons
why they should have done this, why they should add at least
twelve miles to their journey. We have to remember that for the
first fifty years of the pilgrimage to Canterbury the month of
December, in which Becket died, was the prime occasion of the
veneration of the saint. In that month it was always possible
that after days of rain or snow the river would be swollen and
perilous, the valley flooded, and ferry-boats untempting. At
Rochester, however, there was a bridge, and there a man might
cross the Medway in safety. This, however, was not the only
reason why pilgrims made the long detour from Birling. At
Rochester there were also monasteries and nunneries and a
welcome for such travellers as they, and further, there was the
cathedral, in which after the year 1201 the shrine of Saint
William of Perth was to be seen and to be revered. This shrine
alone would be enough to bring to Rochester those pilgrims
who were anxious to include in their pilgrimage as many such
holy places as they could conveniently manage.

In order to reach Rochester we have to pass through Upper Halling, Cuxton, and Strood. From Lad's Farm north of Paddlesworth the road is surfaced all the way, and at Bores Hole near Cuxton we join a main road, the A228, which a little farther north crosses over the M2, the Medway towns by-pass.

At Upper Halling cross-roads, Chapel Houses, apparently a row of cottages, is in reality the transmogrification of a medieval chapel of Saint Laurence, as you may see by a more attentive look—the high gables and the steepness of the roof are enough to mark these as no ordinary cottages. Several dead chalk quarries about the village present bleached and ghastly faces, and Upper Halling and Halling itself, down by the river, are quarry villages, with dismal industrial housing of the nineteenth century, some of it teetering on the quarry brinks. Nearer the river are ancient saltings, in which salt was produced by evaporation of the tidal waters of the river. That was probably in the days when the bishops of Rochester had a manor-house here, a manor-house of which nothing remains but a section of thirteenth-century lanceted wall in the churchyard. The manor was given to the bishops by King Egbert in the ninth century and was in use by them until the Reformation, as a country retreat from the thicker air of Rochester. They grew grapes here, too, in a vineyard by the river, and sent quantities of them to the table of Henry III. The climate was milder in those days, it is said, but it is possible to grow grapes in England in the open air even today. The chancel of the neighbouring church is also of the thirteenth century, and perhaps the nave too, but the nave was altered when aisles were added in the fifteenth century, and the whole church was considerably restored in 1885. The most interesting thing inside is the brass of a lady called Silvester, who married as her second husband the topographer William Lambarde (whom I have frequently quoted) and died in childbirth of her fifth child in 1587. She appears on her brass sitting up in bed, on a pile of cushions, her children round her, in a room with a bare tiled floor. Her children by Lambarde were christened Multon, Margaret, Gore, and Fane.

At Cuxton, the next village to the north, there was some kind of Roman building, and there is still a fine Tudor house of brick called Whorns Place, once famous for its gardens terraced

16. *An open stretch of the Way above Birling*

17. *A fine timbered house at Snodland*

18. *The Norman cathedral of Rochester*

19. *Hall of the Knights Templars at Strood*

down to the river. It was the home of the Leveson family and the carved arms of Sir John Leveson, quartered with those of his two wives, are still to be seen high in the gable facing the road.

Farther north the over-restored church of Cuxton, dug into the hillside, looks out on to a wide panorama in which the gravid, shining Medway cuts through a level land littered with pylons. Beyond the river and beyond the river-side Wouldham Marshes, the land rises again to Wouldham Downs, where we shall have to go to pick up the thread of the Pilgrims' Way once more. Upstream is the efficient but thin and spidery and far from beautiful Medway bridge carrying the M2, along which modern travellers who are not pilgrims to anywhere travel at speeds that leave them in ignorance of the countryside through which they pass and of the ancient city of Rochester, to which the river winds two miles to the north.

The river divides the suburb of Strood on the west bank from Rochester on the right. Eastwards, Rochester without pause becomes Chatham and Chatham with scarcely more division becomes Gillingham, and so here we have an extensive conurbation bordering a sharp loop of the Medway. That loop from ancient times has provided safe harbour, and across its narrows, since Rochester was the Roman town of Durobrivae, there has always been a bridge.

The pilgrims we follow, trudging along the highway, or cheerfully jogging on horseback, would pause at Strood to look at and perhaps to visit the preceptory of the Knights Templars (*plate* 19), the order founded for the protection of pilgrims in the Holy Land. The Templars were granted the manor of Strood Temple in the reign of Henry II and on it they raised a good building of stone. Such centres were for the management of the estates that contributed income to the order. Founded in France about 1119 by eight knights, the Company of the Knights Templars, or the Poor Knights of Christ and of the Temple of Solomon, quickly grew to be anything but poor. With many munificent gifts and bequests it became so very rich and so powerful that kings began to take fright of its power as much as at the same time they coveted its wealth. Charges of the unholiest kind were levelled against the knights by king and pope, and in particular by Philip IV of France, whose

PPW

life the Templars had once preserved, in Paris, by giving him asylum from a mob. Base plots and terrible tortures were brought to bear to make individual Templars confess to witch-craft and other crimes, and so to incriminate their order and give the king excuse to suppress it. The grand master, Jacques Molay, under extreme torture, made some such confession, and was sentenced to death; but on the scaffold, in front of Notre Dame in Paris, before he could be stopped by the executioner, Molay publicly retracted his confession and declared his and his order's innocence. It was too late. The order of the Knights Templars was forcibly dissolved in many countries throughout Europe, and in England among their other properties the preceptory at Strood was seized. The year was 1314.

Edward III gave the Templars' estate to Mary, Countess of Pembroke, who used it to found an order of Franciscan nuns, which continued here until the Reformation. Afterwards the estate and the buildings passed through several hands and the Templars' thirteenth-century house was altered and extended. Eventually, it became a simple farmhouse, until it was bought by C. Roach Smith, a well-known Kent antiquary, who preserved it as well as he could. It is now in the hands of the Department of the Environment, and stands in a little green plot beside the railway line, in an estate once the farm-lands of the Templars, and now given over to light industry. The Templars' thirteenth-century stone-built hall remains, on a vaulted undercroft, with Tudor brick additions at each end.

Pilgrims coming from London and from Halling would converge on the bridge and they would see across it a grouping of buildings that was as remarkable in their day as it is in ours. In the foreground stood the small and modest bridge chapel, built in 1387, where one gave thanks for the crossing of the river and a journey so far safely completed—the chapel is now the boardroom of the Bridge Wardens' Trust, which was founded in 1391 to manage the bridge. Near the chapel rose the huge and sullen walls of the Norman castle, erected by Bishop Gundulph, of hard Kentish ragstone, with an emphatic keep more than a hundred feet high soaring above the high walls of a bailey resting on the infrastructure of the Roman fortress. Beyond the castle walls the towers of the cathedral, also built by Gundulph, pricked into the air. Around about and in every nook and cranny the timber houses of the inhabitants presented pointed gables to the streets.

Few towns in England can claim to be older than Rochester. The Belgae, those part-Saxon, part-Celtic town-dwellers, had a town here before the Roman conquest, as may be deduced by the derivation of the name Durobrivae, which is not Roman but Celtic—it means the bridges of the stronghold—where there was a bridge there was also generally a settlement or town. The present name is post-Roman; it comes from a Saxon called Hrof, who had his fort or *caestre* here. The town was of sufficient importance by the year 600 to merit an enclosing wall, and within that wall in 604 Ethelbert, King of Kent, built the first cathedral to serve the see founded by Augustine.

The Norman castle is only the latest of a series of strongholds built at Rochester, beginning with the Celts and continuing through the Romans and the Saxons, and the story of Rochester is in part one of sanctity and of the cathedral and its monastery, and in part one of violence and military clashes and sieges. In the dark ages Rochester was beset in turn by Saxon kings and by the Danes, the latter being driven off in 888 by King Alfred. William the Conqueror gave the new fortress built for him by Gundulph to his bastard half-brother Odo, who held the titles of Bishop of Bayeux and Earl of Kent (he should be best remembered for his having ordered the making of the Bayeux tapestry). But Odo was ambitious and untrustworthy and for his treachery he spent six years in prison, from which he was released only by a death-bed pardon from William. Odo then joined his nephew Duke Robert, eldest son of the Conqueror, in a siege of Rochester castle. Robert should have inherited the throne, but he allowed his younger brother William Rufus to take it and failed to dislodge him. Robert had a second opportunity when William Rufus was 'accidentally' killed by that glancing arrow in the New Forest, but he was then out of the country and the throne was usurped by another of his younger brothers, who had hastily galloped from the forest to have himself crowned in Winchester as Henry I.

In the Barons' War, King John managed to capture Rochester castle, and was about to have the garrison hanged or skewered, as the custom frequently was, until he was dissuaded by some of his nobles—not on the score of humanity but because such an act was likely to be revenged on royal castles reduced by the rebellious barons and their supporter Louis, Dauphin of France. The dauphin in fact took Rochester the following year.

Today Rochester castle, like other such strongholds, is a dead bone of a tumultuous past, rising gauntly from a bailey set out as a flower garden. The interior of the keep is empty, but you may climb to the top for an enchanting view over the countryside and the town, and downwards, as it were at one's feet, of the roofs and pinnacles of the cathedral and its precinct, and the park, still called the Vines, where the monks had their vineyard.

The cathedral has an uninterrupted history of more than thirteen hundred years. How many times the Saxon church may have been rebuilt cannot be known with certainty, but it is improbable that the first church remained unaltered between 604 and 1066. The foundations of an apsed Saxon church are known to lie under the north-west corner of the present cathedral (*plate* 18), which was consecrated in 1130. Fifty years later part of this Norman cathedral was rebuilt, probably because it had been damaged in some of the fires to which medieval towns, with their jostling timber-built houses, were subject, their inflammable structures always likely to burst into sudden uncontrollable conflagration from some minor cause.

In the thirteenth century the monks, feeling rich from the contributions made by pilgrims to the shrine of William of Perth, and taken with the new pointed style that had begun at Saint Denis in the Île de France and at Sens, and which had been brought to Canterbury by William of Sens, began to rebuild their cathedral, starting, as was the custom in building churches, at the east end. But funds began to run out, Saint William presumably not living up to expectation as a source of income—the monks were constrained to melt into coin the silver shrine of Saint Paulinus. It was not enough for the work to continue and the church remains Norman in the nave, except at the east end, and Early English in the choir and chancel.

I would not have it otherwise. Rochester is not the only cathedral where such a conversion was never completed—Canterbury is another—and it is to be valued as one of those in which the Norman style is seen at its best and the transition to first pointed gothic is both a progress and a contrast.

The monks had good reason to believe or to hope for a continuing flow of money. True, the old shrines of Saint Paulinus, one of the early bishops, and of Ythamar the Englishman, so called because he was the first native-born bishop, were not as productive as may have been foreseen, but in addition, from 1201, they had the tomb of William of Perth, and he, more recent in time and more akin to the common man, could have been expected to be popular. William was a pious baker of the town of Perth in Scotland, who gave every tenth loaf to the poor. He decided to go to the Holy Land, fitted himself out as a pilgrim and took the required vows, and set off for the south. On the 20th of May in 1201 he presented himself at the door of the monastery attached to Rochester cathedral and asked for shelter for the night. In the morning he departed, to continue his long journey. He elected to go, it appears, not by the direct route along Watling Street to Canterbury, but south and by the ancient way, the Pilgrims' Way, which he would join at the foot of Bluebell Hill. He had scarcely got clear of the town when he was attacked and stabbed to death, by some person unknown, say some accounts, by his servant say others. The body of William was brought back to the cathedral, where it was given a decent burial by the monks. Before long the usual miracles began to occur that identified a man as a saint and people began to come in increasing numbers to pray at the tomb of this Scottish baker. A special shrine was built, as was customary on the north side of the church (in the north choir transept), and pilgrims came to it through the main north transept and along a passage up a short flight of steps, which, worn and irregular from the pressure of so many bony knees, are now covered with wooden treads. The story is thin, the canonization uncertain, and not obviously deserved for a man whose sole claim was the gift of loaves to the poor, and the shrine of William of Perth never became an important competitor with that of Saint Thomas at Canterbury. Nevertheless, his story

and his death and the miracles attributed to him did bring
many pilgrims to Rochester. Look around you, at the tall
arcades and the graceful pointed arches with their nail-head
ornament, the slender pillars, single and multiple, and the high
rib-vaulted roof: in these you see the true memorial of William
of Perth and of the belief of the monks and of pilgrims in his
sanctity.

There is a great deal in Rochester that is of deep interest to
archaeologists, to ecclesiastical and secular historians, to
students of architecture, and to readers of Dickens—Dickens
lived and worked here as a boy and spent his last years at Gads-
hill three miles along the Watling Street towards Canterbury.

Near the castle is Satis House, in which Queen Elizabeth I
lay for a night and expressed her opinion in the one word
'satis'; and near Satis House is the Old Hall, in which her father
Henry VIII met and saw for the first time the amiable but
unprepossessing girl who had been brought all the way from
Cleves to be his wife, that Anne whom we found, after her
divorce, living so happily at her house in Bletchingley. The
Bull Hotel or the Royal Victoria and Bull (unlikely conjunction!) has been an inn for more than four hundred years, and
may have been an inn in the later days of the pilgrimage.
The George Hotel stands on vaults of the early fourteenth
century and so reaches back farther than the Bull. Some
remains of the priory are to be seen, and lengths of the medieval
town wall, its lower courses Roman, while in the High Street
Saint Bartholomew's church, built of flint as the chapel of a
leper hospital founded in 1078 by the energetic Gundulph,
keeps its Norman apsed east end. For the rest, much is outside
our period, but in all periods Rochester is a place of delight,
or would be so if it could solve its serious traffic problem. Along
the High Street there is an enchanting medley of different
styles and periods, of houses with timber frame, of old houses
with classical or Georgian fronts, and such satisfactory buildings as the Guildhall and the Old Corn Exchange, whose over-
hanging clock cannot but remind one of the more elaborate
Guildhall clock at Guildford. The Old Corn Exchange was
built by Sir Cloudesley Shovel, mayor of Rochester and Admiral
of the Blue and of the Red in the Navy of William and Anne;

he died miserably, as many believe, at the hands of some atrocious hag when he was cast up helpless on a beach of the Isles of Scilly after the wreck of his flagship the *Association*—the woman wanted the jewelled rings from his fingers. The admiral's body was taken away to be buried in Westminster Abbey, while his flagship and other ships, after two hundred and sixty years in the sea, are now yielding to skin-divers the treasures that were appropriate to an admiral of that time. These things are for a different book than this, as are the many nooks and corners in Rochester connected with Dickens and the characters of *Great Expectations, The Pickwick Papers, Edwin Drood,* and others of his novels. We follow the pilgrims, and turn off in the town, skirting the cathedral, whose beautiful west doorway is famous for its ornament, and looks out on to a half-reclining catalpa tree. We go down Saint Margaret's Road, which shortly becomes Borstal Road—an association that need not detain us—and then passes under the M2 and divides into Wouldham Way and a road officially called Pilgrims' Way. Both of these are surfaced roads. The Pilgrim's Way runs, as we have frequently seen, along the mid slopes of the downs, and it has admirable views of the Medway valley and of the hills above Snodland and Halling on the far shore; but this is a section, some two miles only, that I would not follow of preference, if I had to choose at all, because the lower road, the Wouldham road, is the more interesting. It runs just above the marshes of the river side and passes Starkey Castle Farm which lies at the end of a short, straight drive between the road and the river. The author or reviser of the *Little Guide to Kent* must have received a dusty answer here to his request to look over the house, and it would not be surprising if such an answer were given today. People who live in picturesque old houses such as this must be constantly plagued, until their patience wears thin, by casual visitors knocking at the door. Starkey Castle, however, may be seen plainly from the road, as my picture shows (*plate* 20). It was not a castle but a fortified manor-house, the home of Humphrey Starkey, who was chief baron of the Exchequer in 1483 and was knighted by Richard III. The present farmhouse retains many of the features of the original house.

We come next to Wouldham, where the ferry that formerly worked here has been abandoned for years. Wouldham is another quarry village, with glum cottages and terrace houses for the men who worked in the vast chalk-pits between here and Burham and for the cement factories that converted what was dug out. Pits and factories on the east bank died when the railway company decided to run its line on the west bank of the Medway.

Wouldham is mentioned as early as 751 in a charter of King Ethelbert, and possibly there was a church here at that time. A new church was built in 1058, eight years before the Conquest, and this in turn was rebuilt in the late Norman and Early English periods. Those pilgrims who crossed the ferry from Halling would have visited Wouldham church and might have witnessed a strange and comic scene—the priest, wielding a rod, chasing an adulterer round the churchyard and whacking him as often as he could—this punishment is recorded in 1325 and again in 1348. In the churchyard is the grave of Walter Burke, purser of the *Victory*, who held the dying Nelson in his arms; Burke's cottage in Wouldham was dismantled between the wars and was taken away for re-erection in Sussex.

At Burham, in the low-lying land by the river, the Romans had an underground chamber in a position that suggests a ferry over to Holborough. The building has been described as a temple to Mithras, and alternatively as no more than a store-house. Nothing of it is to be seen today.

Just as obviously postulating a river-crossing is the site of the old church at Burham. The church is now abandoned and derelict but it is still roofed; entry through the graveyard is hindered by breast-high weeds that hide the tombstones. In the echoing spaces of the roof birds flutter and call, desperately seeking a way out—why do they never remember where they got in? The Normans built this church as near the river as they could find ground firm enough to support it, and surely there must have been a damp little village around it then. It welcomed travellers coming by the ferry from Snodland, that sometime village turned into industrial town, whose factories and tall chimneys seem only a short stone's throw distant. Burham, presenting its fifteenth-century west tower towards the river, embodies thirteenth-century work and some re-windowing in the Perpendicular period. Travellers crossing the muddy river or the doubtful ford came by it and passed on towards the east to climb the hundred feet or so up the down to the Pilgrims' Way, where now we find the 'new' church and the 'new' village of Burham. We are once more on the main line of the Old Road, the road that became the Pilgrims' Way, and here we complete the Rochester diversion and enter upon a new chapter.

13 *Burham to Charing*

16 MILES

This, the penultimate of our stages along the Pilgrims' Way, runs in a direction generally south-east, parallel with the A20, whose traffic is often in sight and distantly heard. We pass by a string of villages, some of which are close to the Way, and others lower down in the valley, beads along the thread of the main road. There is one large town, Maidstone, which was a centre of the archbishops of Canterbury, with an important palace and monasteries, which would have been an attraction for our pilgrims, bringing them down for a night or two from the bleak and ancient path. But the palace of the archbishops at Maidstone is only one of the latest of a series of antiquities along this stage of the Way, a series surviving from several periods in which the Old Road was the principal highway between east and west. Standing-stones and ruined dolmens signal the passage of men of the stone age, of the bronze age, and of the iron age, Roman or Romano-British sites have been uncovered where villas or other buildings once stood, and in places isolated objects have been found after lying for eighteen or nineteen hundred years since they were lost or cast away by their former owners. There are legends, some with a basis of fact, concerning the battles of the Celts against the Saxons, of the Saxons against the Danes, of the clash of arms and the cries of violent men and dying men. And along the Way there were the monasteries and churches, palaces and manors, many of which flourished from a time before the death of Thomas Becket.

The argument that the crossing of the Medway from Snodland to Burham was the original crossing of the ancients is supported by the fact that it is undeniably the shortest practicable route between the megalithic structures of Coldrum and Addington west of the river and those of Kit's Coty and the Countless Stones on the east side. That there was some special relation between these monuments and their sites that we do not know and probably never shall know may easily be believed, and if that is believed then one must admit the importance of communication between the two groups across the river. I think it certain that what is to be seen today in these two places is only a part, and perhaps a minor part, of what there once was. I do not argue that there was here in Kent an equivalent of Stonehenge or of Avebury; those two great monuments were evidently national and perhaps international centres. Everywhere a megalithic monument is to be found it is probable that there were once many more, which through the centuries have fallen to tomb-robbers breaking in for gold and silver and whatever else of value was to be found beside the bones or the ashes of the dead; or to farmers anxious to clear hindrances from their lands; or to builders or road-makers who regarded the ancient structures as no more than handy quarries. Where circumstances have combined to preserve them, circumstances such as ignorance, the awe of later generations and of superstitions and legends, or inaccessibility, or simply the sheer labour necessary for their destruction, megalithic monuments have survived in large numbers. At Carnac in Brittany there are long lines of stone rows preserved either from superstition or simply because there was no profit in removing them, and at Carrowmore in Ireland, below Knocknarea, some twenty dolmens have survived in an area known to have had at least sixty. A cairn on top of Knocknarea illustrates another force for survival, the difficulty of taking down such a structure, of thousands of tons of stones, without danger and without a large force of labourers and a parallel supply of money. Here by the Medway there were so many of the huge sarsen stones scattered about the landscape, lying like sheep in the fields, that the district became known generally as Greywethers. Sarsen stones occur naturally in the Reading Beds and in the greensand and it cannot certainly be said of any group of them that they were once part of a megalithic construction, just as it cannot be said with certainty that they were not, since ancient man generally employed such stones as he found there, without chiselling the surface or altering the shape.

Where men of the stone ages and of the ages of metal chose to live and to die the Romans or their Romanized dependent peoples also found genial country. There are so many sites of

Roman buildings or finds of Roman goods within reach of this stage of the Old Road that a connection with that road must be accepted. Farms and villas must have been linked with the road by lanes and drives, exactly as the case is with roads and farms today. There was, indeed, such traffic along the Old Road between Burham and Canterbury that that road has never been lost and it may today be followed with ease and with little doubt, except for the interruptions of enclosed parks.

The road from Snodland ferry through the hamlet of Burham is firmly marked. It crosses the soggy marshland in the shortest possible distance, that is to say in a straight line. This suggests to me that under the modern surface there must be an ancient causeway running from the river bank and past the old church. As it approaches the higher land the road turns southwards so as not to affront the slope in too steep a gradient. It climbs up above the hamlet of Eccles, whose name suggests a church; here there was a palatial Roman villa with wall-paintings and a bath. Above the hamlet the side of the downs has been dug out, and the lower land too, in huge yawning chalk-pits, long since dead and disused, with the old houses of Great Culand and Little Culand on their margins. At 150 feet we join the Pilgrims' Way coming from Rochester, and pass the site of the Coffin Stone, a large recumbent stone that has gathered hazy and uncertain legends about it. Near it stood a chapel of Saint Stephen, which we shall shortly mention again. The road comes to a junction from which depart two other roads and two footpaths. The road to the south leads past the Countless Stones and comes in a mile and a half to Aylesford, where, in a sandpit next to the church, a boy's discovery of some bronze objects led to the uncovering by Sir Arthur Evans in 1890 of an iron-age urn-field cemetery and a hitherto little-known late Celtic culture in Britain.

In this neighbourhood, that is around Aylesford and its ford over the Medway, battles were fought between Briton and Saxon, between Saxon and Dane. Here Hengist and Horsa, invited into this country by the British king Vortigern or Vortimer to assist him as mercenaries, saw their chance and took it to gain the Kingdom of Kent. At Aegelsthrep, that is Aylesford, in 455 AD they defeated the Britains but Horsa was killed in the fight. Hengist took his prize and perhaps extended his conquest far to the west, for his name is found in Hengistbury Head near Bournemouth.

Whether Hengist and Horsa, the stallion and the horse, ever existed historians doubt, but that there was a battle one day or another, and that the Saxons obtained the Kingdom of Kent, is sure enough. Those who would like to believe in these Saxons with the queer names point to Hengistbury and also the hamlet of Horsted, where the slain Horsa is said to have been buried, and to Kit's Coty House, which some early chroniclers ascribed to the memory of Catigern, brother of Vortigern, who was also killed in the battle. What is clear is that any invader into north Kent would have to fight for, and the native ruler would have to defend, the ford in the Medway at Aylesford, and any invader who got past it and was subsequently defeated would have to fall back to it in order to escape annihilation on the west bank of the river. Alfred in 893 chased the Danes across the ford and into Thanet, and in 1016 Edmund Ironside defeated a Danish force at Otford and drove it into flight over the river and through the streets of the village. The crossing of the Medway here was also, as I have already said, convenient for certain of the pilgrims, in particular for those coming from the nunnery of West Malling. There was a bridge here at an early date, and this would have given Aylesford an attraction only second to that of Rochester.

The present bridge is not the first bridge, but it is medieval and after the manner of medieval bridges it is both humped and narrow, so narrow that it is not wide enough for two cars at once. The village, with its bridge and with the tower of the church rising behind, above sharply gabled roofs of red tiles, makes a sentimentally pretty picture that in one composition or another has appeared in all sorts of guises—in magazines and in guide-books, on calendars, and so forth, and I make no apology for including it also in this book (*plate* 22), for it retains its charm, however familiar. The changing light, the gleam of the water, the colour of stone, timber, and leaf, and the protean sky make Aylesford perennially attractive.

In the narrow village streets and the sloping triangular

place (for it is not a green and certainly not a square) old houses of timber frame nod their gables above advancing jetties. The Old George, dated 1714, but beneath its plaster a jettied house of at least a century earlier, is no longer an inn. It guards the entrance to the bridge, facing another old timbered house. The Little Gem tearoom claims the date 1106—but that is too ambitious. Westwards the village street climbs round a bend in front of the Chequers up to the high knoll on which the church is set. The church was built originally by the Normans very likely in place of a Saxon one (which one may assume existed because the village was of such account in Saxon times), but only the lower part of the tower remains from the Norman church; the rest is of the fourteenth and fifteenth centuries. The plan is unusual, in this part of the country at least, though familiar enough in the Welsh valley of the Clwyd. The interior is divided down the middle by arcades, fifteenth-century in the nave and fourteenth-century in the chancel. The effect is that of a double church, of two equal naves and chancels side by side. I suppose that this schizophrenic pattern had some advantages, if only in the reduction of the number of columns compared with an ordinary aisled church, and the consequent effect of spaciousness; but it must also have had disadvantages.

At the east end of the church there are highly interesting monuments. The vaunting, grandiloquent memorial of the Banks family in the north-east corner dates from the 1690s and commemorates a family who lived at the Friars, a converted Carmelite monastery. Two mourning characters, stock figures, stand either side of a large urn, against a thickly draped sheet that in itself expresses, in repeated folds and drapes and in its knotted apex, the restlessness of the baroque mood. South of the Banks monument stands the tomb of the Culpepers or Cole-peppers, an old Kentish family. Sir Thomas Culpeper, who died in 1604, was a great man in these parts. He lies in plate armour with his wife Margaret beside him on a tomb-chest on which appear his children and the proud blazonry of his arms. Margaret wears a remarkable head-dress (*plate* 23), pleated and gauffred into the form of a scallop shell. I am undecided whether this recall of the old symbol of pilgrimage is accidental or deliberate, a quirk of fashion. This head-dress must have been uncomfortable to wear, in constant danger or disarray, or even of collapse, if it were not generously stiffened with wire or bone; it could not have been everyday wear. Ladies of the time, and of other times, on such funeral monuments as this, liked to face their maker in their best clothes, doing to God an honour and stateliness that they put on only for their most important occasions. Sir Thomas and his lady lived at Preston Hall, a house now replaced by another, which has become a sanatorium. The funeral armour hanging in the church belonged to the Culpeper and Banks families, with some additional pieces for Heneage Finch, one of three of that name whose family held the earldoms of Aylesford, Winchelsea, and Nottingham; we have met them before, at Albury.

The best bib and tucker and the finest armour are seen again in a brass on the floor beside the Culpeper tomb. It was engraved for John Cossington or Cosenton, who died in 1426. Sir John appears in good plate armour with circular shoulder pauldrons and at his side is slung a fine two-handed sword, while his feet rest on a lion, symbol of strength and ferocity. Sarah his wife wears a simple canopied head-dress, perhaps a little *démodé* in her time, as country women would be likely to be, even so near to the capital, and she has on a long loose gown with drooping over-full sleeves and many folds about the feet; she could never have walked in that gown without constantly practising that feminine grace of lifting the hem clear of her steps. Sir John's house, Cossington, lies up towards the Pilgrims' Way, set in a glen in orchard country. His ancestor, Sir Stephen de Cosenton, founded that free chapel of Saint Stephen that we have already noticed as having once stood near the Coffn Stone.

Outside the church, at the east end, are three worn wedge-shaped coffin lids bearing defaced floriated crosses. Such stones are not uncommon. Nearly always of the twelfth or thirteenth century, they are mostly anonymous, so that one may attribute these examples according to fancy: to the graves of pilgrims (improbable), of crusaders (unlikely), of Carmelite monks of the nearby monastery (possible), or of vicars of this church (probable).

From the raised terrace of the church you may see to the

west a grey building that might, at this distance, be a factory. It is a monastery of Carmelite friars, indeed the mother house, the first of this order in Europe. Here on Christmas Day in the year 1240 a shivering little group of hermits led by Saint Simon Stock, brought from Mount Carmel in the Holy Land by the cruasding Baron Richard de Grey of Codnor, entered into the land and the manor provided for them by de Grey. Here they evolved into an order of mendicant friars known as Carmelites from their original home, or as Whitefriars from their whitish habits. Here they built up their friary and their church and had a guest-house where pilgrims were welcome and were sent on their way comforted and rejoicing; and from here the friars sent out small bands to found daughter houses.

The friary was dissolved by Henry VIII in 1538, its surrender being received by Richard Ingworth, Suffragan Bishop of Dover, who wrote to the king's minister, Thomas Cromwell: 'My synguler goode lorde in my umble man pleseth you to understande that I have receyved the house of the whyte fryers in Aylysforde into the Kings hands.' Together with Boxley Abbey and the nunnery of West Malling, the Carmelite friary was granted to Sir Thomas Wyatt of Allington Castle, poet, statesman, and reputedly, in his younger days, lover of Anne Boleyn before the desires of Henry VIII fell upon her. Had this reputation been known to Henry Sir Thomas would have received the axe (as he very nearly did) and not the property of dissolved religious houses. He died in 1542, having enjoyed his new properties for only four years. His son, another Sir Thomas, in 1554 joined a Protestant revolt against the proposed marriage of the Catholic Queen Mary of England to Philip of Spain, and for his pains he lost his head. On the scaffold he publicly proclaimed that the Princess Elizabeth, Mary's half-sister, had not, contrary to the suspicions of Mary, been privy to the rising.

The former friary thereafter passed through various hands, including those of the Banks family, whose exuberant monument we have seen in the church. In March 1688 Pepys made a journey into Kent and took it into his head to call on Sir Joseph Banks, but found him not at home. He consoled himself by buying in Maidstone a dish of fresh fish, which he

20. *Starkey Castle Farm, once a fifteenth-century chapel*

21. *A surfaced part of the Way near Detling*

22. *Aylesford village and medieval bridge*

23. *The scallop in costume on the Culpeper tomb in Aylesford church*

ordered to be sent to himself at the Bell Inn. He took the opportunity of being in the district to visit an 'old Saxon monument', which he believed commemorated a king: it was Kit's Coty House.

The friary, after neglect of many years and a disastrous fire in 1930, was bought back by the former owners, the Order of Carmelites, and the friars entered again into their ancient house on All Saints Day in 1949. There was a great deal of restoration to be done, and it has been done, with the addition of some modern buildings. In the friary have been gathered many old and modern works of art in sculpture, painting, and stained glass: but go and see for yourself, for the Friars, as it is now called, somewhat unsatisfactorily (why not 'the Friary'?), is frequently open to visitors. In 1951 the body of Saint Simon Stock, who died at Bordeaux in 1265, was brought back to the house he had founded, and it now lies in a shrine of modern, and to me at least repellent, design in a special reliquary chapel. The ancient guest-house, the Pilgrims' Hall, was restored and over the door was set a statue of Thomas Becket.

The Friars is open to visitors of any faith, as worshippers or simply as tourists. It is a house that travellers on the Pilgrims' Way should see, for its modern presentation of the monasteries that lay like a string of jewels along the line of the Way and along other pilgrim routes, and on which pilgrims depended for rest and food, for they could not have carried a lot of money with them. The suppression of the monasteries was the decisive factor in the cessation of pilgrimage in England, with the destruction of the shrines to which the pilgrims directed their steps.

The re-establishment of the Carmelites at Aylesford has been followed by an event that deserves the hackneyed description of an ironic twist of fate. We have seen that at the Dissolution Sir Thomas Wyatt of Allington Castle received the friary from Henry VIII. In 1951 the Carmelites, needing another house to extend their activities, were able to buy the castle, to take over the home of the man who had taken over their friary four hundred years earlier. Allington Castle (*plate* 25), which is also open to the public, is now a retreat or rest-house, in which persons of any faith may find a period of peace and calm for as long as they need to stay.

QPW

Allington stands in a loop of the Medway north of Aylesford, on a site that has been occupied since the stone age. The first castle here was built in the reign of Stephen, when strife was frequent and landowners felt the need to protect themselves behind strong fortifications. Thomas Becket would have known the castle, just as he would have known of the church and village of Aylesford, and he may have stayed at one or the other. But the castle was adulterine, which is to say that it had been built and fortified without licence of the king. Henry II, with a firmer grasp of the realm than his predecessor Stephen had had, demolished these adulterine castles; Allington fell to the pick and the axe in 1174. In 1281 Edward I granted a licence to crenellate, that is to fortify, the house at Allington in a document that survives in the Public Record Office; it was granted to *'nostro Stephano de Pencester et Margarete uxori eius'*, that is, to Stephen of Penchester and his wife, and the work went forward at once. The castle built then, in 1282, forms part of the present courtyard structure. The owners of Allington before and after the Wyatts do not concern us, until we come to Martin Conway, who bought the castle in 1905 and then spent years and a great deal of money in restoring it and in providing for it a collection of notable works of religious art, which he brought from many parts of the world and which, in many instances, he cemented into the walls so that in effect they became part of the castle. As the castle guide-book points out, Lord Conway, though not a Catholic, could have served the present purpose of the castle no better than if he had foreseen what it was to be and had worked intentionally towards that end.

The castle today stands complete and bright among lawns and gardens (*plate 25*). It has a wonderful romantic air, that touch of unreality, of the stage that one sees in the newly washed façades of town buildings. In the courtyard, reached through an impressive gatehouse, a number of small brown pigeons strut and coo; they are of a breed said to have been introduced here by the poet Sir Thomas Wyatt and to have been brought, like the original Carmelites, from the Near East.

The Pilgrims' Way is reached once more from Aylesford by going along Wood Road, which climbs steadily and passes on the right the grove of trees in the shade of which lie the Countless Stones (*plate* 24). The adjective is a challenge and I know of no one who comes here who does not try to number them, with no more likely success than the baker who is said to have attempted it by putting a loaf on each stone to make sure he missed none and counted none twice; he might have succeeded had not the Devil frustrated him. The difficulties arise from the stones, a collection of large sarsens, lying one over the other in a tumbled heap, so that one cannot see clearly which end of a stone belongs to which. The stones are the ruins of a collapsed burial chamber, a dolmen. From the year 2000 BC or thereabouts this dolmen remained intact, until in 1690 it was destroyed by a farmer who supposed that he would make money by selling the stones as road metal; but either he had no customers or he had no further energy, and the stones remain now as he left them, with no evidence to show how they might originally have been arranged.

North of the Countless Stones, Wood Road comes to the junction of roads and paths we have already seen and directly opposite Wood Road a path climbs through a narrow tunnel of bushes and trees to Kit's Coty House, another neolithic dolmen and arguably the best-known dolmen in this country. Its fame does not come from its intrinsic interest, for it is a simple structure with a tripod of three stones supporting a cover stone. The renown of Kit's Coty comes from its intriguing name. Who was Kit and what does 'coty' mean (which seems equivalent to the Cornish 'quoit')? We can put at once out of mind the tradition that this Kit was Vortigern's brother Catigern, for the monument is two or three times as old as the time of the legendary battle in which Hengist gained the Kingdom of Kent. Kit has been said alternatively to have been a shepherd who sheltered under this convenient roof, 'coty' meaning the same as 'cote', a word we still use in 'pigeon-cote'. On the other hand 'coty' has been declared the same as Welsh *coed*, a wood, and that the name of Kit's Coty means 'the house in the wood'. There is no wood around Kit's Coty today, though there are plenty of trees higher up the hill and elsewhere. Instead of trees, what surrounds the megalith now is the Department of the Environment's sharp iron fence, put up to keep the monument from harm by the mindless louts we breed too numerously and treat too leniently, who would derive pleasure from pushing over such a structure as Kit's Coty. What is of interest about this dolmen is that in its present form it could not have served as a burial chamber, for the three uprights make, in plan, a letter H, with the cap set centrally upon them. It is supposed that the structure is only a part of a larger stone chamber, and that the whole thing, as was usual with dolmens, was covered over by a large long barrow, high at the east end and sloping down to the west.

Such a barrow answers the frequent question of how dolmens were erected. The method would be the same as that used by the ancient Egyptians to erect obelisks. The stones were simply dragged up the slope of the mound and tipped into position, and there were propped with earth until the great stone of the roof was also dragged up and laid upon them. The Egyptians cleared their mound away to leave an obelisk standing free. The megalith builders made the mound part of the monument.

The stones of Kit's Coty are sarsens, formations of the Reading Beds, hardened by pressure and natural cements, and exposed to the surface by erosion. Neolithic men in this part of Kent did not have to look far for their stones. Any number of them may be found along this length of the Way and sometimes it is a question whether they have formed parts of megalithic monuments—a circle or an avenue—or whether they lie merely where they have been dragged by farmers clearing their fields of these massive hindrances to the plough.

What great man of his time, what prince or princely family, what priest, perhaps, lay in Kit's Coty no one can now know, and such legends as there are help little; but the information may be somewhere, garbled and changed by the centuries, in that delightful name of Kit's Coty (I think we should drop the 'house'). I remember that in county Cork in Ireland there is a huge dolmen, far bigger than Kit's Coty, though not so high, that is called Leabacailigh, 'the bed of the old woman'. Now 'Leabacailigh' is Gaelic, which was not spoken in Ireland until centuries after that dolmen was erected, but that it meant something sensible, and that it might have been no more than a translation from an older tongue, seems to have been confirmed by the discovery on excavation a few years ago that the dolmen was indeed the grave of an old woman. That discovery emphasized for me the belief that legends, old wives' tales, traditions, and place-names may embody the distant past, a past buried under millennia of years gone by and speaking to us, if only we could understand, through how many shocks and revolutions of language, how many ethnic changes, how many invasions and conquests?

There is another, I think minor, item of interest about Kit's Coty and other such megaliths: they stand generally in positions commanding wide prospects, as though the people buried under those huge stones might want to rise again some sunny day and take time to admire the beauty of the world, or at least of a large piece of it. This is not simply because these megaliths are set on hills; not all positions on a hill or a hillside enjoy notable views. If you think this argument specious, why then, stand by Kit's Coty and look out over the Weald with its beautiful streams and its valleys, its wooded hills and hazy distances, and consider whether after death you too might not sometimes want to come to life just to look at such a view.

We return down the leafy tunnel of the lane to the road junction. The continuation of the Pilgrims' Way, if we can think of such a name here instead of the Old Road of ancient man, the continuation, that is to say, is not any of the surfaced roads but a lane going south-east between them. It leaves to one side the Lower Bell, which is a pub ancient enough, and possibly the Bell to which Pepys sent his parcel of fish (though it must be said here that there was and is a Bell in Maidstone), it leaves aside the site of a Roman building and the line of a Roman road towards Bluebell Hill, and comes to the main Maidstone road, the A229. The Way crosses this and continues on the far side as a lane, signposted the Pilgrims' Way, among hawthorns and field maples. A short way along this lane, among the bushes on the left side, the White Horse Stone stands half-concealed and easily passed by, on the edge of a ploughed field. It is sometimes called the Western Sphinx, but this name is unlikely to have any considerable antiquity—it sounds more like the invention of a country gentleman, or of an amateur country archaeologist, in the early nineteenth century, when things Egyptian were fashionable. The name of the White Horse Stone is better. The stone is a large slab, roughly rectangular and about eight feet long and five feet high, standing on edge. It has holes near the two upper corners, and with a generous exercise of imagination one may see one of these holes as an eye in the vague shape of a horse's head. A number of other smaller sarsen boulders or slabs lie around, some of them at the foot of the White Horse. The White Horse Stone is reputed to be part of another dolmen, possibly having some connection with yet another vanished dolmen to the north, known as 'Smythe's megalith' from the archaeologist who examined it in 1823, and who found within it a chamber seven feet long containing human remains. Another White Horse Stone, lower down the hill, was removed in that same year. As for the white horse and what association there might be, one can only say that the horse was a frequent symbol of the iron age, and today it finds a place in the arms of Kent.

The lane continues for about a mile below the wooded scarps of Boarley Scrubs and Boarley Warren, and becomes a surfaced lane where the road from Boxley Abbey comes up out of Maidstone. The abbey lies nearly a mile south of the Way and two miles farther south rises the important town of Maidstone, where many pilgrims would plan to stop for a night or for longer.

Of Boxley Abbey there remain only ruins, except for a great barn, 186 feet long, that was in its day a guest-house able to accommodate a crowd of visitors. The present dwelling-house, originally Tudor, was built by the Wyatts after the dissolution of the monastery. Boxley was a Cistercian house founded in 1146 by William of Ipres, Earl of Kent, a man of evil reputation who hoped by this good deed to have absolution for his sins. Cistercian Boxley was only the second house of its order, after Waverley in Surrey, in England. The abbot was one of those who hastily interred the body of Thomas Becket in the crypt of Canterbury cathedral. At Boxley, within a long perimeter wall enclosing fifteen acres or more, rose a great church and spacious monastic quarters that one might suppose must have housed a swarm of religious, yet in 1381 Boxley boasted only eighteen monks, and at the dissolution in 1538 the abbot and his monks numbered only ten together. All of these received pensions from the State in return for their yielding their house to the king.

The former monastery became a private house, built by Sir Thomas Wyatt, and a private house it still is, with its drive passing some small cottages and entering the grounds through a ruined arch. The monastic church, with walls still standing to head height, encloses a pretty garden, and recalls the complaint of Henry VIII's commissioners that the monks spent too much of their time and of their income on the cultivation of gilly-flowers and roses. The best-preserved part of the monastery is the great barn, which was in the thirteenth and fourteenth centuries the monastery guest-house; its grey walls and vast expanse of tiled roof may be seen from the M20.

Whatever doubts authorities and historians may have expressed concerning the use of the Old Road in the middle ages by pilgrims going to or coming from Canterbury, in the very extent of the guest-house at Boxley there is circumstantial evidence that pilgrims did come and go past Boxley, that travellers were expected to come and did come to Boxley Abbey, and that the monks took trouble to attract them and to accommodate them. It is true that kings and princes came here, including Edward II, with their trains, but such visits were infrequent and not essentially of importance. It was the general and generous public that the monks wished to draw to them. The abbeys of the middle ages were as anxious to attract attention as the owners of great houses in our day and for the same reason—income—and Boxley had two things that were of potent interest to all who came by the Way to pause at Boxley. They were the marvellous image of the child Saint Rumbold and the even more marvellous crucifix from which the abbey took its name of the Abbatia Santa Crucis de Gracias, the Abbey of the Holy Rood of Grace.

Saint Rumbold was a legendary child of odious precocity, son of a pagan king of Northumberland and his Christian wife. The moment he emerged from his mother's womb he three times declared himself a Christian—and in Latin, too, which no doubt was the tongue one would naturally expect in such a case. During the next three days he instructed the wisest of the district in the tenets of the true faith, and then, having exhausted his purpose, incontinently died. At Boxley a statue of Rumbold was erected, a thing of no great size, for the original of it, remember, was a small child. This statue could be lifted, it was claimed, only by the pure and good, and the lifting of it was a preliminary condition to be satisfied by those who wished to go on to kneel before the Rood of Grace. Whether an applicant might lift it or not depended upon the generosity of his alms, for a monk stood by controlling some kind of hidden catch or spring, and according to what was given he would surreptitiously make the statue immovable or allow it to be lifted. 'In so much, as many time it mooved more laughter than devotion,' says Lambarde, 'to beholde a great lubber to lift at that in vaine, which a young boy (or wench) had easily taken up before him. I omit, that chaste Virgins, and honest married matrones, went oftentimes away with blushing faces, leaving (without cause) in the mindes of the lookers on, great suspicion of uncleane life, and wanton behaviour.' Before they came to try their strength and their chastity with Saint Rumbold visitors had to confess and to be shriven, 'And therefore the matter was so handled, that without trebel oblation (that is to say) first to the Confessour, and then to Sainct Rumwald, and lastly to the Gracious Roode, the poore Pilgrimes could not assure themselves of any good, gained by all their labour.'

The rood came to Boxley by what the monks believed to be miraculous intervention. An ingenious carpenter of this country, taken prisoner in the wars in France, enlivened his captivity by constructing a crucifix with a mechanical figure of Christ. The carpenter, freed from his imprisonment, hoped to sell his rood to some church or monastery, and putting it on a horse he set out as though towards London; but as he rested and drank in an inn his horse, with the statue tied on its back, ran away and did not stop until it came to and entered into the abbey of Boxley, where it trotted into the church. The carpenter, coming after his own, also came into the church, where he found the monks staring with wonder at the horse's burden. The carpenter would have led the horse away, but he found that it would not do his bidding, no more could it be moved by force; it was in short as immovable as was the figure of Saint Rumbold for the ungenerous. There was nothing to be done by the carpenter but to make as good a deal as he could with the monks in exchange for the rood and to take his horse away (which, once the rood was removed, came willingly). Thenceforward the marvellous rood stayed in the church and earned a great reputation among pilgrims in all parts of the country.

The management of the rood was the same as for the statue of Saint Rumbold. The rood was of 'such exquisite arte and excellencie', says Lambarde again, 'that it not onely matched in comelynesse and due proportion of the artes the best of the common sort: but in straunge motion, variety of gesture, and nimbleness of joints, passed al other that before had been seene: the same being able to bow down and lifte up, to shake and stirre the handes and feete, to nod the head, to rolle the eies, to wag the chaps, to bende the browes, and finally to represent to the eie, both the proper motion of each member of the body, and also a liveley, expresse, and significant shew of a well contented or displeased mynde: byting the lippe, and gathering a frowning froward, and disdainful face, when it would pretend offence: and showing a most milde, amyable, and smyling cheere and countenaunce when it would seeme to be well pleased.' The monks could so manage the figure that it was 'froward and disdainful' when the offering was insufficient, and it was pleased when the monks considered that what was given was satisfactory.

The artifice of the Rood of Grace did not escape the commissioner of Henry VIII. If the monks could be faulted for no more than their love of gillyflowers and roses, here was something more substantially wicked and superstitious. He seized the rood and exhibited it in the market-place of Maidstone, demonstrating inside it 'certayn engyns of old wyer with olde roten stykkes', by means of which the monks practised their subtleties. The rood was then taken to London for another exhibition of the foolishness of superstition and the ingenuity of the old carpenter, and then it was ceremoniously broken in pieces and burnt at Paul's Cross.

The town of Maidstone, set where the little river Len falls into the Medway, and on the Roman road from Rochester to the south and the south-east, existed in the days of the Saxons, but came into importance after the Conquest. Henry VIII committed the custody of the standard weights and measures to this town, and thereby tacitly designated it as the county town of Kent, which it has been ever since. A priest's house by the river may have been the house given by the rector to the Archbishop of Canterbury in 1205. It served until the fourteenth century, when Archbishop Ufford began a new manor-house or palace, which was completed by Archbishop Simon Islip. This palace still stands, behind an early seventeenth-century front, complete with strongly buttressed dungeons beside the river. The dungeons undoubtedly found a use from time to time, for archbishops and bishops of the middle ages were secular lords and nobles as well as spiritual leaders of the Church. One of the prisoners in the dungeons may have been John Ball, the mad priest of Kent, who preached social equality, that fantasy of priests and politicians. Three times imprisoned for his opinions, he was on one occasion rescued by the rebel Wat Tyler and his men. It was Ball who led a mob into the Tower of London to capture Simon Sudbury, Archbishop of Canterbury, whom the mob beheaded because he had opposed them. That was in 1381.

The palace of the archbishops, with the dungeons, the old Norman priest's house, the offices and stables of the palace, the buildings of a college of secular priests completed in 1397, and the fine Perpendicular church of All Saints begun in 1395 on the site of a Norman church, all these together form a group of grey, hoary, antique buildings of stone such as you will not easily equal in any other English town. All, or nearly all, are still in use. The palace itself is used by the municipality, the stables facing it contain a fascinating collection or museum of horse carriages, the College of Priests now contains a music school, and the gatehouse is used by the office of weights and measures.

The church of All Saints, of course, continues as a church, its noble west tower of the Kentish pattern, with a distinct stair turret, rising above the old buildings next to it—once it rose more spectacularly, for it had a spire until 1731, when lightning struck it and caused a fire. The broad interior is open, with a fine sense of space. In the church is the table tomb of John Wotton, who was the first master of the college and died in

1417. In the sedilia beside the tomb a wall-painting has survived, showing the presentation of Thomas Becket to the Virgin, a reminder not only of the pilgrimage but also of the dedication of the former church to Saint Mary. A brass indent marks the grave of Richard Woodville, forebear of Elizabeth Woodville, who secretly married Edward IV. Her brother, Earl Rivers, a notable soldier and a writer of excellent English, was a friend and patron of William Caxton. On his return from pilgrimage in Italy in 1476 Rivers handed the printer his own translation of a book that Caxton published in the following year as *Dictes and Sayengis of the Philosophers*; it was the first book to be printed in this country. Rivers chose the wrong side in the dynastic wars of the last quarter of the fifteenth century and was beheaded by order of Richard III. The Woodvilles lived at Mote House, east of the town; rebuilt in the eighteenth century, it is now a Cheshire Home, beside a large, artificial lake in the course of the Len, a lake popular with yachtsmen.

Travellers and pilgrims passing through Maidstone would, if they were not well off, seek out the Hospital of the Newark, or New Work, which was founded about 1260 as a hostel for travellers and at the same time as an almshouse for ten poor parishioners of the archbishop. The chapel of the hostel remains, enlarged in 1836 by the addition of transepts and a new west end, and rededicated as the church of Saint Peter and Saint Paul.

There are many ancient houses in Maidstone and a number of old inns such as the timber-framed Sun. They stand in a medley of timber houses, classical façades, and utterly modern structures. The streets are always busy and crowded with people, confirming that the county town of Kent is a prosperous place.

The road back to the Pilgrims' Way lies over Penenden Heath, now a park but for centuries in the dark ages and the middle ages the moot or meeting-place of the shire. Here in 1075 or 1076 the famous inquiry or trial took place in which Archbishop Lanfranc of Canterbury sought to recover lands and manors illegally appropriated by Bishop Odo of Bayeux, half-brother of the Conqueror no less. Lanfranc brought various witnesses, including the aged Bishop Aethelric of Selsey, who was knowledgeable on the subject of Saxon law and was brought across country in a wagon. Lanfranc won his case all right, to the disgust and fury of the reprehensible Odo.

The lane from Penenden to the north passes over the M20 motorway and comes to Boxley, a tiny village under the downs, which here, covered with trees along the north horizon, have the textured appearance of a loosely knitted scarf. The village of Boxley is a mile from Boxley Abbey, with no more connection between village and abbey than a footpath that starts behind an old pub, the King's Arms, a path along which the Cistercian monks must have toiled on occasions, climbing 120 feet along the chalk slopes. The black and white front of the pub looks along a rectangular green that is like a verdant carpet to the churchyard gate. Along one side, behind a wall, rise the trees of the estate of Boxley House, and on the other is an old farm-house with its barns. The far end of the green is overlooked by the battlemented, high-buttressed church tower, which was built for two thirds of its height in the fourteenth century and for the rest, with the battlements, in the fifteenth century. Above the battlements you can just see the north-east stair turret, rising in the Kentish fashion above the tower roof. A peculiarity of Boxley church is a forebuilding attached to the western face of the tower, and forming a large porch to the west door. Sometimes described as a narthex or a mortuary chapel, it was thought to have been built in the fifteenth century; but the removal of plaster during some work or other in 1921 revealed in the north wall two Norman arches supported by a central pillar. If this feature was built into the wall in the fifteenth century it would be evidence of a very unusual—and unbelievable—antiquarian interest in that time; if, on the other hand, it is *in situ*, we have a Norman porch or forebuilding that formerly had an upper floor and which boasted on its north side a tiny two-bay aisle. Accepting either premise, we are no nearer to the solution of a fascinating little problem that is, as far as I know, unique. What this remarkable aisled forebuilding could have been used for is not at all obvious. It may have formed a small chapel, and indeed it may have been a mortuary chapel where a body could lie before a service in the church. Or it could be that this was a relic chapel, an assumption we may make very readily because of the profusion of relics in the middle ages. If there was some especial relic to be displayed and reverenced here in Boxley village, we have no information to say what it might be; if we knew we would have another small piece of information to bolster the argument that medieval pilgrims did indeed frequent the Pilgrims' Way.

The rest of the church is later than these Norman arches, the nave having thirteenth-century arcades of white clunch, while the windows of the church are later still, of Decorated tracery patterns. On the north wall of the choir is a monument to Sir Henry Wyatt or Wiatt, father of the poet of Allington Castle, whose inscription recalls how, when he was imprisoned in the Tower of London, he was fed by a cat bringing him a pigeon unfailingly every day. Perhaps it was the memory of this event that led his son the poet to bring the brown pigeons from the Orient to live in the courtyard of the castle, where their descendants strut still, untroubled by cats.

The length of the Way from Boxley to Charing continues the character imposed upon it by the increased traffic converging from Rochester and Maidstone, but changes subtly as it follows the scooped flank of the chalk downs under the white blear of quarries ripped into the scarp. North of the Way the contours of the downs are so frilled and ruched that in order to avoid continual winding and stumbling over promontories the Way keeps a little lower down and barely on the chalk. It is in places no longer the boundary between the steeper slopes of the wild scarps and the cultivated fields that sweep over the lower slopes with a grand and female grace. Now it often has fields to the north as well as to the south, and the clearcut line where the corn ends and the scarps begin is now above us. The downs are lower now than they were west of the Medway. They tail away towards the south-east and to that cape or promontory above Kennington, where the hills turn to the north-east and the Way follows them on the last stage to Canterbury.

A few yards north of the village of Boxley and of the Georgian Boxley House (now a country club), the Boxley road joins the Pilgrims' Way. Here, turning sharply to the right, there begins

a long mile of the Way leading down to Detling. This length
is marked on the Ordnance maps, both one-inch and 2½-inch,
as a minor track, but in fact it is surfaced and drivable and has
been so for some time, though in places it is wide enough for
only one car. It runs between hedges that shut off the excellent
panoramas to the south, but field gates provide frequent and
nicely framed views. The road soon loses its southern hedges,
however, and runs unfenced beside cornfields, along the margins of which scabias and other wild flowers seduce brown-
spotted fritillaries (*plate* 21). It is a pleasant, quiet walk on a
fine day, bringing the traveller, however, to a brutality of our
time, the dual carriageway of the A249 from Maidstone to
Sittingbourne. In a loop of this road lies the village of Detling,
like Boxley and some other villages henceforwards, only just off
the Pilgrims' Way.

Detling has been considerably extended in modern times and
has lost some of the charm it once had; but it still possesses
ancient houses and a church of the fourteenth and fifteenth
centuries incorporating Norman masonry. By the churchyard path an unusual monument commemorates a choirboy of
1923, and near by an old yew has a huge bole. In the church
you will find a dug-out poor-box and in a wall an odd monument to a priest of the thirteenth century, with the face recut or
restored. The most important thing here, however, is the fine
fourteenth-century lectern with a pyramid desk and a pedestal
for a candlestick. Its quality led Coles Finch to suppose that it
might have been brought from Boxley Abbey.

Detling Hill, with the bleached gaps of quarries, is steep and
short, and provides excellent views.

Houses line the first part of the narrow surfaced lane by
which the Pilgrims' Way arrives at the next village, Thurnham,
a mile distant. The Saxon name means the 'ham' of thorn
bushes and is not especially applicable today, except for the
remains of Thurnham castle, where nettles, brambles, and
briars flourish and deter. The castle is a kind of motte with some
vestiges of flint masonry, said to be either Norman, or, following
the evidence of various finds of Roman shards, a Roman watch-
tower. Cautious Roman or barbarian Norman enjoyed here as
magnificent a view of the valley and of the variegated slopes of

the downs as they could have wished. The castle may also have served the Anglo-Saxons who buried their dead in the south-east angle of the cross-roads at Thurnham, where previously there was a Roman villa. As there is a record of Thurnham in Domesday Book, it is likely that the Saxons had a church here, but the earliest parts of the present church are of the thirteenth century. Of this period is the deeply splayed lancet window in the north wall closely flanked by later windows of two lights on different levels; in the lancet is a piece of glass possibly also of the thirteenth century, showing a lion's head. The rest of the church is of various periods, and the elucidation of the dates of its elements is an interesting exercise partly confounded by the restorations done in the nineteenth century, when the thickly elaborate east window was renewed.

After Thurnham comes a stretch of nearly three miles of the Pilgrims' Way devoid of villages. The whole of this length is surfaced lane, moving alongside good farming country with many orchards of apple and cherry. At the first cross-roads, Water Lane goes off to the south and Coldblow Lane to the north. These names are significant. Water Lane would mark a place where travellers on the dry downs might descend to find a spring. Coldblow Lane and Coldblow Farm are self-explanatory on these high levels, and the Coldharbour connected with Coldblow by a path must have been one of those shelters by the wayside in which travellers could find a chilly, wind-wuthered night's rest. From the Pilgrims' Way they would climb up by the line of the present lane around the flank of the knobby hill called Cat's Mount.

In the lowlands to the south is the village of Bearsted, the Berghamstyde of the Saxons, part of whose pre-Conquest church is revealed in the masonry of the present church of Holy Cross. The church is largely of the thirteenth century and the four-teenth century, with a typical fifteenth-century Kentish tower, which has strange beasts at the angles of the battlements. But what is most memorable in this village of Bearsted, now become almost a suburb of Maidstone, is its broad village green, which is overlooked by houses of various dates, whose inhabitants enjoy an unrestricted view of the cricket matches for which the green is noted.

Hollingbourne, the next village beside the Way, has a beautiful Elizabethan manor-house of red brick coigned with stone, with a display of mullioned and transomed windows. There are Georgian pubs and older ones, one of which, the King's Head, was formerly called the Pilgrims' Rest. The Old Malt House has a display of fine timber-studding. Edward Hasted, historian of Kent, was for half a century vicar of Hollingbourne's church of All Saints, dying in 1790 at the age of ninety-five. The church, mostly of the Perpendicular period, contains excellent monuments, including in the north chapel a number for a branch of the Culpeper family, who lived at Hollingbourne Manor and at Greenway Court a mile to the south-east; the latter was burnt down in the eighteenth century. A splendid alabaster monument to one of the Culpeper ladies shows her with a ring on her finger tied to a tape or cord that disappears into her sleeve. This is not unique, for I have seen the same device elsewhere, but I have never had any satisfactory explanation of it—it does not seem credible that the cord was merely to secure the ring against loss.

The manor of Hollingbourne was granted to Christchurch priory in Canterbury in 980 by the Saxon Athelstan for the provision of the priory table, and the priors had a house here in which they held their court. The Culpepers built the present manor-house and lived in it for generations. Catherine Howard, whose mother was a Culpeper, is said to have spent her girlhood here, and to be here still, a sad ghost wandering in the rooms and passages in which she lived the happiest part of her life, before she went to Court and attracted the fatal attention of Henry VIII. Here too, three other Culpeper girls, Frances, Judith, and Philippa, during the exile of their father with Charles II, embroidered flowery cloths and hangings for the church, in bright colours and thread of gold, and at least one example of their work, an altar cloth, exists still. The Culpepers, once great landowners in Kent and owners of several houses, including the former royal estate of Leeds Castle, had died out or disappeared by the eighteenth century. Their desirable manor-house of Hollingbourne has in our century been divided into seven flats.

Between the church and the manor-house a spring rises into

24. *The Countless Stones, remains of a dolmen*

25. *Allington Castle*

26. *Gatehouse of Eastwell Park*

27. *War-memorial cross beside the Way above Lenham*

a pool and forms a series of artificial ponds in the stream by which the hollies once grew that gave Hollingbourne its name. It flows through a lower part of the village—Eyhorne Street— to join the river Len south of the A20, a little to the north of the village of Leeds. Leeds whose name (from Hlyde) improbably means a loud brook (the Len) is among the most charming of Kent villages, with its modern additions discreetly at a distance, its old houses a medley of timber-frame, clapboard, and Georgian brick, headed by a timber-studded manor-house. The church has an eleventh-century west tower of enormous dimensions, so large that the interior, despite the thickness of the walls, is as spacious as the chancels of many other churches. The body of the church is of the fourteenth and fifteenth centuries, with some evidence of the thirteenth century. Near the village is an ancient house called Battle Hall, with galleted joints, and to the south stands the gatehouse, but little else, of the former priory of Saint Mary and Saint Nicholas, founded in 1119 by Robert Crèvecœur of Leeds Castle. It was dissolved in 1534, when all it contained were a prior, a sub-prior, and ten canons. Leeds Castle, to the east, a large building partly set on two islands in a lake formed by the Len, partly on the mainland, was originally built by Robert Crèvecœur in the twelfth century and enlarged later. Edward I acquired it and from that time it was one of the royal castles and was visited by several monarchs and their queens. Edward II's wife, Queen Isabella, however, was refused entry by Captain Culpeper, on the grounds that none should come in who did not have permission from the owner, then absent. She complained to the king, who 'levied a power', compelled Culpeper to surrender and hanged him. Henry VIII is said to have housed Catherine Howard in Leeds Castle. She was a cousin of Thomas Culpeper (whom Henry executed for his misdeeds with Catherine). Henry is also said to have wooed Anne Boleyn in the castle's great chambers and gardens. Henry's daughter Elizabeth was kept a prisoner here in the reign of her suspicious and Catholic half-sister Mary, and came here again as queen on one of her progresses. Here in 1665 John Evelyn the diarist was placed in command of French and Dutch prisoners of war.

From the cross-roads at Hollingbourne, the Pilgrims' Way

RPW

continues along a road marked 'No through way', which within about 300 yards becomes a rough track passing between broad arable fields, with the chalk downs, still clothed with trees, standing back a little distance to the north. Soon afterwards, the path continues between wire fences and stands of nettles. This is a pretty part, with occasional glimpses through the trees of cornfields and meadows, and of tall spinneys growing in hollows in the midst of arable fields. Flocks of pigeons and doves, disturbed by our footsteps, scattered from these spinneys as we passed. Meadow pipits rose from the fields to pour their song like falling water from the sky, and then, exhausted by so much singing, dropped like stones after the sound. Partridges hastened off the path before us, leaving behind them scattered floss torn from the bushes. The small pink flowers of the convolvulus lighted a carpet of heart-shaped leaves and opened their faces to the sky. Occasionally we passed companies of a flower too prosaically known as the nettle-leaved bell flower and more aptly as the Canterbury bell. The trees we passed included stands of beech casting with their wide arms a shade tinted brown by the fall of last year's leaves, many kinds of conifers, and quantities of field maple—a tree that Miles Hadfield affirms is rare, but it is common along much of the line of the Way, and frequent between Hollingbourne and Boughton Aluph.

From Hollingbourne the Way has been gently rising from a level at about three hundred feet to reach 425 feet below the rounded breasts of Mile Hill, from which it climbs to 500 feet at the Harrietsham cross-roads.

Harrietsham's church of Saint John the Baptist is nearer to the Pilgrims' Way than it is to the main part of the village. It has the peculiarity of possessing two towers, one to the west, of the fifteenth century and a good example of the Kentish idiom, the other, much lower, on the north side; the latter was probably a two-storey sacristy and seems to be at least as old as the Normans. The rood stair in a polygonal tower on the south side of the nave gives access to a rood loft on the restored fifteenth-century screen. The nave, of the Decorated period, was altered by the insertion of Perpendicular windows; the chancel is earlier, of the thirteenth century. The Norman font, of unusual design, is of marble from the region of Bethersden village, eight or nine miles south of the Way. In the north chapel are monuments of the family of Stede, who lived at Stede Court on the top of the downs north of the cross-roads and of the Pilgrims' Way; one of them, Edwyn Stede, died in 1735 after losing a lot of money running his own cricket team and betting on its prowess. He deserves at least to be counted among the fathers of the game, though in fact cricket can be traced back to the thirteenth century, and Guildford Grammar School has a record of its having been played there about 1550.

South-east of the church, near Spittle Crouch and Platt's Heath, are the sources of the Len, separated by an unemphatic upland from the source of the Stour at Well Street. A superficial view of Kent would suggest that the line of chalk downs should be the logical water-divide, but in fact the rivers are older and cut their way through the downs as those hills rose slowly from the pressure underneath.

The Pilgrims' Way between Harrietsham cross-roads and Lenham keeps for the most part to the 500-foot level, but rises rather higher above Lenham. It begins as a lane, then for half a mile is surfaced along what was a counterchange section such as we saw earlier at Yaldham, but here the lower road has been surfaced too. From here to Charing the Way runs parallel with the A20 trunk road and the sound of cars and lorries is never absent from the air of the downs. The A20, for the greater part of this stretch, must run along the line of a medieval track that came into being as the lowlands became clearer and safer. Every half-mile or so there is a connection between the two roads, which serves to show that for many years the Old Road, the Pilgrims' Way, was not made obsolete by the track in the lower land. As long as the middle ages endured and longer, until roads were hard-surfaced, the lower road would have served in summer for all kinds of traffic of the time, while in the winter, when water and mud made the lower road unpleasant, the upper way would be preferred, for its drier going over the chalk.

Lenham is reached by one of these connecting roads, and also by either of two footpaths through the cornfields. I am undecided whether to call Lenham a small town or a large village. It has the affectionate charm of a village self-contained and full of character, but it also has the comings and goings of a town. It centres on a square round which closes a medley of old buildings, some timber-framed, some of brick with Georgian façades, some very ancient and disguised by later alterations. The National Westminster Bank and a greengrocer share a timbered Wealden house with a recessed centre, whose Georgian windows consort not unhappily with the rustic timber-frame. The Dog and Bear and the Lion are two pubs as old as the eighteenth century on the evidence of their façades, but inside they show work considerably older. On the Red Lion the brewers, Fremlins, have put their name several sizes larger than that of the house, and that seems to me an unforgivable vulgarity. The Saxon Pharmacy (strange name) sports an interesting mullioned window that cannot be younger than the sixteenth century. Just off the square is a short little street with a grassy centre, flanked by eighteenth-century almshouses, on the end of one of which is a brick building with an arched doorway and above it a stubby stone cross; it is said to have been a lock-up. All that is missing from this domestic scene of Lenham is the church, and a church of course there is, a little withdrawn and hidden, but showing its tower, rising above a churchyard bordered by timber-studded houses.

Lenham's church of Saint Mary was a Saxon and Norman building until some disgruntled miscreant set light to it in 1297, a crime so heinous that Archbishop Winchelsea came from Canterbury on purpose to perform the ceremony of excommunicating this anonymous fellow; the incendiary, however, was no jackdaw of Rheims, and there is nothing to suggest that excommunication disturbed a hair of his head.

A large tithe barn (157 feet by 40 feet) near the church is one of the two built by the Abbot of Saint Augustine's of Canterbury as replacements for two destroyed in that same fire of 1297; one of these rebuilt barns was also destroyed by fire—in 1964. A Norman east wall remains to the north chapel of the church, but the rest of the building is of the early fourteenth century, with the tower coming a little later. The church contains a figure of a priest lying as though in his coffin, thought to be one Thomas de Apuldefelde, who died in 1377. Some wall-paintings of the same century include the weighing of souls, with the Virgin dropping her rosary into one of the pans of the scales held by Saint Michael, in order to give weight to a poor soul lacking sufficient substance to counter the pull of devils on the other pan. Another painting dimly shows a bishop. Also to be seen are a fine Elizabethan pulpit and a lectern of the same period and some impressive chandeliers. In the chancel floor is the tomb of Mary Honywood, who died in 1620 at the age of ninety-two, after having had the satisfaction of seeing no less than three hundred and sixty-seven of her descendants—children, grandchildren, great-grandchildren, and great-great-grandchildren.

The Pilgrims' Way, half a mile north of Lenham, turns off the Doddington road by an old quarry, as a drivable track used by the residents of bordering houses. In a short distance the track curves aside and the Way goes on to an iron field gate, through which we pass into a hill pasture dotted with sheep. The open view shows that the steepness of the chalk scarp has been passed and now there is only a rounded slope rising to the north, showing by its contours that we are still on the chalk but with the drama and the height gone by. The Way scarcely shows in the sheep-nibbled grass, and the only thing to do is to go straight ahead parallel with the lower hedge. A huge white cross (*plate* 27) on the hillside, made in memory of the dead of two world wars, shows its bright figure to the un-heeding traffic on the A20 below. The cross seems to have been made, not by cutting into the turf, as the White Horse of Berkshire was made, and as a number of other figures on the chalk downs have been made, but by bringing in chalk rubble and spreading it to shape on the hillside. A small iron-railed enclosure below the cross used to contain a memorial stone or cross but this has now been taken away.

We pass ploughed fields in which the colour of the earth is a rosy brown made hazy and pastelled by the chalk content; later we were to see fields in which the ploughland was a delicate beige. At a wooden gate the Way enters a wood and runs, as it has so often done, just within the trees, with farmlands on the south slightly below the terrace of the ancient path. Presently the Way joins a surfaced road coming up from East

Lenham and the A20 and leading to Warren Street, a hamlet
to the north. It follows this road for a hundred yards or so,
and then when the road bends away to the left carries on ahead
as a rough path to cross another surfaced road, below Lenham
Chest Hospital, into a lane marked by one of Kent's Pilgrims'
Way signs—but this sign, like others, is some distance along the
lane and is no kind of use to anyone on the surfaced road. This
strange placing of the signs for the Way happens frequently in
Kent and one cannot help wondering why. In this area you
may see gliders skimming in the heights of the sky, with only
the humming of the wind in their wires to announce their
presence. Occasionally one may be seen on tow behind an
old biplane.

The Way becomes in places a path along the upper sides of
arable fields planted with barley, corn, or wheat, with few
signs that it is much used. There are occasional groups of
Canterbury bells, of scabias, and hawkweeds, the latter with
their petals sharply square-ended as though cut by scissors.

The path comes to Cobham Farm, which takes its name from
one of the great Kent families, who owned the manor—they
have fine brasses and monuments in Cobham church west of
Rochester and in Lingfield church in Surrey. At Cobham Farm
the path passes through the farmyard and its gates—in wet
weather this is a muddy and odorous experience. A few yards
along the farm track brings us to a rough path leading off to the
left, beside a paling fence. This path is not marked on either
the one-inch or the 2½-inch OS maps, and some writers,
apparently without investigating for themselves, have supposed
that walkers along the Pilgrims' Way must here descend to the
A20 and walk along that for a mile before turning north to
recover the Way at Hart Hill. No such diversion is necessary.
If the path coming to Cobham Farm from the west is the
Pilgrims' Way and the track east from Hart Hill is also the
Way (and both are so marked on Ordnance maps) then the in-
tervening path from Cobham Farm to Hart Hill must also
be the Pilgrims' Way. This length is not much used, that is
evident, and in places it is so bedevilled by nettles and leaning
briars and brambles that a suit of armour might be appropriate
wear. In places the enemy is so dense that it is wiser to walk

along the edge of the arable than on the path. Sometimes the path is shaded by hawthorns, ashes, and field maples, sometimes it runs as though in an avenue of young trees.

Beside the path, on both sides, lie numbers of large sarsen stones, some with the holes that are common in these boulders. It is tempting to believe that here are the remains of a mega-lithic avenue, a link with the distant days when neolithic and bronze-age men walked along these slopes; but I think it more likely that the stones have been turned up in the earth by the plough and have been dragged where they now lie by cursing farmers annoyed by the damage to their shares and coulters. That this path is ancient, as ancient as any other part of the Way, is shown by the fact that it runs on a terrace after the manner of many other stretches of the Old Road.

At Hart Hill we reach another north-south road, which passes between chalk-pits. On this road we have to go downhill for a few yards to find the continuation of the Way as a path on the left, thick with nettles, but bearing a broken sign in confirmation that this is the Way once more.

As the Way approaches the quarry-scarred slopes of Charing Hill, the village of Charing, with its grey church tower and the red-tiled roofs of its houses, is seen across the fields. The village may be reached from the Way by footpath or by road from the point where the Way crosses the A252.

The manor of Charing is said to have been given to the Church in the fifth century. That may be so, but we find it again being given to Augustine in the early seventh century by Ethelbert, King of Kent. Here the archbishops had a house or manor, perhaps the oldest of their possessions outside of Canterbury. The earliest spelling, 'Ciornincge', occurs in a charter of King Coenulf in the year 799. In 1070 the manor was transferred from the see to the archbishop, at that time Lanfranc, and it remained a possession of the archbishops henceforward until Cranmer had to surrender it to Henry VIII. It was there-fore one of the manors of Thomas Becket, and he would without doubt have visited Charing more than once in his movements about his diocese. What house he would have stayed at is not known, but later bishops, from the mid-fourteenth century, resided in Charing's manor-house. This house, which had a late thirteenth-century chapel, was expanded by succeeding bishops until it became large enough to deserve the name of 'palace' by which it is now commonly described, and indeed fine enough for Henry VIII to choose Charing as one of the stages at which he and his monstrous train stayed on the way to the Field of the Cloth of Gold. That was in 1520, when Henry was still welcome at a religious house. The ivied remains of the palace are now in use as a farm, and may be seen on the left side of the street that culminates in the noble fifteenth-century tower of the church (*plate* 11). A broad arched gateway leads into a courtyard around which the archbishops' buildings were arranged, and north of the church may be seen a great barn that was in its day the banqueting-hall of the palace, where Henry VIII ate his meals. This should not be confused with the seventeenth-century Church Barn, which was moved here in 1958 from High Halden and is now the church hall.

Charing church was built in the thirteenth century on a site said to have been given by King Ethelbert of Kent about 597; there is, however, no evidence of a church earlier than the present one. The church was seriously damaged by fire in 1590, when a Spaniard called Dios, out bird-shooting, fired his fowling-piece into the dry shingles of the roof. From long custom the maintenance and repair of the nave of a church were the duty of the parish, while the chancel had to be maintained by the priest. The parishioners repaired their nave at once, and had the beams painted with *trompe-l'œil* patterns that really do look like carving in the wood; the chancel, however, was not roofed until 1620, a delay that suggests parsimony or poverty of the priest. The west tower opens to the aisleless nave by a vast arch that makes the tower space and the nave together almost a single vessel. In the church are some interesting bench-ends, two showing the rural face of Jack in the Green, with foliage about his ears and cheeks or coming out of his mouth. The Jack in the Green, a pagan spirit of nature, according to the church guide, is better said to be or to have become in Christian England a rustic caricature of an ancient village festival of the return of spring. A curious instrument called a vamping-horn, a kind of trumpet, may be seen; it was used in some way not now clear to accompany the choir before the days of organs.

It was at this church of Charing that pilgrims and other travellers in the middle ages could see the very block on which the head of John the Baptist was struck off. The block was said to have been brought from the Holy Land by Richard Cœur de Lion. It may have been successfully hidden in the church at the Reformation; if so it would have been destroyed in the fire of 1590, when even the church bells melted and ran molten from the tower.

The village is a place of delight for the lover of old houses and village character. Timber-frame and Georgian frontages masking timber-frame abound. The rectory by the church was built in the fourteenth century, its old walls now concealed by later covering. The Swan Inn and the King's Head are old enough to have comforted weary travellers coming down from the Pilgrims' Way; but the Swan, still with that indefinable and inescapable air of a pub, is now converted to flats. I knew a man once who bought an old pub and converted it into a house; a disadvantage, he found, was not so much that people tried to walk in, as they did, but that many of them grew bellicose when they discovered that there was no licence and therefore no beer. Perhaps the most amazing of the timber-framed houses, and showing the inherent coherence of such a structure, is the Old House in Station Road, which has looked for many years as though it were about to fall to bits. The best medieval house, however, is one retired behind a wall facing the post office.

This last length of the Pilgrims' Way is for the greater part footpath of varying quality. It begins at an altitude of about 450 feet and maintains this level for the two and a half miles to Dunn Street, where a descent begins towards the valley of the Great Stour and towards the change of direction of the Way from the south-easterly trend to one moving towards the northeast. This change of direction is the result of the necessity of keeping out of the marshy or overgrown valley of the river. For much of the distance the path runs across an upland plain rather than along the flanks of the hills.

Above the village of Charing, Charing Hill rises to 628 feet, its southern face ravaged by the getting of chalk. The hill is worth the effort of climbing it from the Pilgrims' Way 150 feet below, for it is the last high viewpoint on the downs on our way to Canterbury, or the last whose sudden slope dropping away at our feet can induce a marked sense of elevation, both spiritual and physical, of hovering in the cool breeze and the sun above a landscape of such variety and extent that time and space are fused and enhanced and the mind dazzled with what the eye can hold all at once within its little orb. Below us, the noble tower of Charing church rises from the red roofs of the houses with that same emphasis it has had these five hundred years. Away to the south stretch the fields, farms, and woods of the valley of the Great Stour, a country of gentle undulation, through which the river, not clearly seen, unless the light reflects from an occasional reach, wriggles north and east and south, and east again, and then north-east towards Canterbury. There among the lanes and fields are ancient houses of ancient families such as Calehill, home of the Darell family, and the adjoining Surrenden Dering, where the Derings, who have their brasses in Pluckley church, held out from the mid fifteenth century until the twentieth, when their old house became a school. There was a Roman bath-house to the north-west of

Surrenden Dering, near the church of Little Chart. Of that church only the tower and a fragment of wall remain from a direct hit by a bomb in the last war. Julia Cartwright describes how, from Charing Hill, she could see as far as the Channel and the coast from Fairlight above Hastings round to Romney Marsh and Dungeness. I cannot promise you such a view in this hazier time unless you have the fortune to be on the hill on a clear frosty day, or on one of those rare, lucid days in spring before the haze of the heat comes.

From where we left it at Charing, at its junction with the A252, the Way continues eastwards as a narrow surfaced road, which is marked at its opening by one of the Pilgrims' Way signs of the Kent County Council. Chalets and bungalows of the inter-war years line this lane for a short distance, until the lane becomes even narrower between hedges that enclose arable fields in which the ploughed earth is of that beautiful beige colour we have already experienced in the pastel palette of the chalk. A side road leads down to Petts Place, and it is well worth while to add the half mile necessary to see, as you may easily do, the front of this desirable seventeenth-century house of warm brick, with shaped gables. I at least find it desirable, agreeing with someone who bought it at auction in 1969 for the sum of £67,000.

The surfaced lane that is the Way leads past Burnthouse Farm to a large chalk quarry that is still active, and in which in 1935 a bronze-age burial was discovered. The Way continues as an unsurfaced lane in places deeply rutted and in wet weather muddy. Where the trees allowed we saw again the gliders and their tugs such as we had seen earlier, and by the path we found picnicking families come to watch them. The path divides, and the Way is to the right, passing under young beech trees and sycamores along the skirts of Long Beech Wood; many of these trees have been coppiced. An occasional mature beech, whole and unravished, spreads its arms above a ground of golden brown, on which the sun through the leaves scatters a pirate's treasure. At gaps in the southern hedge there are views to the south of a bright landscape of corn and pasture patterned with hedges and trees. Later, a wood entirely of old beeches develops on the slopes to the north, and the path, as it often does, runs just within the margin of the trees, on a terrace in places slightly hollowed. Shortly afterwards the path crosses the rim of a hole in the ground a hundred feet deep and with a sheer drop masked by bushes and the tops of the trees with which this hollow is filled. It is an old quarry, and a surprising one. A little distance beyond this the path joins a surfaced lane coming up from the south and continues on this lane in a descent to Dunn Street, an inconsiderable hamlet of the village of Westwell.

Westwell, whose well is the source of a tributary of the Stour (as also is that of Eastwell), has old houses of brick, among which a mill (now a house) retains its water-wheel, but the village is chiefly interesting for its church, which dates mainly from the thirteenth century and retains lancets of that priod, including a group in the east wall. This too is the date of the tower and of its shingled spire. Massive buttresses of brick lean against the south wall, set there to counteract the thrust of the aisle arcade, a thrust carried across the aisle, inside the church, by flying wooden shores. The arcade leans heavily against these shores and the effect is illusory, as though the whole building were tipping over to the south, as a ship is careened. The chancel has a tall and graceful stone screen, an unusual thing. Its like is to be seen in England in only two other churches that I know of, at Stebbing and at Great Bardfield in Essex. Beautiful sedilia of the Decorated period ornament the chancel south wall, and east of these are the remnants of two arches one within the other, as though the builder had here intended something that got no further. Arch within arch are seen also in the north wall, next to stone benches meant for the singing men, but sometimes perhaps used by the monks of Canterbury, who came here to superintend their possession, for the revenues of this church, from the time of Lanfranc at least, went to supply the refectory of their priory of Christ Church. The east window contains stained glass showing the tree of Jesse, with a huge and massive tree rising painfully from a tiny Jesse to exhibit the descent—or rather the ascent—of Christ. The upper panels of this window come from the thirteenth century, the lower two were made only in 1960. Richard Harris Barham, better known as Thomas Ingoldsby of *The*

Ingoldsby Legends, was curate here for three years from 1814, and a tablet commemorates his son Henry, who died in 1817.

East of Dunn Street lies the extensive Eastwell Park, in which for two miles the line of the Pilgrims' Way is uncertain. A dismembered fragment is shown on the OS maps, beginning in a wood and going from nowhere to nowhere. I suspect that you would be trespassing if you searched for this fragment. It is not necessary to the continuance of our journey, for a yard or two to the north a distinct track is to be found, a track parallel to and within a few feet of the fragment. It serves to take us along the north side of the wood and through the well-kept pastures and arable fields of this model estate. We pass through a series of modern field gates that should be noticed for the excellence of their construction and the variety of their design. The track is clearly marked by the wheels of farm tractors, and for our guidance by a series of wooden arrows that indicate a public way. We come to Home Farm and turn into a drive that descends gently to Eastwell.

From some distance back the tower of Eastwell church, of bright light-coloured stone, rising among trees, has been visible from the path, but the view gives no inkling of what is to come. For Eastwell church, handsomely set, and quite alone on the shore of a large lake full of lilies and swans—and I daresay of fish too—is a ruin. Guns sited near the church during the second world war shook the ancient fabric and made it unsafe and a storm of wind in 1951 toppled the enfeebled structure, throwing down the medieval arches and walls, and leaving little more than the tower standing. Some fine tombs of the Finches and of the Earls of Winchelsea of Eastwell Park were dismantled and taken to the Victoria and Albert Museum in London. With them went a nameless tomb-chest said to have been the grave of Richard Plantagenet, natural son of Richard III, the last of the line of Anjou that furnished kings of England from the time of Henry II onwards, a line longer than any that has held the throne since. Richard Plantagenet, at odds with a country no longer Angevin, worked on the estate as a humble bricklayer until he died in 1550. He was lucky to have his life.

Eastwell House, now demolished, was nearly all imitation

Tudor of the nineteenth century, though some parts of the house built by Sir Thomas Moyle, the employer of Richard Plantagenet and once Speaker of the House of Commons, may have persisted in the structure.

The park has a spectacular, turreted, neo-Jacobean gate-house of flint and stone standing above a green at the road junction of the lake (*plate* 26). Too good to be true, it was built about 1843.

If we were to accept Belloc's theories to the letter, the Pilgrims' Way ought to pass by the south side of Eastwell church, where it would have run through the hollow that is now filled up with Eastwell Lake, which has been formed by a dam in a little stream that goes down to join the Stour. In fact, there is a public way north of the church following a drive of the park, a way that is sufficiently direct to serve our purpose, for we have to accept the probability that the Old Road, crossing such easy slopes as these, would not have been restricted to a narrow line. We pass along a drive bordered by young trees like a road of Picardy, and come out on to the A251 at Boughton Lees. A few yards up this road, on the west side, is a spring said to be near the site of Richard Plantagenet's cottage, and so it is called Plantagenet's Well.

Boughton Lees, an unassuming place of modern houses and bungalows, marks the hinge, the turning-point, of the Pilgrims' Way. Here the Way leaves the south-easterly direction it has pursued since Snodland for a line running towards the north-east. This change is dictated by the formation of the downs and by the gap through them made by the valley of the Great Stour. In the days when the Old Road was trodden out, the valley of this river was spread with marshes, and where there were no marshes trees and undergrowth grew thickly; these were sufficient reason to persuade travellers to keep to the chalk. Marshes no doubt persisted in the days of the early pilgrims, who would follow the dry road already in existence, but by that time farmers had imposed their order on some of the alluvial land. Down there in the valley, on the right bank of the river, is the ancient town of Wye, which flourished before the Normans came, and since no Saxon country town could have continued other than upon the products of the land in which it was set, there must by that time have been good cultivated farmland in the valley and on the slopes rising from it. Wye, a small town today, was an important centre when the neighbouring and now much larger town of Ashford was a hamlet. At that time Wye was fit enough for the entertainment of a king, for here in 1308 Edward II 'held the solemnitie of a whole Christmasse in the house of this Manor'. William I gave the revenues of Wye to his new foundation of Battle Abbey; they remained with the abbot until 1447. Archbishop John Kemp, born at the house of Olantigh a mile to the north, transferred the income to his new foundation, in Wye, of a college of priests and a free school. Teaching and learning have continued in that foundation ever since, though today it has become the Department of Agriculture and Horticulture of London University.

Olantigh, to the north, whose superficially Gaelic name is in fact Saxon, meaning 'holly enclosure', was the home of the Kemp family from 1250 until 1650. Its most illustrious member, John Kemp, held successively the sees of Rochester, of Chichester, and of London; in 1426 he became Archbishop of York, cardinal in 1439, and finally Archbishop of Canterbury. He rebuilt the parish church of Wye to an ambitious cruciform plan, with a central tower and a long chancel typical of a collegiate church. In 1686 people in the church noticed the bell ropes swaying and rushed out of the building in time to escape the fall of the tower. This disaster destroyed all the east end, including the monuments of the owners of Olantigh. The present tower and the apsed chancel were not built until 1706; stones in the churchyard mark the plan of Kemp's chancel and its chapels.

For the rest, Wye is a modest little town, with its streets full of seventeenth-century and Georgian houses. I remember it, however, because of a local man who buttonholed me for no apparent reason and gave me a lecture bitterly regretting the burning down of a brewery more than a hundred years ago, an event he insisted was fraudulent incendiarism.

Above Wye is an old quarry in the down sides, and above that is a crown cut into the chalk by students commemorating the coronation of Edward VII; quarry and crown may be seen from parts of the Pilgrims' Way around Boughton Aluph.

Brook, to the south of Wye, has a Norman church of Saint Mary not much altered, save for the insertion of some Early English lancets and a pretty Decorated window of the four-teenth century; its enormous flint tower, which stares across the valley, contains an upper storey with a thirteenth-century mural of Christ, his hand raised in blessing. Brook was one of those manors whose revenues contributed to the maintenance of the table of the refectory of the monks of Canterbury.

Between Wye and Brook, Saint Eustace's Well, blessed by a French priest, Eustache, in the thirteenth century, and said to cure anything, may have attracted those ailing pilgrims for whom the miracles of Saint Thomas were ineffective, as they returned from Canterbury saddened and disappointed.

A four-armed signpost at the cross-roads at Boughton Lees points plainly to the Pilgrims' Way, along the bungalow-bordered road to the north-east. We follow this lane for half a mile, and a little beyond the drive to Brewhouse Farm turn off on to a path to the left. It leads between orchards and fields of strawberries and across the margins of arable fields directly to Boughton Aluph, whose honey-coloured church tower soon comes in sight. The path by which we have come leads straight into the churchyard.

The several parishes of Boughton take their name from Saxon boc-tun, the tun or settlement where beech trees grew, and their second names from their former owners, as Boughton Malherbe (south of Lenham) from a notable Norman family, who chose to suffer an uncomplimentary description that might have better suited a Borgia. The manor-house, Boughton Place, c. 1550–75, next to the restored fourteenth-century church of Boughton Malherbe, was the birthplace in 1568 and home of Sir Henry Wotton, poet and diplomat, who was host here to Queen Elizabeth I.

Before the Conquest Boughton Aluph was part of the property of King Harold, who died at Hastings, and later it was one of the many manors of that richest of women, Juliana de Leybourne. About 1211 it was in the hands of one Alulphus, who has left his name. I enquired locally for the correct pro-nunciation. 'Bawton A'llup' said a man with great certainty.

28. *Thirteenth-century chancel of Boughton Aluph church*

29. *Old houses in the square at Chilham*

30. *Thomas Becket in thirteenth-century glass in Canterbury cathedral*

31. *The murder of Thomas Becket shown in one of the Miracle windows in Canterbury cathedral*

'Bawton A'lluf' said a woman equally positive. Both pronuncia-
tions are, I find, current, but 'A'lluf' is the more common.
The lonely church of All Saints, set high and solitary, with broad
and benignant views towards Wye and Brook over the Stour
valley, is one of great size and great beauty, with an echoing
interior of light-coloured stone under a massive central tower.
It is lighted at the east end by two large Perpendicular four-
and five-light windows. These windows are only the more
recent additions to a church basically of the thirteenth century
for the chancel and fourteenth century for the nave. The
curious arrangement of the sedile, piscina and aumbry in the
south chancel wall (*plate* 28) is in itself a little history of change
and superimposition, the simple and graceful sedile Early
English, the piscina, with its crocketed triangular canopy,
Decorated, and the plain rectangular recess above, with which
the canopy interferes, of any earlier period. The north and south
porches of brick were added later; the south porch may have
been, not a porch, but a vestry or private room, for it has a
large fireplace—the fire in it must have made this little chamber about as comfortable as the inside of an oven. It is believed
locally that the south porch was used by pilgrims, who gathered
here in the warmth until there were enough of them to brave
the robbers who haunted King's Wood.

There are some pleasant monuments. One for Priscilla
Moyle (1661) remembers a lady who was like Anna for hos-
pitality at home, like Martha for good works abroad, and like
Tabitha in fear of God. The lettering is rustic and the use of
capitals is arbitrary. Another monument of 1631 for Amye
Clark has a figure with graceful, realistic drapery and a verse
of uncommon merit:

> To the tender trust
> Of that sadd earth
> Which gave it birth
> We recommend this sacred dust:
> The pretious oyntment of her name
> That had no taint, that had no soyle,
> We keep to oyle
> The wings of fame.

> The higher storie
> Of her rare soule
> The heav'ns enroule
> In sheets of glorie:
> If perfect good
> Did e'er reside
> In common flesh and blood,
> In her it liv'd, with her it died.
> Reader tis thought our universal mother
> Will hardly ope her womb for such another.

Amye Clerk died giving birth to triplets and two girls and a boy appear at her head and her feet.

Hilaire Belloc found some difficulties in tracing the line of the Old Road beyond Boughton Aluph, difficulties concerned with the disappearance of the path beneath the plough and its diversion by the contours of the hills, but he makes no mention of the problems of private land with no right of way. In short, he treats this section so learnedly, as though he knew it by experience, and yet so summarily that it seems he had not walked the whole length of it. Let us take it in rather more detail.

A fragile stile on the far side of the surfaced lane east of the church of Boughton Aluph gives access to a field in which no apparent path exists, but we go straight ahead to a gate and then along the margins of ploughed fields with recent stiles in the wire fences to confirm the direction. In this country the Way cannot be said to be on the side of the down, but rather over a rolling plain, with a low wooded hill to the north and broad distances to the south. The path through the field ends at an iron-barred gate leading into a short, tree-lined lane full of weeds and nettles. This comes out on to the surfaced lane called White Hill. Cross this lane a little to the left and then right into a gravelly drive beside a bungalow. This drive or lane leads down to the derelict Soakham Farm, set in a hollow, and passes between a barn and the silent house. Beyond the farm we find a rough sign on a tree indicating the direction of the Way. The Way, in fact, begins to climb the downs and Belloc explains this, correctly, I think, by saying that it needs to avoid a combe too inconvenient for a primitive path to negotiate. Hereabouts, the Way is in a deep hollow; many feet trudging up the slope have indented the chalk and formed a miniature canyon, which is now hampered by bushes. We come up beside a wood, and just inside this wood is the combe (or 'ravine') Belloc mentions, full of trees, and certainly, trees or no trees, obstacle enough. An apparent stile into the wood misled us and caused us to wander uncertainly among the trees for a time until we had the sense to return to the field and try again. The thing to do is to ignore this stile and to continue in the field up alongside the wood to a barred gate. This gate brings us into a distinct lane between coppices of sweet chestnut. A short distance along this lane, a sign confirms our conclusion that this is indeed the Pilgrims' Way. The coppiced chestnuts, on both sides of the track, are to accompany us now for miles, their bunched and slender stems smooth and bright and their indented lancets rustling in the breeze, for now we are fairly on the summit of the downs at about 500 feet and the path is mostly level, with only occasional undulations. We are aiming directly for Canterbury, and according to Belloc you should be able to see the cathedral from a point on this lane, the first view of that building and of that city we have come so far to visit. I believe that Belloc looked for a view he had been told should be there, and he says that he could not be sure but that a slight hazy mark in the far distance was the tall tower of the cathedral. I do not think that you can see it today. The chestnuts, with occasional larger trees, prevent it.

The land to the east belongs to Godmersham Park, and the Way forms the boundary between that estate and Challock Forest. A footpath leaves the Way to descend in a mile past Godmersham House to the church. The house, a Palladian mansion as plain outside as many houses of this style are, was built in 1732; its chief interest is that it once belonged to Edward Knight, brother of Jane Austen, whom we have met earlier on our journey, at Chawton. Godmersham House was part of the inheritance for the sake of which Edward Austen changed his name to Knight. Edward is commemorated in the church, which stands a little way upstream by the Stour, and another monument refers to his benefactor Thomas Knight and his wife Elizabeth. Of much more intense interest is a bas-relief of Thomas Becket on the chancel south wall, dating from about the year 1200, and therefore one of the earliest representations of the archbishop. He appears seated, in his vestments and wearing his mitre, but blurred, like a photograph out of focus. For the first time in our journey we see here the low, sensible mitre of his period such as we shall see again in stained glass in his cathedral in Canterbury (*plate* 30), very different from the comic, towering mitres that in our day Archbishops of Canterbury and Popes of Rome bear uncomfortably on solemn occasions. Thomas Becket's mitre is nearer to the Christian spirit of humility; but these were the early days of this kind of hat, and the shape and the size of the mitre perhaps grew with the increasing complexity of the Mass and of those other liturgical or processional occasions for which it was used. The mitre actually worn by Becket, and apparently the original of these two representations, survives, with his vestments, at Sens.

Godmersham church, is, or originally was, Norman, and in the base of the tower the east apse of the Norman church may still be seen. The thirteenth century rebuilt the chancel, and there were other changes before the middle ages came to an end in the Reformation. Nothing was done then, however, as insensitive as the work of the Victorian restorer who attacked the church in 1865. He took carved Norman stones from the fabric and distributed them elsewhere, setting a number in the blocked west doorway.

Guidebooks mention a thirteenth-century house as standing next to the church, a house that was once the manor-house from which the monks of Christ Church of Canterbury managed this property for the benefit of their priory, and to which they came for change and relief or retreat from the city. Julia Cartwright says she saw here a ruined gable remaining from this house of the monks, which had otherwise been demolished in 1820. She describes a figure of a mitred prior and identifies the subject as Prior Henry de Estria, who rebuilt the house in 1290. This figure sounds very much like the relief in the church now said to represent Becket. I poked about and stumbled for some time in a wood of young saplings trying to find some sign of this house, with no success. I was told later that the remains were demolished more than twenty years ago.

The Pilgrims' Way on the track between the trees on the north side of Godmersham Park becomes in parts very cut up by tractors, and in wet weather it must be unpleasant for walkers; but for us the ridges of whitish mud were iron-hard after weeks of sunny weather. The track passes between woods of conifers, and all along its length, between coppice, conifers, or beeches, there is a sense of enclosure, as though one walked in a tunnel. Here and there yews of no great age throw their dark shadows on the Way, and occasional large beeches spread their muscled grey-green arms. The track joins a lane and we turn to the south-east, but a few yards along in this direction we discovered a footpath* turning off to the left that restored our north-easterly trend and brought us back to a lane of which it may be said that it enjoys the Ordnance Survey's blackletter identification as the Pilgrims' Way. There was no reason to doubt otherwise, for the lane leads directly towards Chilham.

I should draw your attention to this lane because, though not itself private, it appears to lead only to land that *is* private. In order to avoid trespassing you may ignore the footpath I have marked above with an asterisk and continue down the lane there to turn off towards Mountain Street, at the head of a public road that winds downhill and then rises briefly into Chilham. We did not do this—at least not originally. Instead we followed the footpath into the trees, beside a wire fence, and presently found ourselves in another lane very similar to the first, which took us through the palings of Chilham Park and on to a stretch of track marked by the Ordnance Survey as the Pilgrims' Way. There was no one about to chide us, no one to deter or banish us, and in fact we had seen no person whatever since leaving Boughton Aluph. So we marched on and soon found ourselves in front of a well-made barred gate giving access to a broad field sloping away from us down to the Jacobean house of Chilham Castle, beside which, rising from the trees, a fragment of the octagonal Norman keep just showed.

According to the OS map the Pilgrims' Way should go straight ahead and down to the old keep and the Jacobean house and out through the main gate of Chilham Park, into the square of Chilham village. Hilaire Belloc was equally positive that the Old Road followed this line, but he made no mention of private property, even though on some previous occasions he had indicated when he trespassed. He passed so briefly over this section that I cannot help wondering if he walked through the park at all. We might have trespassed ourselves, ready with apologies if any should question us, but it seemed that some kind of garden party was going on in the distance beside the house, which we did not wish to interrupt, and so we turned to the left along the fence on a clear track and, descending a hill, came to a gate tied with string, which we untied and tied again behind us, and made our way among farm buildings and estate cottages below the castle. Within three minutes we were stopped twice by amiable farm employees, who told us firmly but politely that we were on private land. We made our apologies and continued down to the main road, where we turned right and ascended into Chilham.

Chilham appears as the ideal English village and the very pattern of the manor-village relationship. There is the great Norman castle keep (built on the site of a Saxon hall), the later large manor-house, and at the gates the houses of the villagers and the inn, with the church tower peering across the roof of the inn to the castle gates. The inn, the White Horse, claims to have been founded in the fifteenth century, and that may well be true enough, though the present building appears as Georgianized seventeenth-century work. The houses of the square are mostly of timber-frame, with white-painted infilling, in some instances over a lower storey of red brick; other, and later houses, are all of brick (*plate* 29). Inn, houses and castle gates are gathered round a square that was once the village green and is now always full of cars. It all seems too good to be true, like a film-set, but the hint of aspic really comes from the excellent maintenance and preservation of the houses, and the discouragement of any modern building out of key as out of time.

A famous heronry that has reputedly existed at Chilham since 1280 is in the grounds near Godmersham Park.

The garden party we had seen from the upper end of the home park turned out to be people taking advantage of the opening of the castle gardens to the public. The castle is now opened regularly to visitors. The Jacobean house, built by Sir Dudley Digges in 1616, is traditionally, and certainly wrongly, attributed to Inigo Jones. The garden gates look across the square to the White Horse Inn and the fine Kentish tower of the church, with its Georgian clock. The church contains monuments of the Digges family and of later owners and inhabitants of the castle. A sculpture of two small boys, who died in 1858, shows them with a book, *Babes in the Wood*, and beside their feet a battledore and shuttlecock; it is guaranteed to draw sighs from sentimental visitors. Sir Dudley Digges employed the best sculptor of his time, Nicholas Stone, to make a monument to his wife, Mary, who was a Kemp of Olantigh; its Corinthian columns and polished stonework are very handsome. Digge's sister, Lady Margaret Palmer, who died in 1619, has a monument with blunt obelisks rising above an architrave of classical pattern, with that uncomprehending mixture of gothic and classical common to the period.

At the dissolution of the monasteries the ornate shrine of Saint Augustine, made for Saint Augustine's priory in Canterbury, was dismantled and brought to Chilham, where it was hoped that the bones of the founder of Christianity in the south of England might remain in peace. Why Chilham was chosen for this purpose is not clear. The move was, in any case, fruitless, for the reforming Archbishop of Canterbury, Thomas Cranmer, compelled the removal of the shrine from the church. It may then have been broken into fragments, as so many other shrines were, or it may have been hidden away in the earth and its hiding-place forgotten. Some restoration work in the church in 1860 brought to light a large sarcophagus of Purbeck marble, a find that at once provoked speculation that the bones of Augustine had been uncovered. Alas, the sarcophagus was empty. The lid, with its worn floriated cross, was removed again in 1948, apparently to make sure that the discoverers of 1860 had not missed anything. All that was found was a record of previous openings in 1883, 1904, and 1914 by inquirers who had been equally reluctant to believe that the sarcophagus was really and truly void. I find that humorous.

Not the least beautiful of the houses of Chilham is the vicarage, built in 1746 beside the churchyard, but taking no part in the general effect of the square. Its red brick is warm and mature, its hipped and tiled roof a darker red, and the façade is embellished with a pedimented doorway and a Venetian window.

Chilham Park is the last of the places where the Old Road, the Pilgrims' Way, has been absorbed into private property. It is surprising that in a hundred and twelve miles there are not more instances of such absorption than there are. Albury, Gatton, Titsey, and Chevening are the other places where the road passes into private land and where it is not accessible without trespass. Together they account for only five or six miles of the Way. Belloc adds Denbies by Ranmore, but that is on a doubtful line of the road, and in any case much of the grounds of Denbies has been open to walkers since the house was demolished. Eastwell may be added for that odd length of the road marked on the OS 2½-inch map, based on what evidence I know not, but the parallel path is only a yard or two from it; and then we should add the later length of the line through Eastwell Park, which may not be the same as the present public way described in this book.

Henceforth we are free, but we are faced at once with a strange circumstance. The line of the road after Chilham looks, on the map, as though it ought to go directly north-east by Mulberry and Bowerland to Mountsford and then to Nickle Cottages (which Belloc calls Knockholt, but I give the spelling on the modern map). In fact the map marks the Pilgrims' Way as running more directly north along the road to Old Wives Lees, where it turns at a cross-roads and passes North Court, and continues with the surfaced road round a bend to the south-east. A footpath is then taken on the left to lead in a few yards to Mountsford and Shalmsford Manor. This is in fact three sides of an irregular rectangle. This is the only occasion on which the Old Road describes a line so wasteful of space and of effort, and Belloc can only suggest that, if the tradition that this is the Way can be trusted, as he thinks it should be, then there must have been some special reason for the pilgrims coming so far out of the direct line, some such reason as a shrine, for instance. There is, however, no tradition of a shrine, no tradition of a holy well even, that might have exerted such attraction. Nor is there any evidence in place-names. Old Wives Lees was once Oldwood's Lees; in this form the name means simply clearings or fields within an old wood. That suggests no clue to me. Sir Dudley Digges, incidentally, founded an annual race to be run here by bachelors and maidens of good conversation, who were to compete for a prize of ten pounds for each sex. Possibly even as late as the early seventeenth century there was some tradition that made Old Wives Lees the obvious place for such an event. Today the place is simply a modern settlement and no more attractive or important than others of its kind.

It may be that there was some structure of prehistoric origin on these hills to correspond with the long barrow called Julliberrie's Grave on the opposite slope east of the Stour, as the megaliths of Addington and of Greywethers seem to correspond. An old tradition says that Caesar during his second expedition to Britain fought a battle here and that the barrow was the tomb of a Roman tribune killed in that battle. His name, mangled into Julliberrie, was Julius Laberius. The tradition comes via Camden, but it is probable that he merely repeated what he heard. Those traditions were not untrustworthy, for when the barrow was opened in 1936–38 four Roman burials were found, not of a Roman general, but Roman nonetheless, though a century later than Caesar's day. Those burials, for me, are enough to complement the value of tradition. There is just a hint in the name Julliberrie, or Julaber, of the Gaelic word 'leaba' for 'bed' that is found in Leabacailigh in county Cork, which I mentioned earlier in connection with dolmens, but beyond this fortuitous syllabic similarity I am unable to go.

At Mountsford the Old Road joins a lane and at once emerges on to the main road, the A28, alongside the Stour. It follows this road for about half a mile to a lane marked 'private road to Nickle Farm'. Private or no, this lane has to be taken to reach a footpath turning off to the right and going north-east on the line of the Way. It passes over the railway on to a track going by the slopes of Fright Wood to join a surfaced road at Chartham Hatch.

The village of Chartham is a mile to the south, set astride the Stour. It has a famous paper mill, a huge mental hospital of Saint Augustine, and a notable church exemplifying in its windows the style of medieval tracery peculiar to Kent and so called by its name. The church was built about 1300, aisleless but cruciform, with an astonishing timber roof in which scissors beams or ribs join at an oak-leaf wooden boss in the centre over the crossing. The parish, however, is much older than this church, for a Saxon noble gave it to Christ Church in Canterbury so that its revenues should contribute to the clothing of the monks. There are interesting monuments and several brasses, the best of which is a life-size figure of Sir Robert de Septvans, constable of Rochester Castle, who died in 1306. He appears in full armour, with his shield on his arm and a long sword in its scabbard at his side, but he wears no helmet, and his pleasant face is outlined by his bobbed and curled hair. Strange, bell-like objects shown on his shield are winnowing-fans, the 'vans' or vanes of his name. A similar symbolism appears on a small brass of a rector, Robert Sheffelde, who has a wheat-sheaf, from 'sheaf-field'. The Kemps of Olantigh also used the symbol of sheaves, in reference to their name, which was derived from 'champ', the French for a field, and in turn from the Latin 'campus'. The notable stained-glass designers of the end of the nineteenth century, the two Kemps, also used the wheatsheaf as their sign-manual, sometimes hiding it in the design, as they did at Kennington, north of Ashford.

The road from Chartham Hatch runs through the heavy woods of Howfield, and converges on Watling Street, by which most of the pilgrims of London came to Canterbury; but before the two meet, the Old Road passes through an old fort, the tree-covered Bigbury Camp. Built in the iron age as a defence against invading tribes, Bigbury in all probability had to face a more disciplined enemy, the seventh legion of Julius Caesar, who in his second incursion in 54 BC, with five legions and two thousand cavalry, penetrated through Kent and into Middlesex. There, Cassivellaunus, if he did not defeat the Romans, so harassed them that Caesar thought it better to withdraw, with the solace of a tribute that was readily agreed but was never paid. In his passage through Kent Caesar would have considered it necessary to reduce Bigbury Fort, and he does indeed mention a strong native camp which he had to storm and overcome. Unexpected and therefore interesting is the fact that nearly all the objects found in excavations at Bigbury have been of a domestic or peaceful character, with little to suggest the turmoil and danger against which such a camp was built and defended.

Bigbury marks a junction of alternate ways.

Alternative 10a. The direct route
This goes by the footpath beginning at Bigbury Cottages, crossing fields below the village of Harbledown, and then entering a lane that soon becomes a street in a modern housing estate and debouches on to the dual carriageway of the A2 east of Harbledown. This is the most direct line from Bigbury to Canterbury, and is marked as the Pilgrims' Way by the Ordnance Survey, but it has the disadvantage of ignoring Harbledown.

Alternative 10b. By way of Harbledown
At Bigbury Camp take the surfaced road to the left to join the A2, and turn east on this road up into Harbledown, a village set on the slope of a hill, near the summit of which stands the church of the former lazar-house of Saint Nicholas founded by Archbishop Lanfranc in 1084. As was often the case with leper-houses, the site was fixed sufficiently far from the city to be neither an offence nor a peril to the citizens, and perhaps the summit of a hill was chosen so that all might see the archbishop's benevolence and at the same time be warned of contagion. The Norman chapel, which survives to this day, is built with the floor sloping down to the west door; the incline follows the descent of the hill, but it is probable that the slope was adopted, as it was in some other lazar chapels, so that the floor might at intervals be conveniently washed down with water. Henry II, in his penitential pilgrimage to Canterbury, descended from

his horse at Harbledown and walked the rest of the way to the cathedral; but before he set out on foot he knelt and prayed in the chapel and gave a grant of twenty marks of rent to the inmates. Edward the Black Prince is supposed to have drunk of the pure water of the leper's well on his visit in 1357 and to have sent for some of it as he lay dying in 1376, a tradition sufficient to confer on the well at Harbledown the name of the Black Prince's Well. The prince would have remembered how he had come to Canterbury in triumph, bringing with him from the fantastic English victory at Poitiers Jean, King of France, in a fine procession through Harbledown on the Watling Street; and that earlier victory of Crécy, when, at the age of sixteen, he had commanded the right wing of his father's army; and the procession of 1361 in gay panoply, when he came to found a chantry in the cathedral on the occasion of his marriage to his cousin Joan the Fair Maid of Kent; and the passage of Roncesvalles and the defeat of du Guesclin at Nájera in 1367; and the sun of Spain, where he had taken a wasting disease. It was this disease that killed him nine years later. In the summer of 1376 Harbledown saw its prince again, but a dead prince borne from Westminster along the Watling Street, on a hearse with the horses nodding sable plumes to the beat of muffled drums.

At Harbledown there were, too, relics to be honoured. One of these was a portion of a shoe, framed in brass and crystal, that had belonged to Thomas Becket and this was presented to be kissed by pilgrims on their way to Canterbury, together with an offertory almsbox on a pole. The shoe was offered to Dean Colet, who came this way with Erasmus. 'Pshaw!' said the Dean, or something like that, and he rejected the object with such vigour and repulsion that Erasmus felt compelled to give a larger donation, by reason of the ire of his friend, than he had previously intended. You may see the alms-box today, with some other objects of interest, in the almshouses that were built in the 1840s on the site of the lazar-house.

The Norman church or chapel of the lepers was enlarged in the late twelfth century by the addition of a north aisle and tower and enlarged again some two hundred years later. A second church at Harbledown on the other side of the road, away from the lepers, was for the parishioners; the present building is of Victorian date and of little interest.

Geoffrey Chaucer came by Harbledown to Canterbury and mentions it at the beginning of the Manciple's prologue:

> Woot ye nat where ther stant a litel toun
> Which that ycleped is Bobbe-up-and-doun,
> Under the Blee in Caunterbury weye?

The little town was Harbledown, and the 'Bobbe-up-and-doun' refers to the steep hill on which the village and its lazar-house stand, the last hill before Canterbury and the first place from which pilgrims would see truly and clearly the roofs and chimneys of the city and the splendour of the cathedral rising above the houses, in front of the tall church of the abbey of Saint Augustine. Nowadays the view includes an over-prominent gasometer. The 'Blee' refers to the Royal Forest of Blean to the north.

The line of the Pilgrims' Way to Harbledown, the last mile, is now overlaid by modern extensions of the city. It is not the line of the A2, which is a modern street not leading to any of the main gates. The pilgrims passed through the West Gate, so they must have come from Harbledown off the A2 and somehow on to what is now the A290. They passed through the arches of the overwhelming grey tower of the West Gate into Saint Peter's Street and the High Street and so to the centre of the city.

15 Canterbury

The Pilgrims' Way leads directly to Canterbury in the valley of the sub-dividing Stour; but exactly how it accomplished the last few hundred yards is not clear. The present motor road comes down to a modern roundabout and to Rheims Way, the latter part of a modern circular road round the city, running outside the circuit of the ancient walls. We cannot find the footprints of the pilgrims or of the Old Men here. In any case, a consensus of opinion agrees that pilgrims, whether coming by the Pilgrims' Way or by Watling Street, entered Canterbury by the West Gate, one of the six gates in the city walls (and the only one in existence today). Now the West Gate, which is in fact if not in name the north-west gate, is to the north of Rheims Way, and of the present Canterbury end of Watling Street (the A2). Somewhere east of Harbledown the Way leaves the line of the modern road to come into the Whitstable road and what has since the middle ages been St Dunstan's Street. The 2½-inch map shows a street (called Queen's Avenue) following this line, but breaking off half-way. The line the pilgrims followed would have been the shortest that was practicable. No modern street quite does this, and we therefore have to come into Canterbury by whatever route, over these last few yards, may be most convenient. We pass over the Stour, which was as a moat to the gate, and through the gate itself into the city.

Since the Old Road is ancient beyond knowledge, so too in all probability is the city or settlement of Canterbury, and a sure sign of its ancient importance is that it is now, as it always has been, a focus of all ways from the sea and its harbours, of Celtic trackways that became roads, of Roman roads that followed and amended where the Celts trod, and of the miry and untended ways of the Saxons and the middle ages. It was the royal city of the Saxon Kingdom of Kent, and it was the centre from which Christianity spread over the southern half of England. It is today the seat of the primacy of the Anglican Christian church in this country and abroad, wherever the English have established themselves.

The Romans neither invented nor founded the city of Canterbury, but they walled it round and rebuilt it to their own pattern. They called it Durovernum Cantiacorum, revising the name from some Celtic original that seems to have meant 'the Kent men's fort in the marsh' or the 'marsh by the fort of the Kent men'. That name says clearly enough that the iron-age Celts had a fortified place here, which took advantage, for defence, of the swampy or marshy nature of the valley of the Stour.

It has been suggested that Bigbury, or Bigberry, Camp represents the Canterbury of the iron age, that this was the 'big bury' or borough of the men of Kent. I do not think that this can be so. The camp, as we have seen, certainly stands astride the Old Road and would therefore be known to every traveller along that road, but look as you may, you will not find evidence that Bigbury was ever a focus of tracks from the surrounding coasts or from the west, as I think it must have been, even at so early a period, if it were truly an iron-age or earlier metropolis. The town of Canterbury, on the other hand, though it stands in a valley more difficult to defend—and how difficult it may have been we cannot know in the absence of more detailed knowledge of the extent of the marshes—appears as a natural centre, easily reached from almost any point of the compass.

The Romans were content to accept it as such. If the Seventh Legion overcame the fort on Bigbury Hill, the Romans then left that fort as of no value to them, but the town in the valley they turned into a real Roman town, with streets laid out, after the manner of Roman town-planners, at right angles, forming neat square blocks of buildings. There was a large theatre, and a forum, and no doubt there were temples, and all the other qualities of an important Roman provincial centre. The full story of the Romans in Canterbury cannot be known because their streets and sites have since the middle ages always been built over and one cannot knock down existing buildings for the sake of completing an archaeological record; but much valuable evidence was revealed by the bombs of Hitler's Luftwaffe and the consequent excavations before rebuilding of the city centre.

When the Romans at last marched away to defend their constricting empire on a smaller front that excluded Britain, the town in some manner lost its Roman shape and plan. As Silchester did, it may have become within its walls a space of ruin and desolation, its broken buildings perhaps inhabited by beggars and the poor. I base this supposition on the fact that the regular Roman street plan has scarcely survived. A segment of the Watling Street coming to a gate in the east wall is all that is clearly recognizable, with its continuation beyond the walls as the straight Old Dover Road. This disappearance of the Roman plan is not to be explained by the superimposition of a new plan, but rather by the casual and haphazard building of Saxon shacks and houses over Roman sites and streets that were by then imperceptible or wrecked.

For Saint Augustine and his companions, who arrived in the year 597, Canterbury was the capital of the pagan Kingdom of Kent, ruled by a king called Ethelbert. Augustine came as a missionary to convert the Saxons (or Angles, as he may have thought), but the popular notion that he introduced Christianity into England is wrong. Irish missionaries had been busy for years converting the north of England, and even here in the south there were Christian churches that had survived from the Christianity of the Romano-British period. Moreover, Ethelbert's queen, Bertha, was already a Christian, and she and her confessor worshipped in a Christian church, the church of Saint Martin, on a hill to the east and outside the walls. Saint Martin's still stands, perhaps the oldest church in this country in which Christian worship has gone on uninterruptedly for so long. Another church stood within the walls, where the cathedral now rises. Augustine at first centred his mission on Saint Martin's but later chose to use the other church, which had a position more conveniently at the centre. There he established a monastery, and the old church became his cathedral and the centre of his see. There he preferred to continue even though he had been instructed by the Pope to make London the centre of his ministration. In later days the monastery became a priory, governed by a prior, with the archbishop as titular abbot.

Augustine also founded a second monastery, in 602, outside the walls, between the priory and Saint Martin's. This second monastery was dedicated to Saint Peter and Saint Paul, but it became better known as Saint Augustine's Abbey and so it remains known to this day. These two large Benedictine foundations existed side by side, as priory and abbey, throughout the middle ages, constantly vying one with the other. Saint Augustine's had the right to claim the bodies of the archbishops for burial within its walls, but this was not always granted without disagreement and in the end the archbishops were laid to rest in their own priory. Each house had its relics and each welcomed pilgrims. In 1170, however, the abbey sheltered the conspirators who had come to murder Becket. It is unlikely that the abbot or his monks knew the true intentions of the knights, although their behaviour was not that of peaceful men. The murder of Becket and the subsequent cult of Saint Thomas gave Christ Church permanent supremacy. The visible result of this is the fact that today Saint Augustine's is an utter ruin, church and abbey, while Christ Church, despite its grievous losses, remains in part, gathered about its noble and intact cathedral.

Thomas was not the first saint of the priory of Christ Church of Canterbury. An earlier archbishop, the reforming Saint Dunstan, was accounted a saint and enjoyed a cult; a kinsman of Dunstan's, Alphege, was another. Dunstan, who had had his education from Irish pilgrims at Glastonbury, was an amiable man who in his youth had loved books and song and was good with his hands. He reformed the English Church and established the strict Benedictine rule in the somewhat haphazard Saxon monasteries, and in 988 died peacefully in his bed. Alphege had been a monk and an anchorite before he became archbishop in 1005. Five years later he was captured by the Danes and was held prisoner for seven months while his captors tried to get him to agree to a ransom. This he would not do and the exasperated Danes at last set him up at Greenwich as a cock-shy and killed him by pelting him with beef bones and whatever else they could find to hand. These two saints were already the object of pilgrimage when Thomas Becket became archbishop in 1162, and their shrines and remains continued to

TPW

be visited throughout the three and a half centuries of the cult of Saint Thomas. The body of Alphege, whose death had touched the popular imagination, was first buried in London, but in 1023 Canute had it exhumed and conducted in solemn state and ceremony to Canterbury.

The numbers of pilgrims these two saints attracted to Canterbury were considerable enough, but they were nothing like so large as the crowds who came to visit the shrine of Becket at the height of its popularity in the middle of the fourteenth century. Then, enormous sums were received in donations from pilgrims, sums that would have to be multiplied by a very large factor to express their equivalent in our debased currency. Whatever may have been the primary attraction that called them, the pilgrims would worship at as many shrines and as many objects as might be presented as worthy of their attention, their reverence, and their prayers. Every church and every cathedral had, as we have seen, a collection of old bones, of shreds of garments, of vessels, and of other things that were believed to have acquired sanctity by having belonged to or having been used by a saint, and no pilgrim, having come so far, would neglect paying his respects to any person who might be supposed to have had merit on earth and therefore enjoyed influence in Heaven.

For few, it should be remarked, came to worship at shrines and relics out of pure love of religion and simple piety. Many came, as people go to Lourdes and other places today, to seek divine intercession for the cure or relief of maladies, and some to ask for success in worldly ventures. Others came to ensure as well as they might their eventual entry into the materialist bliss of a materialist Heaven, or at the least some protection from the flames or torment of Purgatory or of Hell, the fearful roasting and consuming of the physical flesh by fire.

As the centre of pilgrimage, the chief centre in England, Canterbury had to look to its accommodation, just as any other town in modern times that has a seasonal attraction or event. I have already spoken of the variety of places and houses in which pilgrims stayed. As anywhere else, pilgrims in Canterbury were of all kinds, the rich and the poor, the mean and the generous, and of all shades in between. Those who were either notable or well-off were accommodated in superior guest-houses, in which, however, only the most favoured would have a room to themselves. The monastery guest-houses included hospices meant for the poorer classes. Among these was one in the cathedral precincts, reached by the fine Norman stair that still stands. The Meister Omers, east of the cathedral, was a house for the better-off. Among guest-houses for the moderately affluent was the Chequer of the Hope at the corner of a narrow street or alley called the Mercery leading from the main street to one of the principal gates of the cathedral precinct. The Chequer of the Hope, built by Prior Chillendon about the year 1400, was the inn to which the author of the sequel to *The Canterbury Tales* conducted his party. From here, in the evening, his pilgrims went off severally each to his own pleasures. The knight and his son went to see the fortifications, the Wife of Bath to walk in the garden with the prioress, and the pardoner to find some pleasurable amour. This house was regrettably burned down in the mid nineteenth century, but the vaulted cellar remains beneath the timbered and jettied building, now a bookshop that stands in place of the inn.

There were guest-houses also at Saint Augustine's, of course, and at the various other religious houses within or without the walls.

One of the earliest guest-houses founded for the use of pilgrims to the shrine of Saint Thomas was Saint Thomas's Hospital, or the Eastbridge Hospital, which was built about 1157, in an important position in the main street, beside and in part over the eastern branch of the Stour. It remains in use to this day, but now as a home for old people. It has a splendid Norman crypt, which you may enter freely. South of this and also over the water stands all that remains of the Franciscan house called the Greyfriars, the building taking its name from the habit the friars wore. Near this is the Poor Priests' Hospital, founded soon after 1200 and partly rebuilt in 1373; it was meant for poor and ailing priests, a purpose that may have included assistance to priests who had come to Canterbury as pilgrims and who had fallen sick on the way or in the city. The hospital now contains the regimental museum of the Buffs and some offices of the city health department. Dominicans, or Black

Friars, had a house north of the main street, also on the river, where the refectory notably remains, with a shallow tower or bay to accommodate the pulpit from which one of the friars read to the company during meals. The lower floor of this building is now a Christian Science reading-room. The Augustinians also had a house in Canterbury, but nothing remains of it.

In addition to the religious houses, there were various inns or hostelries of differing quality, in which even a poor man who did not care to take the charity of the religious guest-houses might for a small coin or two find rest on the straw-covered floor of a communal dormitory.

Just as in a modern resort all kinds of trumpery rubbish are displayed for sale, so too was the case in Canterbury during the days of the pilgrimage. Especially in the Mercery, through which most pilgrims would pass at some time, there were shops and stalls selling such wares. Here the pilgrim could buy, and undoubtedly he was charged too much for, little keepsakes and mementoes and religious symbols made of tin or of lead. Brooches or badges showing a figure of Saint Thomas were popular and could be had here by the dozen, and there were in addition tiny flasks to be filled in the cathedral with the saint's blood, or in later days from a holy well to which the powers of the blood were in some manner believed to have been transferred.

The culmination of the visit, of the pilgrimage, was in the cathedral. The pilgrims were marshalled into an orderly file or procession, led by a monk, and this procession entered the north transept through the door by which Becket had entered on that fatal December afternoon of the year 1170. Through this door his murderers pursued him, with a crowd of citizens pressing in to see what would happen when these violent men came face to face with the archbishop—for by then it must have been known all over Canterbury that a monstrous evil was about to take place. The pilgrims, with the vision of that encounter in their minds, skilfully coloured by their guide, looked on the stones where Becket had stood and where Becket had fallen. They knelt and said their first prayers in the cathedral before the Altar of the Sword's Point, on which lay the shattered end of de Brito's sword, the sword which that knight had wielded with such force that the blade had cut straight through Becket's skull and struck and broke on the stone floor. Scarcely a pilgrim would not have shuddered and felt a chill as that stroke was described, with the vision of Horsea flicking out the white brains from the skull that had been opened like an egg.

Next the procession ascended to the high altar, up the stairs leading from the well-like transept, to look on the sacred place where Becket's body had lain throughout that night of his death. The file of pilgrims then descended once more to enter the crypt and the culmination of their journey, the miraculous tomb of the saint. What it looked like we can see high up in one of the tall Miracle Windows in the Trinity Chapel. The tomb or shrine was strongly built of stone, hard mortar, and metal, but there were holes in the side of the structure through which the coffin might be seen and touched, and even kissed—for there was mystical benefit to be had in such a touch or a kiss of the coffin of a saint. It was into one of these holes that Henry II in 1174 thrust his head, kneeling, while the monks whipped him with leathern thongs to drive out of his body all taint of the sin he might still have in his soul as the result of the hasty words he had uttered on that day in Normandy—words that had led directly to the death of the archbishop before whose body Henry now abased himself.

The three stations of the reverence of the saint were accomplished in this way until the body was translated in 1220 to the shrine behind the high altar. In the interval a great deal had happened. The Norman cathedral begun by Lanfranc about 1067, after a fire had destroyed the previous one, was itself attacked by fire and the whole of the east end was burnt out. This was four years after the death of Becket, whose tomb in Lanfranc's crypt was not damaged. The prior and the monks decided to replace the ruined Norman choir with something more up to date and they sent to Normandy for William of Sens, who had built the cathedral there in the new style of the tall pointed arch. The new fashion was what we in England call the Early English style of architecture or, more rarely, first pointed. Not long after beginning his work, William, climbing about among the builders' scaffolding, as architects will who are anxious to see that each detail is properly done, fell off and dropped fifty feet to the floor. He was succeeded by another William, known as the Englishman, who also worked in the pointed style and must have learned it from the first William. The refacing of the walls of the transepts and of the choir aisles are the work of William of Sens; the Trinity chapel east of the presbytery and the circular tower (Becket's Corona) at the east end are the results of William the Englishman's design.

The new chapels were ready before 1220, and are much the same now as when they left the hands of the two Williams. The prior and the monks were probably delighted, as indeed they should have been for so delicate and so enduring a masterpiece of architecture, and if by the time it was finished the fashion was no longer new, for by then it had travelled far and wide in this country, that was no matter—it was still à la mode. The tall windows were filled with brilliant glass in the scenes of which the story of Thomas Becket was told (plates 30, 31).

With the new work completed, the cathedral authorities began to plan for the translation of the body of Saint Thomas Becket out of the crypt and into the new Trinity chapel behind the high altar. The preparations were elaborate, long, detailed, and needlessly expensive—they included wine and food free to all for the asking at the monastery gates and at stages along the road from London to Canterbury. On the 7th of July 1220 the ceremonies and the festivities culminated in the translation of the saint. Solemnly the body was lifted out of the shrine in the crypt and was borne aloft by monks chosen for their transparent holiness, up the steps from the crypt, up the further steps to the choir, and then up steps again to the Trinity chapel where the new shrine stood. Among those who watched was Henry III, thirteen years old and impressionable, in this church where his grandfather had yielded to the saint.

Nothing of this newer shrine survived the destruction of Henry VIII's commissioners, but clues to its appearance can be found in the writings of various persons who visited it before 1538. It seems, and I find it astonishing at this date, to have been of Norman or Romanesque design, with a pair of round arches. The arches supported a level slab on which rested a gabled casket containing the body. This casket was covered with gold leaf or gold plates, over which was spread a covering of gold wire. Fixed into this were all the costly objects given by pilgrims—thousands of jewels of various sorts, precious things of gold, silver, and rare stones, so many that in the end they hid the gold background almost entirely. This casket was covered at those times when it was not being shown by a bottomless wooden box or cover of similar shape, which was let down from the roof on ropes. The whole shrine stood on a tessellated floor, in which you may still see the hollows worn by the feet and by the knees of a procession of pilgrims thirteen generations long. The glitter and the gaudiness, the magnificence and sheer lavish wealth of the shrine now made it something to be seen of its own, for the wonder and the admiration it evoked. The more pious and reverent perhaps perceived through all this rich hoard of gleaming treasures the holiness of the saint shining from the old, dried-up bones inside. The more worldly saw no more than unimaginable treasure.

The translation was undoubtedly planned to take place in July in order to provide for the saint a festival in the kindlier days of summer, which would bring more pilgrims to Canterbury than did the shorter, colder, and wetter days of the month in which Becket died. And the reasoning was right. The shrine of Saint Thomas Becket became one of those of international rather than merely national fame, and the numbers of visitors increased. The receipts began to climb, not at once, but gradually and encouragingly.

There were now two more stations of the pilgrimage of Saint Thomas in the cathedral to be added to three that had sufficed for fifty years. The tomb in the Norman crypt was retained, and here a piece of Becket's skull, mounted in gold, was presented to be kissed and revered. Then there was the tomb, now different, to see which the pilgrims ascended all those stairs, with effect growing upon effect as they rose beneath the soaring pillars and ribs of the high vaulted roof. As they gathered around the shrine the wooden cover was drawn up to reveal the treasure within. One can hear, even at this distance of time, the sudden hiss, the intake of breath as the whole splendour burst upon their eyes, the precious, scintillating, gleaming shrine of the saint, rich beyond all calculation, beyond all the gold of Midas, Erasmus declared. The descriptions that have come to us from those who saw it make it appear, to our tastes, very vulgar in its display, but we are members of a more material age, with less wonder and less gusto, and we lack the mystical reverence of the middle ages for its saints and what surrounded them. If we have gained in reason we have lost a great deal else.

The guide touched with a white wand the various parts of the shrine, and all the larger jewels one by one, saying what this or that was, and who had given it. It was a roll-call of kings and queens, of princes, barons, and knights of many countries, and of some of their ladies. The most remarkable of the jewels was a large ruby, of the size of a thumbnail, which had been given by a King of France—and not altogether willingly given, for it was said that it had jumped from his finger of its own accord as he knelt in prayer, and adhered to the shrine so that no device could manage to recover it. The king was Louis VII of France, who had supported Becket in his exile because it was politically convenient for him to do so. The ruby shone with an internal red fire even in the dimness of the chapel; so, at least, one visitor declared.

The other of the two additional stations was to be found in the rounded chapel that forms the easternmost part of the cathedral. This chapel was in the base of the tower called Becket's Crown, and here the actual crown of Becket's head, the occiput sheared off by de Brito's sword, richly mounted in precious metals, was reverently exhibited and might be kissed.

The five stations completed the pilgrimage; other relics in the cathedral might be viewed and revered, but none with the emotional effect of the stations of the round of Saint Thomas. The more religious would come again another day, to double their piety and their prayers, and yet again, but for all the rest it was time to disperse, to begin that day or another day the long journey back to their homes. Some, like the palmers, simply packed up and left to undertake another pilgrimage elsewhere.

Every fifty years a jubilee of the translation of the body was held to celebrate the saint with especial reverence. In the jubilee years Canterbury bulged out of its gates and over the countryside with the press of its visitors; pilgrims found accommodation in every kind of house, from rural shacks and cottages upwards. In those times among the crowds who came to Canterbury to make the rounds of the saint were kings, princes, barons, and knights, and various degrees of priests, monks, and nuns. At the last of these jubilees in 1520 there stood and kneeled among the worshippers a wide and brawny figure: Henry VIII had come to take part in the reverence of a saint who had quarrelled with and defied a king of England. Henry was twenty-nine.

By this time the pilgrimage to Canterbury and indeed pilgrimages in general had long been in decline, with the numbers of pilgrims and the value of their gifts tailing off to meagre figures that scarcely made the maintenance of the shrines possible. With the fall in the numbers of pilgrims there was a corresponding fall in the number of monks in monasteries —not enough young men were coming forward to join the monastic life. In some monasteries the numbers of religious were ridiculous in relation to the size and maintenance of the buildings they occupied. The cause of the decline was the same in both cases. The Reformation and the Renaissance were in the air and men were beginning to think more objectively and to examine beliefs with more candour and more courage. Was Henry, as he moved around the cathedral, already thinking of the enormous wealth the monasteries owned, wealth they could no longer effectively apply for want of men? Did he already suppose or begin to suppose that that wealth was part of the national wealth and that it ought to be given up for his administration? Did he already feel the beginnings of anger as he looked at the stained glass, the sculptures, and the paintings showing the apotheosis of a common man and contrasted it with the degradation of a king? His decision to dissolve the monasteries in England was yet some years ahead, but as he knelt in Canterbury on the worn mosaic pavement before the wealth of the shrine of Saint Thomas, Henry may have begun to plan what he should do and to wonder if he had the courage to do it.

He saw in the cathedral two of his ancestors, lying either side of the Trinity chapel, in splendid tombs, of course, but in tombs outshone by the lavishness of the shrine. On the south side was the resplendent tomb and the recumbent armoured figure of Edward the Black Prince, heir to a throne he never lived to occupy, but a great man none the less, who had fought bravely in his father's victory at Crécy and a few years later at Poitiers had utterly defeated the French army, capturing, as we have seen, the French King Jean and leading him a prisoner through the streets of Canterbury. Without doubt Edward would have taken John into the cathedral to visit and to revere the shrine, before they left through the West Gate—an earlier gate than the present one—and jogged away along Watling Street towards London. Edward had a special affection for Canterbury and in his will he desired to be buried in the crypt. The monks thought that for so noble a prince, so great a soldier, burial in the crypt would do insufficient honour and they placed his tomb and his body in the Trinity chapel, where Henry VIII saw it and where we see it still.

Edward's son came to his grandfather's throne as Richard II and for a few years ruled in absolute power, declaring that the laws of England were in his mouth. He was deposed by Henry of Bolingbroke and, as some say, was horribly tortured and murdered at Pontefract. Bolingbroke succeeded as Henry IV. Henry's life does not here concern us, but his death does. On the 20th of March in 1413 he fell in a faint while kneeling in prayer in Westminster Abbey, and he died that same evening. A day or two later another sombre procession, like that of the Black Prince, set out from Westminster towards Canterbury, where the king had desired to be buried, and a fine tomb was prepared for him in the Trinity chapel opposite that of the Black Prince. Saint Thomas now lay between two royal tombs and outshone them both and Henry VIII must have noticed this and remembered it. His view of Thomas was to prove very different from that of his predecessors.

It appears that certain visitors to the cathedral were shown more relics than the general public might be allowed to see. These hidden things were got out for the visit of Erasmus and Dean Colet. Colet had already shown, at Harbledown, limits to his patience with the veneration of relics, and here in the cathedral he and Erasmus were shown arms, legs, bones, ribs, and other pieces of genuine human or doubtfully human anatomy. These relics were presented with reverence and the expectation that the two men would put their lips to them in a holy kiss. Colet revolted against a special piece to which the dried flesh still adhered, and when a moment later a filthy rag was presented as the handkerchief with which Becket had wiped away the blood of the first stroke of the sword, Colet refused it in disgust. Erasmus feared for this evident discourtesy, but the monk with them affected to take no notice, and put the bones and the rag away.

This was already in the late evening of monasticism in England and Colet could not have been the first to hesitate before unsavoury relics. The last of the notable pilgrims to the shrine was a Frenchwoman, Madame de Montreuil. She was of sufficient status for the king to put a knight, Sir William Penison, at her service as a guide, and for the prior to receive her personally and to send to the house in which she stayed wine, fish, and capons for her supper, more than she could possibly eat. In the cathedral she looked with interest on the shrine and the relics, but she would neither kneel to the saint nor kiss the detached pieces of the skull; she came, it seems, as a sightseer. That was in August 1538. How near it was to the Dissolution may be seen on a page of the king's account or expenses book, where the payment of £40 to Sir William Penison for his services comes only a few lines above the record of payments to Wriothesley, the king's commissioner.

Within a few weeks men like Wriothesley were knocking at monastery gates throughout England, with workmen at their backs to strip out all that was valuable, even to the lead on the roofs.

Saint Augustine's Abbey was razed to the ground, except for some parts that were to be converted into a posting-house for the king, to serve him as he travelled around this part of his kingdom. At Christ Church Wriothesley and his men bundled up the treasures of the priory and of the cathedral and carried them away in a veritable fleet of wagons—twenty-six wagons, say some, forty-two say others. The gold and the jewels of the shrine were prised off and crammed into two huge chests, which proved so heavy that six men or eight men to each one staggered under their weight as they carried them out of the cathedral to a waiting wagon. How much private pilfering went on, how many unregarded pieces valuable in themselves but minor in comparison went into the pockets of workmen and of the commissioners will never be known, but in the general scramble for these riches some pieces assuredly went astray. As for the rest, of all the great wealth that no Christian church had any business to own and which was now taken from it and sent to the king's treasury, a large part was squandered by the king or given away to favourites and fawners. No gentleman, however noble, thought it undignified in that time to ask the king for favours, for monastic land here or there, for this building or that. Out of all Canterbury's riches Henry remembered in particular that great ruby, the Regale of France; he made sure that this stone came to him directly, and he had it set in a ring, which he wore on his thumb.

The archbishop, Cranmer, made no protest. He was a king's man, who had come to royal notice and favour by his discovery of a means by which Catherine of Aragon could legally be divorced to allow Henry to marry Anne Boleyn. He was so much a king's man that when in turn Henry desired to be rid of Anne Boleyn, it was to Cranmer he turned, in expectation that Cranmer would reverse all his previous arguments, as indeed the archbishop did. Here was no stubborn Thomas Becket, no courageous martyr to deny the justice or legality of Henry's policy.

The cathedral in which Henry knelt and which he later despoiled was not the cathedral that Thomas Becket knew. The east end, as we have seen, was rebuilt in the first pointed style by William of Sens and William the Englishman. The nave remained as Becket knew it until the fifteenth century, when it was rebuilt in the Perpendicular fashion of the day by the mason Henry Yevele. The Norman central tower was probably low with a pyramid roof; by the year 1500 this had given way to the tall and pinnacled Bell Harry tower that is now one of the glories of the cathedral and its principal accent. The southwest tower was built in 1460, and the west end remained until the nineteenth century with one tower of the Perpendicular fashion and the corresponding north-west tower still of Norman design and build. This Norman north-west tower was taken down in 1840 to make way for one to match the south-west tower and to provide the symmetry that the Victorian architect felt sure must have been in the mind of the prior in 1460.

The one part of the cathedral that Thomas Becket would know again if he could return, that perhaps his spirit, still suffused in these stones, finds gratifying, is the Norman crypt, built by Lanfranc. There the round arches and stone vaults that echoed Becket's step echo still, and the carved capitals to the pillars please our eye as they pleased his. At the east end he would pass into strange territory, into the extension of the crypt built by William the Englishman, with pointed arches and more graceful vaults, ten years after Becket's death.

Some other parts of the cathedral of Lanfranc remain. A capital or two may be seen in a dim corner, as in Dark Passage, and there are also the west wall of the cloister and the lower storey of the round water-tower north of the north transept. If the present cathedral, however, is not the one in which Becket prayed and met his death with so much obstinacy and courage, it is, in one part or another, and in almost the whole, the building seen by generations of pilgrims. Except for the nave, it is much the same today as when Chaucer's pilgrims arrived, though the distant view from Bobbe-up-and-doun would have lacked the emphasis of the Bell Harry tower and of the pinnacles of the west end; but there *was* a tower, and on it rode a gilded angel.

We came into the city by the way that Chaucer's pilgrims came, and by which all the other pilgrims from London and the west must have come, that is along what is now Saint Dunstan's Street to the West Gate. Near the outer edge of the city we passed the Tudor brick gateway, mouldering now, with the bricks powdering, that prefaced the house of the Roper family. Margaret Roper was the daughter of Sir Thomas More, a man who had disagreed with Henry's divorce and was outrageously framed and beheaded as a result. Margaret, courageous and clever, somehow rescued her father's head from the spike on which it had been fixed on London Bridge and had it decently buried in the church of Saint Dunstan lower down the street.

Saint Dunstan's church is a plainish gothic building today, much restored, but it retains signs in its large corner stones of Saxon workmanship. It was at this church that Henry II, coming on foot from Harbledown, changed his clothes for the sackcloth of a penitent and took off his shoes to walk barefoot the last stage of his journey to the shrine of Saint Thomas Becket. He could never have dreamed that dead Thomas would become so great an influence, and as he stumbled along over the rough cobbles, Henry must have remembered that other Becket, the gay and open-handed chancellor with whom he had been so close in friendship, who had hunted with him in the royal forests, who had shared adventures and frays at home and abroad. I doubt that Henry had got over or ever did get over what appeared to be an utter change of character. It seemed to him that the man who had been chancellor had died and that Thomas Becket the archbishop was another person in the chancellor's body.

We passed by inns and houses whose nodding gables and timber frames retain the flavour of another age, neither Becket's nor ours, and came to the huge grey West Gate, with its two tall cylinders of stone pressing in upon the arched opening between them. This fine gateway, among the best town gateways in the country, was built by Archbishop Simon Sudbury in 1380 as part of the defences intended to keep the city safe in a troubled time. It served in the rising of Wat Tyler, to which those troubles led. Tyler's men caught Sudbury in London, and, believing him their enemy, beheaded him; you may see his severed head still, dark and desiccated, in Saint Gregory's church in his home town of Sudbury in Suffolk.

Just within the gate is the church of Holy Cross, which was originally on top of the gate and was rebuilt here by Sudbury. It is too much restored to be of interest now, and it is desecrated too, to serve as something else than as a church. It was, in fact, superfluous in this age of unbelief, as others of the many churches of medieval Canterbury would have been had they survived. Of those that do remain, the most interesting are the oldest, Saint Martin's, which still serves after sixteen hundred years or more, Saint Peter's with a tower possibly Saxon, and Saint Mildred's, which was rebuilt after a fire in 1247, keeping only a few stones of the previous Saxon church. Saint Mildred's stands down by the battered, disembowelled keep of the Norman castle, which in its time has served as a dump and as a coal store.

About half of the medieval enceint of the walls remains, and we walked along the allure, the broad path on the top, looking down on the traffic of modern Canterbury spinning along the outer circular road, and on the inner side on the green lawn and comparative peace of the Dane John gardens. In these gardens there is a monument to a famous son of the city, Christopher Marlowe, who died so strangely in a brawl in Deptford. Some say he did not die at all but was a spy and had to leave the country and forgo his name, so that plays he wrote thereafter could be published and acted only under an allonym, that of William Shakespeare. The Dane John itself is a large pudding-shaped mound of unknown origin, but evidently older than the Roman wall, which turned an angle to go around it. 'Dane John' is really *donjon*, the French and medieval word for what we call a keep; the latter name was not known to those who put up such strongholds. We walked by the Stour, where monks and friars and pilgrims walked, and came back to the High Street to enter the Mercery, which was blocked by a single van delivering something or other. Beyond it rose the Perpendicular Christ Church gateway leading into the cathedral close, where, as impious pilgrims who had come the length of the Pilgrims' Way, we entered the cathedral.

Appendix

The North Downs Way

In the last few years a number of long-distance walking routes have been planned under the terms of the National Parks and Access to the Countryside Act of 1949 and the Countryside Act of 1968 and these have been or are being put into effect by the Countryside Commission. Rights of way are negotiated, where necessary. The Pennine Way, the Cleveland Way, and the Pembrokeshire Coast Path are now in existence. The North Downs Way from Winchester to Canterbury and on to Dover is planned but at the present moment it is not open along its entire length—a number of rights of way are still to be cleared. The Countryside Commission's sign, a silhouetted acorn, is used at intervals along the walks as a waymark. I do not remember having seen these waymarks along the Pilgrims' Way.

The North Downs Way coincides only in places with the Pilgrims' Way. It seeks to avoid motor roads as much as posssible by using a series of paths, tracks and lanes. It is, as one would expect, not as economical of space and energy as the Pilgrims' Way is.

From Winchester the North Downs Way follows the Nuns' Walk to King's Worthy and then takes the footpath south of the A31 to Martyr Worthy, Chilland, and Itchen Abbas. Then it cuts across the railway to go north-east to Abbotstone, from which it follows an irregular route to the north of and parallel with the A31, but distant from it some three or four miles, by way of Wield, Bentworth, and Shalden, beyond which it is to be joined by a track or way coming from Inkpen and the Ridgeway on the Berkshire border. The North Downs Way continues north of Froyle and Bentley, co-incident for a time with the Hoar Way, with which it crosses the Surrey boundary into Farnham.

After Farnham it follows the lower alternative course of the Pilgrims' Way, south of the Hog's Back, past Crooksbury Hill and the village of Seale, to Puttenham. In the steps of the pilgrims it reaches the river Wey below Saint Catherine's Hill, where a footbridge is proposed to take the place of the defunct ferry. Still with the pilgrims, it climbs to Saint Martha's church, but then cuts off to Newlands Corner, and so through the woods of Netley Heath and Ranmore to the A24 north of Dorking. The Mole is crossed by the existing footbridge or the stepping-stones and the route then ascends Box Hill. Henceforward it touches or follows the Pilgrims' Way along the Buckland Hills and Colley Hill to Reigate and the A217, which it crosses to go along Wingate Hill. Still with the Pilgrims' Way, the North Downs Way passes Gatton to Merstham church and the A23 and keeps with the pilgrims by White Hill and Gravelly Hill to the A22. Crossing the road by a footbridge (to be built), it follows along the slope of the Downs to the Kent boundary south of Tatsfield.

In Kent the North Downs Way follows the mid-slopes to Chevening Park and so to Dunton Green and across the Darent to Otford. It then follows a somewhat winding path above the Pilgrims' Way to Wrotham, and next by lane and path partly on the Pilgrims' Way comes towards Birling, where it turns north-east to Rochester.

East of the Medway it goes along Wouldham Downs and by way of Bluebell Hill above Boxley to Detling. From Detling the path runs at a higher level than the Pilgrims' Way, which, however, it joins at Hollingbourne and follows the Way to Charing.

The route then goes through Boughton Lees north-eastwards, skirting Godmersham and Chilham Parks, to the village of Chilham, and so through Harbledown to Canterbury.

Beyond the city the route continues by way of Patrixbourne and Barham Downs to Shepherdswell and so through Waldershare Park along the Roman road to Dover.

A branch from Charing leaves Canterbury aside, crossing the Stour to climb the downs above Hastingleigh and then by Stowting, Etchinghill, and Cheriton Hill and other hills to Folkestone and at last along the cliff tops to Dover.

UPW

Bibliography

Anonymous, *Informacōn for Pylgrymes into the Holy Lande*. Fifteenth century. Replica of 1498 ed. published 1824 by Shakespeare Press (William Nicol). New edition, edited W. Gordon Duff, 1893

Anonymous, *The Tale of Berwyn, with a prologue of the merry adventure of the Pardoner with a Tapster at Canterbury*, re-edited from the Duke of Northumberland's unique manuscript by F. J. Furnival and W. G. Stone. London: Chaucer Society, 1887

Anouilh, Jean, *Becket ou l'Honneur de Dieu*. La Table Ronde, Paris. Première at the Théâtre Montparnasse-Gaston Baty, 1959. English translation by Lucienne Hill. London: Methuen, 1961

Aubrey, John, 'Perambulation of Surrey' in Richard Rawlinson's *Natural History and Antiquities of Surrey*, 1719.

Belloc, Hilaire, *The Old Road*. London: Constable & Co., 2nd ed. 1910

Borenius, Tancred, *Saint Thomas Becket in Art*. London: Methuen, 1932

British Regional Geology. London: H.M.S.O.
　London and Thames Valley, R. L. Sherlock, 3rd ed. 1960
　The Hampshire Basin, R. W. Gallois, 3rd ed. 1960
　The Wealden District, R. W. Gallois, 2nd imp. 1965

The Buildings of England Series. Ed. Nikolaus Pevsner. Penguin Books.
　Hampshire, Nikolaus Pevsner and David Lloyd, 1967
　Surrey, Ian Nairn, 1962
　Kent, 2 vols, John Newman, 1969

Cartwright, Julia (Mrs Adie), *The Pilgrims' Way*. London: 2nd ed.

Chaucer, Geoffrey, *The Canterbury Tales*, Ed. F. N. Robinson, in *Works*. London: O.U.P.

Cobbett, William, *Rural Rides*. London: Dent, 1948

Cochrane, C., *The Lost Roads of Wessex*. Newton Abbot: David & Charles, 1969

Daniel, Glyn E., *Prehistoric Chamber Tombs of England and Wales*. London: O.U.P., 1951

Eliot, T. S., *Murder in the Cathedral*. London: Faber, 1938

Erasmus, Desiderius, *Pilgrimages to Saint Mary of Walsingham and Saint Thomas of Canterbury*. Ed. J. G. Nichols. London: John Murray, 2nd ed. 1875

Giles, J. A. (ed.). *Life and Letters of Thomas à Becket*, 1846

Green, W. Carter, *Old Cottages and Farmhouses of Surrey*

Grinsell, L. V., *The Archaeology of Wessex*. London: Methuen, 1958

Hall, Donald J., *English Medieval Pilgrimage*. London: Routledge, 1966

Hasted, Edward, *The History and Topographical Survey of the County of Kent*, 12 vols, 2nd ed. 1797

Heath, Sidney, *Pilgrim Life in the Middle Ages*. London: T. Fisher Unwin, 1911

Knowles, Dom David, *The Religious Houses of Medieval England*. London: Sheed & Ward, 1940

Leland, John, *Itinerary*, 1535–43. Ed. Lucy Toulman Smith, London: Bell, 1907. Ed. L. T. Smith, London: Centaur Press, 1964

Malory, Sir Thomas, *Morte d'Arthur*

Maynard-Smith, H., *Pre-Reformation England*. London: Macmillan, 1938

Morris, John, *The Relics of Saint Thomas of Canterbury*. Canterbury, 1888

Oursel, Raymond, *Pèlerins du Moyenne Age*. Paris: Fayard, 1963

Parker, Eric, *Highways and Byways in Surrey*. London: Macmillan, 1966

Pont-Maxence, Guernes, *La Vie de Saint Thomas Becket*, 1172–4. Ed. Walberg, 1936

Snowden-Ward, H., *The Canterbury Pilgrimage*. London: A. & C. Black, 1904. 2nd ed. 1927

Textus Roffensis

Timperley, H. W., and Brill, Edith, *Ancient Track Ways of Wessex*. London: Phoenix House, 1965

Victoria County Histories: *Hampshire, Surrey, Kent*

Wall, Frances, *Canterbury Pilgrims and their Ways*. London: Methuen, 1917

White, Gilbert, *The Natural History of Selborne*, 1789

Wood, Eric S., *Collins' Field Guide to Archaeology in Britain*. London: Collins, 2nd ed., 1968

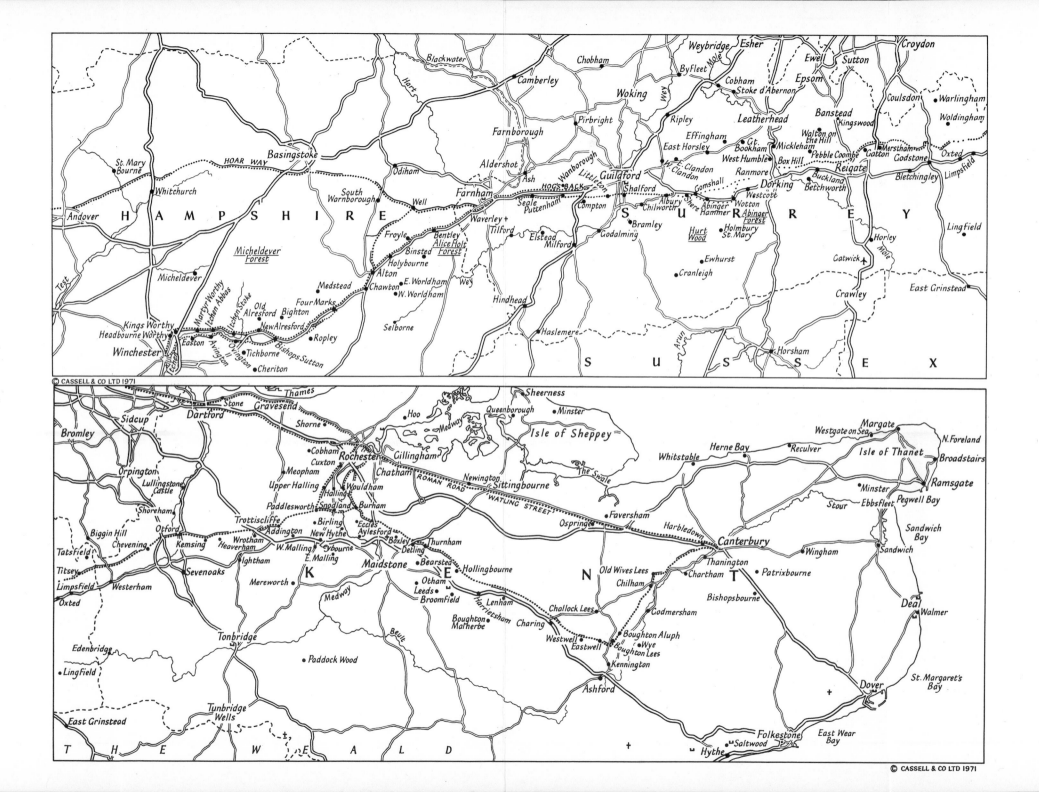

The Pilgrims' Way

Scale
0   2   4   6   8   10 Miles
0   2   4   6   8   10 12 14 Kilometres

.... The Pilgrims' Way
━━━━━ Trunk Routes and Motorways
━━━━ Primary Routes
──── 'A' Roads
▪▪▪▪ Places where the Pilgrims' Way follows surfaced minor roads or lanes
─ ─ ─ County Boundaries
✝ Cathedrals and Abbeys
🏰 Castles

Index